# EARLY MODERN ASCETICISM

## Literature, Religion, and Austerity in the English Renaissance

# Early Modern Asceticism

## *Literature, Religion, and Austerity in the English Renaissance*

PATRICK J. McGRATH

UNIVERSITY OF TORONTO PRESS
Toronto Buffalo London

Toronto Buffalo London
www.utppublishing.com

ISBN 978-1-4875-0532-5

Publication cataloguing information is available from Library and Archives Canada.

University of Toronto Press acknowledges the financial assistance to its publishing program of the Canada Council for the Arts and the Ontario Arts Council, an agency of the Government of Ontario.

Funded by the Government of Canada
Financé par le gouvernement du Canada

*For My Parents*
*In Memory of Jeanette Nugent Meola* (1918–2015)

# Contents

# Acknowledgments

This book could not have been written without the help of Feisal G. Mohamed, Ryan Netzley, Regina Schwartz, Anne Chandler, Curtis Perry, and Catharine Gray. At Southern Illinois University Carbondale, Ryan Netzley has been a tireless advocate for this project and an unfailingly supportive colleague. Anne Chandler read several chapters with great care, precision, and astuteness. Dave Johnson read all the Greek and Latin in this manuscript, saving me from many errors; and I am grateful to Clayton Killion for introducing me to Gerhard Kittel. At the University of Toronto Press, Suzanne Rancourt has expertly shepherded this book through the many stages of review and publication. Brooke Conti and James Kuzner, the Press's anonymous readers who have since yielded up their identities, provided invaluable advice that improved the argument greatly. My thanks to Eric Song, Lori Newcomb, Bob Markley, and Angelica Duran for the support they offered at key moments in this book's composition. Revised portions of the introduction and chapter 3 first appeared in *Prose Studies* 34 (2012), and of chapter 4 in *The Andrew Marvell Newsletter* [now *Marvell Studies*] 5 (2014). I am grateful to the journals for permissions to include these revised portions. While writing this book, diversion, companionship, and comic relief were supplied by Kev, Sara, Mikey, Layla, and Harley. The book is dedicated to my parents, Robin and Kevin McGrath, whose encouragement and support remain unceasing; and it is dedicated to my late grandmother, Jeanette Nugent Meola, whose boundless intellectual curiosity continues to inspire my own.

# EARLY MODERN ASCETICISM

## Literature, Religion, and Austerity in the English Renaissance

# Introduction

## I Woodstock, 1631

In August of 1631, Charles I made a public declaration in favour of clerical celibacy. William Laud, his Bishop of London and soon-to-be Archbishop of Canterbury, may have done the same.[1] For some, this must have caused considerable alarm at the blatant popery of the new-fangled religion; for others, it confirmed that Laudianism was reclaiming the precious grain of traditional religion winnowed with the chaff by an overzealous reformation. Whatever the interpretation, one thing was clear: the church of Charles and Laud – and all the innovations they introduced or traditions they were recovering – was invariably associated with asceticism.

Peter Heylyn, a royal chaplain and Laud's eventual biographer, offers this account of the Woodstock meeting:

> In the late Agitations at Woodstock before the King, he [Laud] let fall some words, which were interpreted to the disparagement of the married Clergy. He was a single man himself, and wisht perhaps as St. Paul once did, That all men else (that is to say, all men in holy Orders) would remain so likewise. And some occasion being offered at that time to speak about the conveniencies or inconveniencies of a married Clergy, he made some declaration of himself to this effect, that in disposing of all Ecclesiastical Promotions he would prefer the single man before the married, supposing the abilities of the persons were otherwise equal; which limitation notwithstanding it gave much matter of discourse, and not a little ground of scandal to many very honest and well-minded men, who began presently to fear the sad consequents of it. This general murmur could not but come unto his ears, and found him very sensible of the Inconveniencies which might grow upon it.[2]

One can sense Heylyn's unease with Laud's comments and, more largely, with the celibate principle they maintain. With the reference to St. Paul, a marginal note directs the reader to 1 Corinthians 7:7: "For I would that all men were even as I myself. But every man hath his proper gift of God, one after this manner, and another after that."[3] A certain grammatical slippage exists whereby Heylyn's parenthetical, "(that is to say, all men in holy Orders)," qualifies not only Laud's attribution of celibacy to every man, but also St. Paul's. It is almost as if, in the face of direct textual evidence to the contrary, Heylyn would revise Paul's position, limiting its broad applicability ("all men").

The fullest account of the meeting at Woodstock, Bodleian Jones MS 17, does not attribute to Laud the comments that Heylyn associates with him.[4] Rather, Charles I makes them in response to the circumstances that had occasioned the Woodstock meeting. Giles Thorne of Balliol was an Oxford MA accused of publicly denouncing Laudianism; he had preached about idolatrous altars in a sermon on Kings 13:2. It was also alleged that he had "out of private malice … abused the head of his house [Dr Carkhurst]," even making disparaging remarks about Carkhurst's wife. In his defense, Thorne claimed that his comments were not personal, only meant to indicate how he found it "unfitt" that "Colledge busines should be governed by heades of houses wifes." Charles I took the opportunity to opine.

> Whereuppon the King was pleased to say that he himselfe wisht that noe heades of houses were married, nor noe other in Orders and that if other thinges were equall in preferment which hee bestowed hee should respect those that were unmarried before those that were married, but told him that that was noe fitt matter for him to meddle with in the pulpitt.[5]

Charles's and Laud's comments contain several striking verbal parallels: "noe other in Orders" (Charles) and "all men in holy Orders" (Laud); "if other thinges were equall in preferment" and "supposing the abilities of the persons were otherwise equal"; "respect those that were unmarried before those that were married" and "prefer the single man before the married." Is Heylyn simply wrong as to who said what, later putting the words of Charles into Laud's mouth? This is why Heylyn's unease with Laud's comments matters. *Cyprianus anglicus* (1668) is, in the words of Anthony Milton, "a sustained apology for the life and policies" of Laud (*ODNB*). The apologetical nature of Heylyn's work and his discomfort with Laud's remarks would have made them easy to omit had he doubted their validity.

Charles's speech does seem to invite a response, one that the scribe has perhaps not recorded. The King carefully defers to Laud on the matter of preferment ("which hee bestowed"), and he concludes by soliciting Laud's response: "that was noe fitt matter for him to meddle with in the pulpitt." One can imagine an expectant Charles turning to Laud to have his opinion ratified, and the obsequious Laud obliging, perhaps only by a gesture of assent (hence the parity in their remarks). A sense of a *quid pro quo* informs the exchange, whereby Charles affirms church autonomy and anticipates an affirmation of his own. While there is no definitive way to prove that Laud participates in the conversation, his participation in fixing the controversy arising from it is clear.

Heylyn also details how Laud addressed the backlash resulting from the Woodstock meeting:

> For he soon wiped off that reproach, by negotiating a Marriage between Mr Thomas Turner, one of his Chaplains, and a Daughter of Windebanke his old friend, (at whose house he had so long lain sick, as before is said.) And that the satisfaction in this point might appear the greater, he officiated the whole Service of their Marriage in his own Chappel at London House, joyning their hands, and giving the Nuptial Benediction, and performing all other Ecclesiastical Rites which belonged to the solemnization of Matrimony by the Rules of this Church. This was the answer which he made to his own Objection, and indeed it was so full and home, that the Objection seemed not to require any further answer.[6]

The wedding's elaborate choreography suggests that Laud's church was seen as potentially inhospitable to clerical marriage. The intricate staging reads as a kind of damage control intended to contain a public relations disaster. In short, it may have been Charles's comment, but Laud was responsible for fixing it.[7]

In order to understand why Laud went to such spectacular effort to fix the controversy – and, more broadly, why Laudian asceticism struck a sensitive nerve with Protestants – here is how one Reformation scholar describes just what clerical marriage came to symbolize:

> The evangelical defence of clerical marriage was part of a broader effort to redefine the nature of priesthood and the clerical estate, to undermine the sacramental theology which underpinned the sacerdotal caste and demanded celibacy of those who served at the altar, to prioritise the word of God over the laws of man, faith over works, and to reclaim the history and heritage of the primitive church from the pages of monastic chronicles.[8]

The reach of clerical marriage extends even into the fundamental principles of the Reformation: a priesthood of all believers, the primacy of faith, a return to primitive Christianity, and the centrality of scripture. Favouring clerical celibacy could seem to some, then, like goodbye to all of a very considerable *that*. The issue of a celibate clergy in England does not disappear at the advent of reform.[9] The Act of Six Articles, Mary's reign, and Elizabeth's grudging acceptance of a married clergy constitute but a few qualifying events. To a certain extent, though, these events belong to the formative years of reform, when it was proceeding and retreating fitfully, by stops and starts. When Joseph Hall published *The honor of the married clergy* in 1620, he was responding to the Jesuit Edward Coffin's attack on an "Apologeticall Letter for the Marriage of persons Ecclesiasticall" Hall had written twelve years earlier.[10] While Hall was forced into print by a frontal assault from Rome, he could not have envisioned the surprise attack that would come some ten years later from within his own ranks. Hall (and others) must have responded to the insurrection with disbelief. Had not John Jewel offered a persuasive defense of a married clergy, of the proposition "that Matrimonie is Holy, and Honorable in al sortes and states of Personnes: as in the Patriarches, in the Prophetes, in the Apostles, in the Holy Martyrs, in the Ministers of the Churche, and in Bishoppes"?[11] Had not John Foxe and countless others effectively decried the "Sodomiticall feditie and abhomination, with other inconveniences, [that] did spring incontinently" from the "Diabolicall doctrine" against priests' marriage?[12] Had not the reformers been successful in working tirelessly to restore matrimony's reputation, after centuries of popish neglect and aspersion, to a state in which "vertue is mayntayned, vice is exchewed, houses are replenished, cities are inhabited, the grounde is tylled, scienses are practised, kyngdoms floryshe, amite is preserved, the publique weale is defended, naturall succession remaynethe, good artes are taught, honest order is kepte, Christēdome is enlarged, Goddes word promoted, and the glory of GOD hyghely avaunced and sette forthe"?[13] No, the late agitations at Woodstock suggested, they had not.

## II Early Modern Asceticism

The agitations at Woodstock illustrate the persistence of asceticism long after the institutions and devotional practices associated with its pre-Reformation existence had disappeared. That does not mean, of course, that asceticism persists unchanged or that fundamental assumptions about its use and definition go uncontested. After the Reformation, the traditional forms of ascetic life – monasticism, virginity, corporal mortification – were variously rejected, reformed, and reinvented. They were revised with this question in mind: Is asceticism primarily a spiritual or physical process? If the end of asceticism is spiritual, then should not the means to achieve it be similarly spiritualist? Is that not precisely what Roman Catholic asceticism got wrong – or did it? For many of the early moderns discussed in the following pages, a wholly spiritualist revision of asceticism went too far. The body had an important role to play in worship and devotional life: its disposition bore directly on the soul. Bodily austerity reflected and increased internal piety. These early moderns, who generally identified as Laudian or High Church English Protestants, recovered many of the ascetic practices the Reformation jettisoned. They revived them according to their own theological predilections, especially Arminian theology and the liturgical principle of "the beauty of holiness" (Psalms 96:9). And the recovery proceeded under the chastening and often hostile scrutiny of those emphasizing the spiritual nature of asceticism. This is because for many early moderns, a wholly spiritual revision of asceticism went just far enough. Corporal austerity idolatrously externalized an internal process, and every drop of blood spilled by fanatical ascetics was an affront to the sufficiency of Christ's. Traditional asceticism struck spiritual ascetics as legalistic and Pharisaical, constraining what Christian liberty set free. Was not all this physical austerity a return to a salvific economy of good works, a captain back into Egypt? Most troublingly, this asceticism smacked to many early moderns of popery. Those adopting these views were, on the whole, the godly, puritans, and Calvinists (three separate designations that could very well describe one individual).

While the conflict over spiritual and physical asceticism is partly explicable by confessional (Roman Catholic and Protestant) and intra-confessional (Laudian and godly) allegiance, it also results from a paradox at the centre of all ascetic activity. This paradox derives from a seemingly straightforward dichotomy. Asceticism is one attitude towards the relationship between the body and the soul. It conceives of that relationship in hostile, dichotomous terms: the body versus the soul. The soul needs to overcome the body. The overcoming might happen through prayer and self-denial or physical action. Whatever form it takes, the same problem arises: embodiment. Prayers against lust are prayed in the vessel of it; the body is both agent and object of mortification. Since the soul resides within the body, it must – paradoxically – overcome the body *through* the body; this can perpetuate, rather than escape, the problem. Far from resulting in the elimination or the total subordination of the body, asceticism effects a supersession of the body that also preserves it.[14] An attempt to assert the independence of the soul results in recalling its dependency on the body. Carnality is a permanent partner in ascetic endeavour. This permanence could drive one away from the body (spiritual asceticism) or it could encourage ever more strenuous exertions to overcome it (physical asceticism).

This book argues that the tension between spiritual and physical asceticism became a major theme in the literature and religion of the period as authors attempted to negotiate the tension, to find their way around or through it, to throw their lot in with one side, to reconcile one side to the other, or to question the intellectual and spiritual bases of the tension altogether.[15] In so far as this tension responds to and questions the body's role in asceticism, it is not entirely new. Basil of Caesarea had felt it, and no doubt countless other Church Fathers, desert anchorites, and medieval monks.[16] But the tension was *renewed*, and with a particular intensity, during the Reformation because of how asceticism adumbrates the larger issues of reform: works and grace, free will and predestination, the sanctity of marriage, sacrilege, idolatry, religious ceremony, and the role of the priesthood. This book employs the rather fungible term "tension" precisely because elaborating the complexity of ascetic practice requires that flexibility. While ascetics might conceive of asceticism in primarily spiritual or physical terms, ascetic expression does not always cohere into such self-contained categories. Purely spiritual and physical asceticisms often represent polemical idealizations and not practical realities. Physical ascetics fret over the popish connotations of corporal austerity; spiritual ascetics cancel and conserve bodily severity. The following paragraphs document both the polemical idealization and practical reality. They begin with a discussion of physical and spiritual asceticism by authors who conceive of them as largely self-contained and separable categories. The section ends with the example of two individuals, William Laud and "Eliza," who collapse these categories.

Instead of punishing the body, the godly advocated self-denial, the predominant version of spiritual asceticism.[17] Though we will find this pre-Cartesian "self" defined in several ways, writers of the era associate it with "affections" that can include self-absorption and willfulness, as well as one's sense of personal identity, what Timothy J. Reiss refers to as "who-ness."[18] Protestant distrust in externals to work spiritual effects represents the single greatest inducement for this internalization of corporal austerity. As William Gouge declares, "external and carnal things cannot work internal and spiritual effects."[19] John Tombes is similarly adamant about external ineffectiveness: "All which reach no further then the body, cannot rectifie or amend the Soule: and make it more like to God."[20] These axioms are put into practice by Thomas James who, while distinguishing Protestant from Roman Catholic repentance, relocates external asceticism inwards: "Their penance consisteth in outward affliction of the body, and maceration of the flesh: our repentance is inward, and spirituall in the grace, and faith of Christ."[21] Radical divisibility between physical and spiritual could push one towards corporal austerity as a way of making the body more habitable for the soul. But considering the inability of externals to effect internal spiritual benefits, such divisibility could just as easily reorient an asceticism of the body inwards.

In addition to challenging the role of externals in religion, spiritual ascetics urged self-denial for reasons polemical and theological. They associated bodily ascetic acts with Roman Catholicism, and they sought to reverse what they perceived as a medieval and Roman Catholic bias against holy matrimony.[22] Moreover, the belief in human depravity held by many spiritual ascetics limited the extent to which the sanguine goals of bodily asceticism (virginity, suppression of all lust) were even achievable.[23] Extreme forms of physical asceticism also prevented one from performing his or her calling and vocation; they offended, with their strictures and potential vows, the largesse of Christian liberty. And, most troublingly, extreme ascetic acts denied the sufficiency of Christ's sacrifice.[24] To describe this version of asceticism as spiritual, internal, or virtual is not meant to be euphemistic. In many ways, spiritual ascetics discipline the self with the same severity that bodily ascetics punish the body. The "irrational self-torture" that Max Weber deplores in physical asceticism does not disappear following the Reformation but switches the object of its austerity.[25]

Christopher Wilson's *Self Deniall: or, A Christians Hardest Taske* (1625) illustrates how spiritual asceticism redirected austerity inwards and intensified the attention that Roman Catholics and some English Protestants wasted on the body.[26] In the work, Wilson disparages a long list of innovations in the church, including "Solitary life, Abotts, Monkes, Friers, Pilgrimage, Purgatory, Fastings, Difference of meates, and Dayes, Distinction of Clergy, and Laitye, Single life."[27] About all of them, Wilson argues, "they have a shewe of carnall wisedome; and are measured, grounded and guilded over with witty reason."[28] Wilson uses the bad example of "will-worship" and "selfe-will" in Roman Catholicism to illustrate the hardships of a self-denying religion:

> This shewes us the difficulty of true Religion; for what can bee harder to man then to overcome himselfe, to deny his owne reason and choice, and wholly to subiect himselfe to Gods; to renounce his owne will, and to chuse and doe the will of God.
>
> This is harder then to offer all outward sacrifice, then to undergoe the severest penance of whip and sack-cloath.[29]

The penance of whip and sackcloth that punishes the body does not compare in ascetic severity to the spiritual self-denial Wilson advocates.

A telling expression of the higher level of difficulty appears in the verbs accompanying Protestant and Roman Catholic asceticism: "overcome" versus "undergoe." The impressionable passivity of "undergoe" pales in comparison with the heroic activity, the godly exertion, of "overcome."

Later in the tract, Wilson conveys the existential pain of self-denial, as "our affections" are pulled sharply in two directions:

> As on the contrary, when our affections carry us to the mislike off [sic], and flying from a thing as grievous, yet to imbrace that with joy and delight: o how happie a thing it is? this is a worke farre passing the severest Popish discipline, which in their blinde devotions men inflict on themselves: As to wallow in the snow, and to cast themselves into the cold of waters, or to lye in hayre cloath, or in shirts of male; yea or with Baals Preists, to lanch their own flesh.[30]

Contempt for Roman Catholic ascetic practice as a kind of passive endurance (rather than active accomplishment) is evident in "wallow"; these ascetics loll about in the snow. In two of the examples, external conditions provide the tools of ascetic discipline. The individual is acted upon instead of acting to generate ascetic self-denial from within. Expressing the shift from corporal to internal asceticism, Wilson locates the severest form of ascetic activity – not in the body's subjection to climatic extremes or intense pain – but in disciplining the affections. The description of self-denial as at once "happie" and "a worke farre passing the severest Popish Discipline" illustrates its paradoxical rigours. The stark irreconcilability encloses the demands – logical and otherwise – self-denial imposes on its practitioners.

Wilson's generalized message is clear enough. But the specific practice of fasting – always a favourite of the godly – reveals the complicated relationship spiritual asceticism had with acts of corporal austerity. A considerable variance existed among the godly as to what part the body should play during fasting.[31] No one less than Thomas Cartwright, whom Patrick Collinson dubs the "true progenitor of English presbyterianism" (*ODNB*), embraces the "corporal exercises" of watchings, "abstinence" in apparel, and abstaining from sex during times of fasting in *The holy exercise of a true fast* (1582).[32] Cartwright's view is the exception to the rule, however: most godly writers pit a spiritual version of fasting against an inferior physical peer. In *The doctrine of fasting and praier* (1633), Arthur Hildersam cautions, "bodily exercise profiteth little … But godlinesse (whereof the inward afflicting of the soule, and mortifying of our lusts is a chief part) is profitable unto all things."[33] With a similar nod to 1 Timothy 4:8, Humphrey Chambers asserts in a 1643 sermon before Parliament, "true it is, that the substance of the duty of religious fasting stands not in these, or any bodily acts, and exercises whatsoever."[34] Considering their concerted effort to avoid making fasting about bodily exertion, it is no wonder the godly rejected extreme fasts. In William Attersoll's "The conversion of Nineveh: opening the doctrine and practise of prayer and fasting, as also of faith and repentance" in *Three treatises* (1633), he asks about severe mortification, "what commendation of patience can arise to them, that afflict themselves, and suffer willingly from their owne hands?"[35] In *Compunction or pricking of heart* (1648), R.J. derides the "civill formalist, superstitious and meriting Papist who spares not his own body, but macerates it with whippings, fastings or pilgrimages."[36] Samuel Smith's *The Character of a Weaned Christian* (1675) argues that Paul "censures all monastic, self-imposed Severities, which spare not the Body" and includes under this censure "immoderate Fastings."[37] Attersoll, R.J., and Smith roundly reject such immoderation.

Spiritual ascetics were so anxious about avoiding these "immoderate Fastings," and the will-worshipping idolatry of Roman Catholic practices, that they could make the body completely disappear during fasts. For instance, in *The Christians sanctuarie vvhereinto being retired, he may safely be preserued in the middest of all dangers* (1604), the Calvinist George Downame includes a treatise on "The Christian exercise of Fasting." In the treatise, Downame rejects corporal practices such as "sitting in the ashes, the renting of their cloths, their girding of themselves with sackcloth, their putting of earth upon their heads, and such like" as obsolete Old Testament ceremonies that have a popish connotation.[38] Instead, he articulates a conception of fasting in which the body fades into obscurity. Advancing the idea that "the fasts of Christians are rather spiritually to be observed, than carnally," Downame ventures one step farther, suggesting that the very term "fast" need only be used metaphorically: "Wherefore let us principally fast from sinne … principally therefore let our mind fast from evill."[39] Defining fasts as an abstinence from sin obviates the need for any bodily expression at all. Downame leaves it entirely up to the individual godly believer whether any exercise "to observe the outward fast" is even required.[40] Downame's fasting technically allows Cartwright's "corporal exercises." But one wonders if that robust observation of the outward fast might not seem to Downame to miss the point of fasting or, even worse, to impede it.

Laudians expended no less intellectual energy in their attempts to arrive at an authentic concept of asceticism. To many Laudians, corporal asceticism made good sense in three ways.[41] Asceticism corresponded to the Laudian desire to style itself as authentically apostolic. Laudians sought precedent for many of their ascetic beliefs in the writings of the

Church Fathers, especially Jerome and the Greek Fathers.[42] In so doing, they plundered a corpus of ascetic literature that Protestants often regarded with suspicion if not outright derision.[43] Arminianism also supplied a controversial basis for the Laudian emphasis on asceticism. The belief that one could remain virginal, suppressing lust and carnal desire, exhibited a more optimistic view of human nature and the will's efficacy than Calvinists possessed.[44] For Laudians, asceticism demonstrated the will's power. Enduring the pain that severe ascetic acts inflicted on the body manifested willpower.[45] The ascetic body in pain would seem to have little truck with the sumptuous devotional style of the "beauty of holiness." In fact, a sympathy between holy beauty and painful asceticism offers the third and final way austerity fits into the Laudian program. Ceremonial worship and austere asceticism shared an underlying principle: the body disposes the mind towards – and through austerity becomes a vessel of – piety.[46] Ascetic practice embodied the corporal discipline that ceremonial worship valorized.[47]

A number of the motivations for Laudian asceticism appear in the work of William Watts.[48] Watts's *Mortification apostolicall* (1637), an extended justification of physical asceticism, explicitly urges the "apostolic" provenance of austerity while implicitly sanctioning an Arminian view of the will's power.[49] The tract begins conventionally enough, with Watts arguing for the holiness and necessity of mortification. He describes those mortifying as destroying sin.[50] That description is consistent with most definitions of mortification as killing, or dying to, sin. But Watts does not stop there. The sermon claims that mortification takes place not only in the soul, but also *on* the body. To this end, Watts advocates an unambiguously corporal regimen of mortification consisting of barefoot processions (3, 19, 45); "praying prostrate in Sack cloath and ashes" (4); the hermitic life (10), whether in a cell or in the wilderness (27–28); avoiding all women if one is prone to lust (24); hard labour (30); "extream long fasting" (41); and late watchings and an observance of "Canonicall howers" (46–47). Rather provocatively, Watts offers Origen – notorious for his self-castration – as a paragon of apostolic mortification and virginity: "Take Origens experience, for your encouragement" (9). Origen's experience does not often meet with general approbation. *Christs victorie ouer Sathans tyrannie* (1615), Thomas Mason's abridgement of Foxe's *Book of Martyrs*, succinctly concludes, "and Origen mistooke himselfe when he gelded himselfe, that he might be chast for the kingdom of heaven."[51] Mason criticizes not only Origen's action, but the soteriology behind it; namely, the idea that a work such as chastity can accrue merit for salvation.[52]

Watts, however, remains committed to contextualizing Origen's extreme act within patristic tradition. In the margin adjacent to Watts's remarks about Origen looms an encomium to virginity from Gregory Nazianzen: "Virginitie and single life, is a high matter: which rancks a man in equalitie with the Angels" (6).[53] Such a quotation supplies a textual and visual ratification of the chastity Origen practices.[54] Gregory's praise of the ascetic life is often so pronounced that the Jesuit Girolamo Piatti cites him "formost" while offering "testimonies of the ancient fathers in commendation of a Religious Estate."[55] Perhaps it is Gregory's vaunted place among Roman Catholic proponents of asceticism that leads Gervase Babington to accuse him and other Fathers of Manichaeism for their "misliking of y$^{e}$ ordinance of god against incontinency" and "over great opinion of single life."[56] Watts shows nothing but approval for that "over great opinion." This kind of appeal to patristic example occurs throughout *Mortification apostolicall*, and it is symptomatic of Laudian interest in styling itself as recovering patristic precedent. Jean-Louis Quantin characterizes this patristicism as a movement away from continental reformers back to the Greek and Latin fathers.[57] *Mortification apostolicall* seeks to recover those traditions in all their austerity. As Watts boasts at the sermon's beginning (while justifying a seeming divergence from patristic precedent), "I glory to be an imitator of the holy Primitives" (2). That imitation is crucial when recommending highly controversial practices.

Elsewhere, Watts incorporates the "apostolic" pillar of Laudian austerity while justifying the "beauty of holiness." *The Churches Linnen Garment* (1646), a work Watts wrote in defense of the surplice, illustrates how austerity and religious ceremony reinforce each other.[58] The surplice was a priestly garment that Laud's church required ministers to wear during services.[59] Puritans and anti-Laudians loathed it. Richard Culmer refers to the surplice as a "ragged smock of the where [sic] of Rome."[60] À la Culmer, the spurious *The recantation of the prelate of Canterbury* dramatically imagines Laud confessing, "I will not harbour the least hopes of escape, or think that my Surplice stained with the adulterous spots, of the great whore, can plead favour."[61] Richard Bernard, writing under the pseudonym Dwalphintramis, describes the surplice as "one ragge of the Ceremonies," "of all the Idolatrous Rites not the least," and a "ragge … so infectious in Gods worship, that many thousands of Gods people dare not joyne with it."[62] Against the charge that it is an idolatrous ceremony or a mere rag of Rome, Watts painstakingly traces the provenance of the surplice from the "Apparitions of the glorifyed, the practise of the Patriarches" up to the 1630s.

In particular, he locates the use of the surplice (or a garment from which it was derived) among the primitive Christian ascetics, and explains how the garment signified the rigours of their lives:

> St Marks disciples, & theyr Successors being mortifyed from the world (which was openly justifyed by theyr Habite (b); sayd Cassian, speaking of theyr Colobium, or linnen coate: they thought they appeared the liker unto deade bodyess. & in particular, unto theyr Saviours: being thus like his, wrapped up in white linnen. And, indeede, the Father, there, directlye alludes unto our Saviours Wynding sheete. And this symbolicall peece of Theologye, being not typicall, but morale, in the intention: may verye significantlye, allso, goe along with our Albe & Surplice.[63]

Watts uses mortification in two senses: one, as meaning a monastic dying to the world; and the other, as denoting a literal death. In that way, his dual usage of the term both anticipates and annotates the point he makes about the surplice as a "symbolicall peece of Theologye," as "significantlye" various. The surplice – decried by the puritan Henry Burton as of a piece with "Sumptuous Ceremonies," "hypocriticall formalities," "the glaring luster of … externall worship," and "externall pompous service" – has a remarkably less precious and pretentious meaning for Watts.[64] It covers up a corpse. Burton does not necessarily misinterpret what the surplice signifies; rather, he partially interprets it. For him, the aesthetic and ascetic – the lavish and the ghoulish – are incompatible. Not so, *The Churches Linnen Garment* avers: the splendid might sit alongside the morbid.

The foregoing discussion has brought out the sharp differences a Laudian like William Watts and a godly Protestant like Christopher Wilson perceived, and worked hard to present, between physical and spiritual asceticism. It is indeed tempting to follow these partisans' leads in considering each stance as internally coherent and inimical to the other. When the godly preacher William Gouge contends, "external and carnal things cannot work internal and spiritual effects,"[65] and the Laudian Jeremy Taylor calls the body "the shop, and forge of the soul,"[66] these two positions certainly seem to present an orderly dichotomy. Yet the broader premise of this book is to demonstrate that this dichotomy – of ascetic types and confessional allegiance – can be porous and the neat opposition unstable. The instability appears in two examples that follow. Contemporary accounts of William Laud's life attest to the permeability between physical and spiritual asceticism in regard to his personal severity. On the "other" side of the great divide, the scriptural interpretations of *Eliza's Babes*, often assumed to reflect the radical views of its female author, in fact present an outlook on marriage and chastity that would seem to conflict with her religious identity.

Descriptions of Laud's austere personal habits often combine features of both spiritual and physical asceticism. Laud's committed diary-keeping exhibited the intense scrupulosity and painful introspection of the godly. The diary, Kevin Sharpe explains, "a record of dreams, omens and insecurities, of the application of scriptural text to everyday life, has been aptly described as a Puritan document."[67] That level of intense self-scrutiny could be a cause or a symptom of self-denial. Self-denial might also manifest in the austerities detailed by Thomas Fuller in *The Church History of Britain* (1655). Fuller, though a royalist, was no Laudian. As W.B. Patterson notes, Peter Heylyn "attacked the *Church History* in his *Examen historicum* for inaccuracies and bias in taking the side of the nonconformists against the bishops" (*ODNB*). In the *Church History*, Fuller writes that Laud "was very plain in apparel, and sharply checked such clergy-men whom he saw go in rich or gaudy clothes, commonly calling them of the church-triumphant." To fill out a portrait of his abstemiousness, Fuller also recounts that Laud was "temperate in his diet, and (which may be presumed the effect thereof) chaste in his conversation."[68] This type of rigour leads a bemused Fuller to conclude his portrait of Laud by observing how he "wore his hair very close; and, though in the beginning of his greatness many measured the length of men's strictness by the shortness of their hair, yet some will say, that since, out of antipathy to conform to his example, his opposites have therein indulged more liberty to themselves."[69] Fuller's use of "strictness" has two senses: one, referring to doctrinal strictness, so that Laud makes the puritan less of a puritan; and the other to the bevy of fastidious personal habits (plain appearance, temperance, chaste conversation) associated with dour godliness, so that Laud turns the puritan less puritanical. For Laud, celibacy must represent a logical outcome of such strictness. Puritans, perhaps shocked by the implication, disown their own strictness. He encompasses so much of the period's asceticism that Laud discovers a certain porosity in its categories of spiritual and physical.

In other circumstances, it is physical and spiritual asceticism that discover a certain permeability in the categories structuring intra-confessional identity. To that end, asceticism provides the opportunity to adjudicate the religious identity of early moderns in increasingly complex and nuanced ways. Often that identity is a composite of theological positions, all of which do not cohere. For example, scholars have debated the religious affiliations of "Eliza," the anonymous female author of *Eliza's Babes* (1652). She has been described as a radical presbyterian and her theology as Calvinist.[70] An examination of Eliza's ascetic views yields a more complicated conclusion.

In the poem "Luke 20.36. *In that world they shall be equall to the Angels*," Eliza considers the Sadducees' well-known questioning of Christ about a woman who had seven husbands who all predeceased her.[71] "Therefore in the resurrection," the Sadducees ask, "whose wife of them is she?" (Luke 20:33). Jesus responds, "the children of this world marry, and are given in marriage: But they which shall be accounted worthy to obtain that world, and the resurrection from the dead, neither marry, nor are given in marriage: Neither can they die any more: for they are equal unto the angels; and are the children of God, being the children of the resurrection" (Luke 20:34–36).[72] In the poem, Eliza anticipates the angelic condition by importuning, "Here like the Angels let me be,/And as those blessed spirits free:/From vaine engagements let me bide,/And as they with thee still reside" (1–4). According to the verses from Luke, being like the angels entails not dying, yes, but also not marrying. The angelic freedom that Eliza desires, then, refers to an unattached – unmarried – earthly condition. Understanding these lines as being about marriage paints a rather unflattering portrait of the nuptial state: "From vaine engagements let me bide." Reference to these engagements at the poem's end clarifies how indifferently they should be treated: "So shall my soul such sweet joys find,/That earthly things I shall not minde" (11–12). The dual connotation of "minde" summarizes the poem's attitude towards earthly things: they will be tolerated or paid no mind to. Both attitudes continue the diminution of matrimonial honour begun in equating it with "vaine engagements."

Eliza's exegesis of Luke 20:36 devalues marriage and – implicitly – elevates virginity. Her interpretation contrasts with those of the puritan Henry Burton and the ejected minister Joseph Alleine. Each finds a way, sometimes an ingenious one, of compensating for marriage's absence in heaven. To offset any damage to matrimony implied by Luke 20:36, Burton reminds the reader that marriage mystically prefigures – it is a preparative for and precursor of – the believer's divine union with Christ.[73] Alleine is more insistent. He analogizes the angelic condition of Luke 20:36 to marriage with a prince, thereby comprehending the passage by reference to the earthly institution it expressly disallows.[74] Though marriage may be absent in heaven, Burton and Alleine minimize the implications of its absence. If it is characteristic of the hotter sorts of Protestants to resist the demotion of matrimony found at Luke 20:36, then Eliza's demurral of such resistance, given what has been surmised about her sectarian affiliation, is significant.

By contrast, the Laudians William Austin, Peter Heylyn, and Joseph Beaumont accept Luke 20:36's devaluing of marriage or, in the case of Beaumont, extenuate it.[75] The angels in Beaumont's poem "Virginitee" are resigned to "Let dirty wormes below goe wed."[76] Perhaps that seems a bit far from Eliza's "vaine engagements," but she approaches this position in another poem. In "The Bride," she writes, "Sith you me ask, Why borne was I?/I'le tell you; twas to heaven to fly,/Not here to live a slavish life,/By being to the world a wife" (1–4). The phrase "by being to the world a wife" could mean that Eliza rejects living a life of worldliness as the world's spouse; or it could mean that she rejects being considered by the world and those in it a wife. She refuses not only being the wife of a particular individual, but more generally the prospect of being a wife; the latter indicates a systemic critique of the institution of matrimony not wholly unlike Beaumont's.

Eliza's ascetic views do not disprove her radicalism, but they do qualify it, indicating how that label does not quite fit, or fits in certain instances but not others.[77] As Sophie Read writes, "gradations of belief do not always submit to precise confessional categorisation."[78] The examples of Laud and Eliza illustrate that the categories we use in discussing early modern asceticism (physical or spiritual) and religious affiliation (Laudian, radical, puritan, etc.) can misrepresent the convolutions and contradictions of religious identity. This does not demand renouncing those categories, for they clearly structure much of the period's religious discourse. Anthony Milton explains that, "the indivisibility of the one true religion – a concept inherent in the doctrine of the 'Two Churches' and also common to most Calvinist writers – meant that Protestants could not be in a position to compromise on any points."[79] Recognition of the compromises that occur behind an uncompromising veneer means acknowledging that abstract discourse and practical reality do not always correspond. Following the doctrinal complexity of Eliza, and the pan-asceticism of Laud, much of this project will be spent measuring the space between practical reality and abstract discourse.

## III Asceticism and Contemporary Scholarship

The previous pages have outlined the contours of early modern asceticism. The following paragraphs explain how the topic complements and, at times, challenges critical trends in scholarship of the period. Most pointedly, the cultural importance of asceticism frustrates a common assumption in early modern studies: namely, that asceticism disappears with the Reformation, giving way to a modern world of increased bodily liberation;[80] or that the internalization of asceticism (à la Max Weber) removes its pre-Reformation monastic ethos and/or severity.[81]

In *The Unrepentant Renaissance*, Richard Strier contends, "it is only in the Reformation tradition that the attack on Stoicism and asceticism is freed from ambivalence." As a result of this attack, "the whole rationale for asceticism and renunciation of the world disappears."[82] Luther's redefinition of Pauline flesh and spirit represents a key development leading to the disappearance of this rationale. For Luther, flesh and spirit do not mean body and soul.[83] Strier maintains that "fleshliness or carnality, from this point of view, is fundamentally the condition of egotism or self-regard." If fleshliness is synonymous with egotism and the self, this then gives rise to Luther's doctrine of grace: "The doctrine of grace flows from the reinterpretation of 'flesh' and 'spirit' because *it seems truly impossible* to imagine the self willing itself out of self regard" (my emphasis).[84] How does a self escape itself without some kind of divine aid? It cannot, and that is where grace comes in. For Strier, Luther's theology of sin and grace obviates asceticism in two ways. By redefining flesh and spirit as self-regard, it removes the antagonism between the soul and body that forms the basis of asceticism; and, as a result of that removal/redefinition, Luther's theology forces ascetics into a logical bind. While it is one thing to deny the body through the prayerful activity of the soul, "self" is rather all-encompassing: it has no auxiliary to carry out its own abnegation. And yet, this is precisely what self-denial, the spiritual asceticism advocated by the godly, attempts. Rather than undoing the whole rationale for asceticism, redefining flesh and spirit as self-regard merely indicates the inauguration of a new ascetic imperative. As illogically perverse as it sounds, the self denies its way out of itself. The reasonable constraints that Strier imposes on self-denial ("it seems truly impossible") – and that subtend a Reformed concept of sin and grace that would supersede asceticism – are not, in fact, constraining for early modern ascetics.

An unwillingness to imagine a self's ability to deny itself also constitutes the major limitation of Michel Foucault's theory of asceticism in *The Hermeneutics of the Subject*. In these lectures, Foucault distinguishes Christian and pagan asceticism in the following way:

> It seems to me that in this Christian ascesis there is, therefore, a movement of self-renunciation which proceeds by way of, and whose essential moment is, the objectification of the self in a true discourse. It seems to me that pagan ascesis, the philosophical ascesis of the practice of the self in the period I am talking about, involves rejoining oneself as the end and object of a technique of life, an art of living.

Christian asceticism renounces the self; pagan asceticism "involves coming together with oneself … the subjectivation of a true discourse in a practice and exercise of oneself on oneself."[85] Pagan asceticism works on the self, and Christian asceticism denies it. How then to explain Richard Baxter's account of self-denial in *A Treatise of Self-Denial* (1659):

> The illuminated Soul is so much taken with the Glory and Goodness of the Lord, that it carrieth him out of himself to God, and as it were estrangeth him from himself, that he may have communion with God; and this makes

> him vile in his own eyes, and abhor himself in dust and ashes; He is lost in himself; and seeking God, he finds himself again in God.[86]

For Baxter, self-denial does not lose the self; it finds it. Abhorring oneself (can there be a stronger term for self-renunciation?) leads to the constitution of the self. In this way, early modern asceticism joins together what Foucault relegates to either pagan or Christian asceticism. This would seem to frustrate doubly Strier's claim about the impossibility of the self willing itself out of self-regard. Here, the self not only denies itself, but denies itself back into itself.

Max Weber's theories have also contributed to a sense of the demise of asceticism in early modernity. This project challenges Weber's analysis in two ways. It contends that Weber's notion of internalized asceticism as more rational and less severe misrepresents self-denial, and it resists Weber's conception of the Renaissance as closing the door on the monastery, to use his famous phrase.[87] Weber's attenuation of monasticism leads scholars to assume that it actually disappears in early modernity. Weber's overstatement informs, for example, Thomas Rist's conclusion that "Protestantism espoused and encouraged a mentality that was anti-ascetic in the traditional sense." The "traditional sense" includes a rejection of monasticism: "English Protestants were not merely anti-monastic, but were against any practices perceived as 'monkish.'"[88] Another analysis of early modern asceticism along Weberian lines echoes Rist's claim. "The Reformation," Thomas Nipperdey writes, "did away with monasticism ... The religious life was, thereafter, no longer a means of escape from the world, religious asceticism was an innerworldly asceticism."[89] In the early seventeenth century, however, self-deniers often describe their austerity as intensifying and correcting the putative rigours of monasticism, as we have seen in the example of Christopher Wilson above. They might disagree with monastic practices, but they give tacit assent to monasticism's rationale: renunciation of the world. This does not do away with monasticism or indicate a chronic, anti-monastic bias. Against all odds, and even if it means resituating the hermitic life within the world, monasticism is retained.

Perhaps most influentially, Charles Taylor's *Sources of the Self: The Making of the Modern Identity* interprets the relation between asceticism and the Reformation through a Weberian lens. The Reformation enabled what Taylor calls "the affirmation of ordinary life," and a key component of that affirmation lies in the following: "The institution of the monastic life was seen as a slur on the spiritual standing of productive labour and family life, their stigmatization as zones of spiritual underdevelopment. The repudiation of monasticism was a reaffirmation of lay life as a central locus for the fulfilment of God's purpose."[90]

A decline in asceticism results in a sacralization of ordinary life and marriage that, in turn, leads to a greater sense of individuality: "The new understanding of marriage naturally goes along with further individualization and internalization."[91] As chapter 5 discusses, individualization does not naturally follow if the spiritual asceticism that the "new understanding of marriage" inaugurates advocates the elimination of subjectivity. Moreover, the generalizations in Weber's and Taylor's narratives of asceticism's demise and/or sublimation into "innerworldly asceticism" are not compatible with the persistence of traditional ascetic modes and early modern Protestantism's agonized deliberation between them. There are simply no clean breaks with an ascetic past in this book, and the transposition of asceticism into something more rational, secular, and manageable does not take place. The object of austerity might shift – from the body to the self – but the resulting asceticism is far from shiftless: it proceeds against the self with a renewed, at times savage, intensity. While Taylor rightly stresses that worldly asceticism "most emphatically doesn't mean a life of asceticism in the traditional sense," that does not alienate self-denial from either the goals or the severity of the traditional sense.[92] Self-denial often represents the pursuit of conventional asceticism by other means. Instead of bringing their bodies into subjection, ascetics bring subjectivity to heel.

While the notion of asceticism's demise informs many scholarly accounts of early modernity, there have nonetheless been several valuable studies of the topic to which this work is indebted. Even so, the existing scholarship on early modern asceticism displays a tendency to internalize a sense of the topic's marginalized position: it often focuses on recusants, a particular revolutionary moment, or monarchs.[93] Exceptional is the rule. This has led to a limited conception of asceticism's applicability and influence in the culture. In her study of queer virginity, Theodora A. Jankowski states that "the only sexual continence that Protestants were willing to accept was that which occurred within marriage."[94] Yet even John Calvin, in Thomas Norton's 1561 translation of *The institution of Christian religion*, writes, "virginitie, I graunt, is a vertue not to be despised."[95] The concession and the grudging litotes encapsulate much of the period's ambivalent attitude towards asceticism. In contrast with Jankowski, John Rogers acknowledges the appeal of virginal chastity. But his argument about the "idealization of virginity in the years of the English Revolution" applies equally well to the Laudian Church and its precursor in what Peter Lake calls early Stuart avant-garde conformity.[96] After all, the effigy in St. Saviour's, Southwark for the intellectual scion of avant-garde conformity, Lancelot Andrewes, includes the following memorial inscription: "He has departed from here, unmarried, to a heavenly crown."[97] More amenable to the approach of the present book, Jenna Lay writes that the asceticism of "Catholic women resisted any easy demarcation between a Catholic, medieval past and a Protestant, reformed present." Yet again, that observation could as easily apply to the conflicted relationship of Protestant England with asceticism.[98] By recovering that relationship, this book argues for a robust asceticism endemic to early modern culture, not one persisting in isolated parts or persons or for ephemeral durations during it.

One might assume that this recovery defines itself in reactive opposition to studies of the body and sexuality. For example, in *The Cambridge Companion to the Body in Literature*, David Hillman senses a potential opposition between ascetic practices and new attitudes towards the body: "But these disciplines [such as asceticism] entail a turning against one's own body; and, as Richard Strier (among others) has recently emphasised, several of the key writers of the period appear to accept an ethic that embraced the embodied passions, an ethic of intersubjective somatic openness."[99] As we have seen, the embrace of embodied passions assumes that a Reformed theology of sin and grace renders asceticism impossible. Asceticism, though, does not have to be written out of the narrative of early modernity to tell the story of changing attitudes towards the body. In fact, queer interpretations of sexuality often have the most profound sense of, and appreciation for, the suspension or subduction of desire integral to asceticism.[100] In *Sex before Sex: Figuring the Act in Early Modern England*, Will Stockton and James M. Bromley describe their project as "contribut[ing] to a history of sexuality that both includes and exceeds a history of sexual identity. It does so through the construction of histories that reshape, expose the limits of, and challenge the dominance of current discourses of sexuality."[101] Many of the literary works studied here issue their own challenges to current discourses by exposing the limits of sexuality and imagining a reality beyond it. Andrew Marvell's *Upon Appleton House*, I argue in chapter 4, tries to locate a reality outside of sexual desire through asceticism. For Marvell, the reason that asceticism fails is that its austerities perpetuate – rather than prevent – the desires of the body. By attempting to escape sexuality and embodiment, asceticism can intensify engagement with, and awareness of, them. This is a point that Bill Burgwinkle makes in *The Cambridge Companion to the Body in Literature*: "Decrying human flesh, as we have seen, usually entails a paradoxical and intensive engagement with that flesh. Condemnation of sensation means a heightening of sensation."[102] To put this in other terms, ascetic engagement with the body equals, and may even exceed, the fixation on it found in scholarly discourses investigating the body and sexuality.

One important area of scholarship with which the aims of the present study are harder to reconcile is Eucharistic poetics, the dominant approach to examining the relationship between early modern theology and devotional poetry.[103] A disparity exists in how theologies of asceticism and of the Eucharist assign value to the body. Eucharistic theology assumes a more positive attitude towards materiality. It yearns for bodily presence, whether that presence is understood literally or figuratively. The "sacramental dynamic," as Sophie Read describes it, occasions a movement from spirit to flesh.[104] Asceticism proceeds in the opposite direction; it imagines an inveterate and intractable conflict between body and soul. In John Milton's *A Mask* (1634), the Elder Brother argues that virginity "turns it [the body] by degrees to the souls essence,/Till all be made immortal" (462–463). Lust, by contrast, "Imbodies, and imbrutes" the soul (468).[105] An ascetic act such as virginity resists such embodying, tending instead towards spiritualization. With its sanguine view of materiality, sacramental poetics obviates the problematic relationship between body and soul that exists as the fundamental condition of asceticism.

Sacramental poetics also ignores the moral gradations of bodily presence in Christianity. This manifests in instances where a desire for the sinless materiality of Christ's body comes to represent a desire for materiality generally. The Body becomes the body when erotic love is described as Eucharistic.[106] To the ascetic, perennially suspicious of bodies, those are two radically different kinds of matter, ontologically incapable of confusion. Caroline Walker Bynum offers an example of this phenomenon – of extrapolating from Body to body – while discussing corporeality in a medieval context: "Those who wrote about the body in the thirteenth and fourteenth centuries were in fact concerned to bridge the gap between material and spiritual and to give to body positive significance. Nor should we be surprised to find this so in a religion whose central tenet was the incarnation – the enfleshing – of its God."[107] The ease with which a theological concept about God becomes a source for body positivity in the culture seems precarious. A scholarly preoccupation with Eucharistic theology and poetics, and the elision of Body with body it invites, occludes the presence of asceticism in early modernity. The purpose of this book is to reclaim it.

Chapter 1 focuses on 15 August 1617, the date when John Donne became, in the words of his first biographer and friend Izaak Walton, "crucified to the world." On that date, Donne's wife, Ann, died, and he resolved never again to remarry – a promise (a vow?) which the 44-year-old Donne kept until the end of his life. The full ascetic force of Donne's decision has not been acknowledged. The reasons that Donne gives for not remarrying – namely, that marriage inhibits the prayerful life and that it opens a door to the flesh, world, and devil best kept closed – do not square well with the Protestant revitalization of marriage as another Eden.[108] And it does not sit well with the picture of Donne as "ostensibly the paradigmatic English poet of heterosexual amour" modern criticism offers.[109] Further exposing the limits of that designation, the chapter asserts that asceticism's relevance to Donne's life and work extends beyond (and before) 1617, to the rake of the *Songs and Sonets* and the anxious quest for patronage during the lean Mitcham years.

John Donne seems an unlikely advocate for asceticism. John Milton, a dour puritan who spent his youth translating the Psalms, seems more like one of austerity's usual suspects. As chapters 2 and 3 argue, however, the corporal inflection of Milton's ascetic views requires rethinking his early religious radicalism. Though physical asceticism is conventionally associated with Laudians rather than with puritan firebrands such as the young Milton, it is nonetheless true that in *A Mask*, the subject of chapter 2, Milton articulates ideas about virginity, the Neoplatonic ascent of ascetic practitioners, and matrimony that correspond to Caroline attitudes. Scholars have often identified an inevitable movement in Milton's masque towards chaste marriage, one that pointedly contrasts with a debauched court culture: Milton's emphasis on marriage, we are told, rebukes the promiscuity of Caroline Neoplatonism. That is false, I argue, on two counts. One, it imputes a universal libertinism to Caroline culture. And two, it assumes that Milton's masque culminates in a mythic vision that presages an imminent (or inevitable) marriage. Chapter 2 recovers the persistence of virginal chastity in the masque's epilogue as opposed to its replacement with nuptial fecundity. Moreover, the chapter examines how Milton alludes to, while also omitting key aspects from, Spenser's Garden of Adonis in *The Faerie Queene*. Milton's selectivity suggests an unease with the explosive sexuality of Spenser's account.

In *A Mask*, Milton hints that the Lady's virginity affords her a unique relationship with the natural world. Chapter 3 argues that such a relationship is integral to understanding the representation of virginity in *Lycidas*. The poem establishes a connection between a consecrated natural world and consecration of the virgin's body. *Lycidas* contains an unacknowledged instance of religious ceremony: rogation. In the poem, rogation precedes and enables the institution of Lycidas as a benevolent, tutelary deity; rogation sanctifies the natural world. That view of sanctification is consistent with the poem's concluding vision of Edward King's virginity; he reaps heavenly rewards (in part) because of a strict adherence to the single life. More broadly, the connection

*Lycidas* establishes between the sanctifying power of both virginity and rogation illustrates how the Reformation's changing attitudes towards the landscape inform its revaluation of asceticism. The Laudian celebration of virginity occurs simultaneously with the reversal of many of the changes the Reformation introduced relating to a sanctified natural world. The chapter shows how *Lycidas* engages both the celebration and the reversal and how, ultimately, that engagement challenges the prevailing critical perception of the poem as radically puritan.

Chapters 1–3 focus primarily on physical asceticism; Donne and Milton make surprising (albeit conflicted) allowances for corporal austerity. Chapters 4 and 5, by contrast, examine spiritual asceticism. That examination begins in chapter 4 with Andrew Marvell's exhaustive and merciless critique of physical severity in *Upon Appleton House*. In particular, the poem attacks what I have referred to as the paradox driving asceticism: namely, that the body is the means of ascetic overcoming and the thing overcome. Marvell rejects this logic and argues that it merely perpetuates the problem (a troubled relationship between body and soul) rather than resolving it. In other words, *Upon Appleton House* claims, asceticism does not deliver on its basic promise. If it were possible to correct the problematic relationship between body and soul, Marvell has a response to this scenario as well. The means to correct the relationship are simply impossible: they demand a perfection of which humanity is not capable and, quite simply, they would require bodies and matter to change substance entirely – to become brittle, inanimate glass. Marvell's dissent is an important voice in this study. He is preoccupied not only with the doctrines of asceticism, but also with its basic metaphysical assumptions. In this way, his critique goes beyond, goes deeper, than the discomfort Donne and Milton occasionally exhibit with ascetic practices.

After Marvell has destroyed asceticism, it belongs to John Bunyan and *The Pilgrim's Progress* to pick up the pieces. To do so, chapter 5 argues, Bunyan switches the object of ascetic discipline from the body to the self. If asceticism loses in its contest against Marvell, Bunyan's insight is to shift the grounds of the conflict (body to self). Bunyan's work represents the most sustained engagement with spiritual asceticism found in the pages of this study. And yet despite his spiritual aspirations, Bunyan's asceticism still exhibits many of the same tendencies found, for example, in Milton: namely, an advocacy of one ascetic type drifting towards the embrace of its opposite. In particular, I argue that the allegory illustrates how self-denial and humiliation – primarily spiritual modes of asceticism – both reinvent and retain corporal austerity. One of the most striking moments in *The Pilgrim's Progress* – indeed, I think in all of early modern literature – occurs when Christian abandons his family, placing his fingers in his ears to drown out their desperate pleas. Paradoxically, Bunyan depicts this moment of exquisite selfishness as a model instance of self-denial. To become dead to one's family, and the worldliness they represent, is to deny oneself. That has monastic connotations. Christian's experience qualifies Max Weber's theory of Protestant ascetic life. Weber argues that puritans close the door on the monastery by accommodating ascetic severity to the logistics of daily living. In Bunyan's work, though, the monastery doors – and all the ascetic severity they enclose – are not shut: they still stand open in the hearts of each individual believer. They have been found closed because the monastic connotations of the self-denial and humiliation Christian undergoes remain unacknowledged. Acknowledging them is one of the ways this book argues for the broader prevalence of asceticism in early modern England.

# 1 John Donne and Asceticism

An "apostle of modern heterosexuality" (Bach), "ostensibly the paradigmatic English poet of heterosexual amour" (Saunders), and "the Heidegger of Renaissance love philosophy" (Kerrigan) are all ways in which scholars have (with varying degrees of skepticism) described John Donne.[1] While some of these statements are hyperbolic, they do not wholly belie the image modern criticism presents of Donne. When one reads that his work makes "sexual love sacred,"[2] that his poems offer radical new visions of sexuality,[3] or that he remains committed to celebrating the body,[4] these exalted titles seem fitting. Casting Donne's eroticism in such grandiose terms, or exaggerating its importance to his work, means denying other aspects of him. It liberates the critic from the unenviable task of having to reconcile (or acknowledge the irreconcilability between) Donne's erotic investments and countervailing ones. The poet of Renaissance amour also wrote that "all flesh is sinfull flesh."[5] A distrust of the flesh informs a statement in a 1620 sermon that "there is a chastity in Marriage: but the chastity of virginity, is the proper, and principal chastity."[6] For that opinion, Donne might have been branded as diabolical by a contemporary. Gervase Babington, the Calvinist bishop of Worcester, traced the elevation of virginal above married chastity to one source: the devil.[7] Moreover, Donne possesses an acute awareness of the basic problem of embodiment that produces an ascetic response. In a 1618 sermon, aptly summarizing what it means to have a body and a soul, Donne writes, "I have not body enough for my body, and I have too much body for my soul."[8] Donne's interest in austerity is not limited to topics (body and soul, marriage) that have obvious ascetic relevance. Processes of transformation – such as death's spiritualization of the body or alchemy's transmutation of metals – that refine, distill, and purify crude materials fascinate Donne.[9] In "An Elegy upon the Death of Lady Markham," he intimates a possible connection among the ascetic discipline of the flesh, alchemical transmutation, and death's sublimation of the body.[10] This chapter collects these suggestive indications of ascetic proclivity into a unified portrait of Donnean asceticism. Indeed, it argues that asceticism constitutes a coherent and under-acknowledged component of his work.[11] There are traces of asceticism even in the characteristic features of Donne's thought scholars associate with sexual modernity.

One of the reasons adduced for that modernity is Donne's treatment of the relationship between body and soul.[12] Some scholars argue that his work depicts a holistic or symbiotic relationship between them.[13] Charis Charalampous contends that the poetry imagines "an ideal union between mind and body, between the spiritual and corporeal."[14] Siobhán Collins discerns that union in "Metempsychosis," a poem that invites "readers to contemplate the relation between, and the mutual interdependence of, body and soul."[15] Ramie Targoff's *John Donne, Body and Soul* makes the most comprehensive argument on behalf of that mutuality. "Donne's expression of his belief in the mutual necessity of body and soul," Targoff writes, "and his obsessive imagining of their parting, is the most continuous and abiding feature of his collected work."[16] This body and soul dynamic holds the danger of imputing to Donne's work an integrated subjectivity that affirms modern attitudes towards sexual pleasure and the body: what is pleasurable for the body is good for the soul.[17]

At times, Donne does offer a fairly positive appraisal of body and soul relations. A sermon from 1622 states, "man is not all soule, but a body too; and, as God hath married them together in thee, so hath he commanded them mutuall duties towards one another."[18] Rather than this mutuality leading away from asceticism and towards sexual futurity, the sentiment enables Donne to enjoin a new form of spiritual monasticism on his auditory. The text of the sermon is John 1:8 ("He was not that Light, but was sent to bear witness of that Light").[19] While discussing John the Baptist's existence in the wilderness, Donne maintains that it "does not imply an abandoning of society, and mutuall offices, and callings in the world, but onely informes us, that every man is to have a Desert in himself, a retiring into himself."[20] The solitude and retirement that were obtained by physical isolation in a monastery are now available through spiritual separation from the world. Too vehemently traducing the body would affirm traditional monasticism. In this instance, mutuality between body and soul serves an ascetic end.

Often, that mutuality turns into outright enmity between body and soul. In "The Anniversary," Donne describes the body as a grave for the soul (20), a description implicit when bodies "like sepulchral statues lay" in "The Ecstasy" (18).[21] Imprisonment represents one of his favourite metaphors for the dynamic between body and soul.[22] It seems facetious to attribute mutuality to the relation between prison and prisoner. For the soul, the body constitutes "Prisons of flesh" ("Metempsychosis," 67). In "To the Countess of Bedford" ("To've written then"), an analogy reckons that "As men to our prisons now, souls to us are sent" (59). To compliment the extraordinary example of Elizabeth Drury, Donne imagines that her "fair body no such prison was" for the soul (*Second Anniversary*, 221). If that seems to yearn for a mutuality between the body and soul, the *Second Anniversary* soon frustrates such a desire, concluding that Drury must simply have been made of two souls (503). The enmity Donne frequently represents between the body and soul explains why, in the stanza on the Holy Ghost in "A Litany," he even tolerates maiming one's flesh (26). As the example of maiming suggests, Donne locates in soul and body relations – whether agreeable as in the 1622 sermon or tumultuous as in "A Litany" – an ascetic imperative. The interplay between body and soul strikes Donne as inescapably ascetic. Dissolving that interplay in a too perfect union obviates the relationship's richly ascetic character. More generally, it obfuscates the presence of asceticism in Donne's work.

The rest of this chapter examines asceticism's influence on Donne by focusing on his three marriage sermons, his decision not to remarry after the death of his wife, and a poem he writes to Edward Tilman after Tilman's ordination. This period, dating from roughly 1615, witnesses an intensification of Donne's ascetic views. The marriage sermons leave open-ended – in ways that contrast with other Protestants – the mortifications that individuals can employ to remain in an unmarried state. Donne's sonnet on his wife's death ("Since She Whom I Loved"), along with Izaak Walton's description of Donne's widowhood, highly value the single life and monasticism. "To Mr Tilman after he had Taken Orders" combines the mortifying intensity of the marriage sermons and a valorization of the single life by alluding to the ascetic requirements of ordination and by imagining a form of procreation outside of sex and marriage. In total, these works demonstrate Donne's commitment to asceticism and its ability to elevate the devotional life.

## I Trying a Little Longer

Several commentators have noted the ascetic character of Donne's three marriage sermons (delivered between 1619 and 1627). While discussing the Nethersole sermon, James Grantham Turner observes that "Donne thus appears to stand in sharp contrast to the 'Puritan' defenders of companionate marriage."[23] Elizabeth M.A. Hodgson perceives not just an anti-puritan severity, but an anti-Protestant one: "The historical argument that Reformed theology made wives, marriage and family life redemptive to replace the Catholic dependence on a salvific priesthood is hardly tenable in light of Donne's marriage sermons."[24] Achsah Guibbory also perceives marriage's lack of redemptive potential for Donne. In comparison with Miltonic sexuality, Guibbory finds that in the sermons "Donne has come out poorly as a conservative exponent of patriarchy, emphasizing wifely submission and even at moments valuing celibacy over marriage."[25] For Ralph Houlbrooke, the attitude in the sermons that could give rise to such a valuation consists of the following: "while marriage is honourable, and indeed an obligation for those who do not have the special gift of chastity, those who can contain themselves should remain single."[26] This section contributes to the study of asceticism in Donne's marriage sermons by uncovering the controversial potential of three of their central themes: one, that continence could be obtained through effort; two, that limitations need not be placed on the strenuous efforts employed; and three (the logical corollary of one and two), that marriage has a limited applicability. These themes illustrate the transgressive nature of the asceticism the sermons advocate.

At a sermon preached at Sir Francis Nethersole's marriage (1619/1620), Donne expounds on Genesis 2:18 ("And the Lord God said, It is not good that the man should be alone"). While considering to whom God's pronouncement applies, Donne references Jesus' observation that some make themselves eunuchs for the kingdom of heaven (Matthew 19:12):

> That some make themselves Eunuchs for the kingdome of heaven: that is, the better to un-entangle themselves from those impediments, which hinder them in the way to heaven, they abstaine from mariage; and let them that can receive it, receive it. Now certainly few try whether they can receive this, or no. Few strive, few fast, few pray for the gift of continency; few are content with that incontinency which they have, but are sorry they can expresse no more incontinency.[27]

Anthony Wotton, in arguing that marriage "is simply better then virginitie," asserts "that it belongs to the perfection of humaine nature."[28] How fallen it is for Donne, where marriage occupies the place of impediment, hindrance, and entanglement. Some unkindness towards matrimony also surfaces in Donne's attitude towards chastity as a gift. At 1 Corinthians 7:7, Paul counsels, "for I would that all men were even as I myself. But every man hath his proper gift of God, one after this manner, and another after that." While accepting that chastity is a gift, Donne still concludes that not enough effort is put into attempting to abstain from marriage: "Few strive, few fast, few pray for the gift of continency."[29] In drawing that conclusion, Donne ignores a default position Protestants adopted while deflecting passages such as 1 Corinthians 7 from seeming to counsel the broad applicability of the single life. While Paul wishes that all men were single, he accepts that "every man hath his proper gift." If the single life is a gift from God, then it may not be in one's power to obtain it. Are not gifts *given* and not laboriously worked for?

The French Calvinist Pierre Du Moulin writes about this issue in *The accomplishment of the prophecies* (1613):

> To urge this yet further we aske if this continent virginitie be the gift of God, or whether it be in our owne power, Bellarmine answers that it is truely the gift of God and yet neverthelesse that it is in our owne power. Which is a plaine contradiction; for if God give it us then is it not in our power, seeing that wee doe not carry the key of his gifts, and that his goods are not at our disposall.[30]

Du Moulin's assertion that chastity is not "in our owne power" echoes the claims of many writers that its obtainment is not a matter of free will.[31] The emphasis on depravity in Reformed religion, Peter Marshall reminds us, suggested "celibacy [was] psychologically impossible for all except a small minority."[32] While Du Moulin rejects the obtainability of chastity because it is God's gift, William Perkins questions that obtainability by taxonomizing God's gifts. In *Christian oeconomie*, Perkins considers the proposition that "he that doth earnestly and from his heart, crave the gift of continencie, God will give it him, and therfore he need not marrie." By way of an answer, Perkins posits "Generall" and "Proper Generall" gifts of God. Continence falls into the latter category. These proper gifts "are given only to some certaine men" and "though they bee often and earnestly asked, yet they are seldome or never granted unto some men."[33] Donne would not claim that single chastity represents an obtainable goal for everyone; it is not just a matter of willpower. But his urging a more strenuous application of the will to resolve chastity's obtainability – "Few strive, few fast, few pray" – does not conform with those who hold single life to be a gift or a remote possibility.

A sermon preached at the marriage of Margaret Washington (1621) illustrates the extent to which Donne finds chastity obtainable. In this sermon, and rather remarkably, Donne adopts an approving attitude towards vows of virginity.

> When men have made vows to abstain from mariage, I would they would be content to try a little longer then they doe, whether they could keep that

> vow or no: And when men have consecrated themselves to the service of God in his Church, I would they would be content to try a little farther then they doe, whether they could abstain or no: But to dissolve mariage made after such a Vow, or after Orders, is still to separate those whom God hath not separated.[34]

Here, Donne speaks to both lay and clerical estates. By adding the proviso regarding the dissolution of marriage after a vow or ordination, Donne reflects a century's worth of Protestant and Roman Catholic disagreement on the subject: he toes a Protestant party line. That only softens the blow. Those trying longer and farther have made vows "whether they could abstain or no." Such vows represent a major site of contention between the Roman and Protestant churches over the obtainability of chastity. Calvin criticizes those who "promise to God perpetuall virginitie, as though they had bargained with God before, that he should deliver them from nede of mariage."[35] God's omnipotence, and man's depravity, combine to produce an even stronger denunciation of presumptive vows in Calvin's sermons on Deuteronomy: "Therefore it is a divelishe arrogancie in a man, to presume that hee hath in him selfe and as it were in his owne sleeve the power of absteyning from marriage. And if hee make a vowe thereof, it is all one as if hee did openlie defie GOD, and say, hee passeth not for him."[36] For Calvin, Donne commits two errors: one, he assumes that the power to contain resides in man; and two, based upon the faulty assumption, he makes a vow out of it, adding insult to injury.

Donne's enthusiasm for the obtainability of chastity in the Nethersole and Washington sermons leads him to tolerate intense measures to maintain it. A sermon preached at the marriage of the Earl of Bridgewater's daughter (1627) recommends "Disciplines, and Mortifications" for those attempting to remain continent.

> For Continency is Privilegium, a Privilege; that is, Privata lex; when it is given, it becomes a law too; for he to whom God gives the gift of Continency, is bound by it: it is Privata lex, a Law, an Obligation upon that particular man; And then Privilegium, is Privatio Legis, it is a dispensation upon that Law, which without that privilege, and dispensation would binde him; so that all those, who have not this privilege, this dispensation, this continency, by immediate gift from God, or other medicinall Disciplines, and Mortifications, (which Disciplines and Mortifications, every state and condition of life is not bound to exercise, because such Mortifications as would overcome their Concupiscences, would also overcome all their naturall strength, and make them unable to doe the works of their callings) all such are bound by the generall law to mary.[37]

Donne qualifies these disciplines by observing that "every state and condition of life is not bound to exercise" them, and that those performing them should not be "unable to doe the works of their callings."[38] George Downame, in *The Christians sanctuarie* (1604), allows for men and women to engage in moral or chaste fasts that "endevour to subdue and chastise their bodies." He cautions, though, that whoever uses "fasting and abstinence" to maintain his single life should avoid "shortning his dayes, and making himselfe unapt for the duties of his calling, and unfit for the service of the Church or common-wealth."[39] Andrew Willet, in *Synopsis papismi*, also worries about exercises designed to preserve the chastity of single life that prevent vocational duties. Monastic exercises, such as covering the body with ice and snow and self-flagellation, do not "subdue and tame the bodie, but … destroy and kill the bodie, and make it unfit for other dueties. The scripture prescribeth no other meanes but prayer and fasting, and labour in our vocation." The limitations that Donne, Downame, and Willet impose on the means to obtain chastity perform two important functions. One, these limitations avoid expressing a too sanguine view about the obtainability of chastity that would be uninformed by Reformed arguments asserting its difficulty or impossibility. For instance, Willet employs the proper gift reasoning about chastity that Perkins espouses.[40] And two, these limitations imposed on the means to obtain chastity guard against the Roman Catholic penchant for austerity. What is significant, then, is that in the Nethersole and Washington sermons, Donne fails to include them.

In the Nethersole sermon, Donne bemoans that "few strive, few fast, few pray for the gift of continency; few are content with that incontinency which they have, but are sorry they can expresse no more incontinency." Here, the intensity of the means employed to strive for single chastity and to abstain from marriage remains unremarked: it is essentially open-ended. The Washington sermon also contains a robust conception of how one might remain single. In addition to the excerpt quoted previously, Donne discusses the matter while interpreting Paul's "better to marry than to burn" (1 Corinthians 7:9):

> As we consider it the first way, In ustionem, every heating is not a burning; every naturall concupiscence does not require a mariage; nay every flaming is not a burning; though a man continue under the flame of carnall tentation, as long as S. Paul did, yet it needs not come presently to a Sponsabo, I will mary. God gave S. Paul other Physick, Gratia mea sufficit, grace to stand under that tentation; And S. Paul gave himself other Physick, Contundo corpus, convenient disciplines to tame his body. These will keep a man from burning; for Vri est desideriis vinci, desideria pati, illustris est, & perfecti; To be overcome by our concupiscences, that

is to burn, but to quench that fire by religious ways, that is a noble, that is a perfect work.[41]

Quenching the fires of the body stands in Donne's estimation as a noble and perfect work. To explain how to quench those fires, Donne offers the example of Paul. The apostle employs "Physick" and "convenient disciplines to tame his body." The "convenient disciplines" recall the "Disciplines and Mortifications" of the Bridgewater sermon. In that sermon, however, Donne limits bodily disciplines to those that do not affect one's calling: "(which Disciplines and Mortifications, every state and condition of life is not bound to exercise ... )." The above quotation offers no such qualification; it does not limit the severity of disciplines employed through a consideration of vocation.[42] To account for this discrepancy between sermons, we can consider how the Washington sermon interprets Paul's remark that it is "better to marry than to burn."

What does it mean to burn? For Theodore Beza, in *A briefe and piththie summe of the Christian faith* (1565), it means being "drawen to evyll thoughtes."[43] In *A booke of notes and common places* (1581), John Merbecke uses Beza's quotation as an epigraph to a chapter on matrimony. In contrast with Beza, Merbecke decides that marriage "is ordained to avoid lusts forbidden in the scripture."[44] Burning means, therefore, not *avoiding* lusts. Avoidance of lust versus being actively "drawen" to it is the standard Merbecke applies for entering into marriage. That places the marital threshold lower than Beza does, with the avoidance of temptation exchanged for compulsion. It is certainly harder to avoid temptation than to resist feeling compelled by it. In short, Merbecke gives the lie to Andrew Willet's attempt to refute the criticism that Protestants think "to burne, is nothing else but to be tempted, because they [Protestants] would easilie picke quarrels to marrie."[45] By contrast, Donne demands a higher threshold for marriage. Instead of broadly applying the directive of "better to marry than to burn," so that matrimony seems like a universal necessity, Donne shrinks it. While "every heating is not a burning" seems eminently reasonable, "every flaming" not being a burning heightens the threshold of marital necessity considerably. One must endure greater heat without getting out of the fire. The temperature of Donne's burning is hotter than most and the "convenient disciplines" more rigorous as a result. Burning's low bar could mean marriage's near-universal applicability and little need for intense disciplines. Merbecke, setting the bar low, writes about 1 Corinthians 7 that Paul "biddeth them to marrie, he biddeth them not to fast, nor to labour, nor yet to weare haire to chasten their bodyes, but alonely to marry."[46] For Merbecke, Paul's counsel to marry is patent and should not be deferred through exertions such as fasting, labour, and hair shirts. Though the Bridgewater sermon also employs Merbecke's cautious approach to Pauline austerity, Donne's Nethersole and Washington sermons come, we have seen, to the opposite conclusions about the obtainability of chastity and the efforts that should be expended in its obtainment. The Nethersole and Washington sermons set the bar for burning quite high, rendering dubious the obviousness of Merbecke's "alonely to marry."

The source of austerity in the marriage sermons lies, of course, in the various scriptural passages and theological propositions they explicate. But it also lies outside of them. To understand the asceticism of the marriage sermons, we must examine the asceticism of John Donne.

## II "A Voluntary Assurance"

On 15 August 1617, Ann Donne died after giving birth to a stillborn child, the couple's twelfth. She was 33. Izaak Walton offers this account of her death and Donne's reaction in his *Lives* (1675).[47]

> Immediately after his return from Cambridge, his wife died; leaving him a man of a narrow unsetled estate, and (having buried five) the careful father of seven children then living, to whom he gave a voluntary assurance, never to bring them under the subjection of a step-mother; which promise he kept most faithfully, burying with his tears, all his earthly joys in his most dear and deserving wives grave; and betook himself to a most retired and solitary life.
>
> In this retiredness, which was often from the sight of his dearest friends, he became crucified to the world, and all those vanities, those imaginary pleasures that are daily acted on that restless stage; and, they were as perfectly crucified to him.[48]

Walton's description of Donne the widower has a number of ascetic implications. These sentences describe an oath Donne makes to his children and his adherence to it over and above his emotional and physical desires. In the sonnet "Since She Whom I Loved" (to be discussed shortly), it is clear that the flesh still retains an allure for Donne. The 44-year-old Donne is not like the impotent hypocrite of one of the sermons: "chastity is not chastity in an old man, but a disability to be unchast; and therefore thou dost not give God that which thou pretendest to give, for thou hast no chastity to give him."[49] Walton's use of the word "subjection" hints at overcoming bodily and emotional desires. In Paul's first letter to the Corinthians, he writes, "but I keep under my body, and bring it into subjection" (1 Corinthians 9:27). Donne's choice against remarriage exemplifies such bodily subjection. Moreover, as Walton expressly connects Donne's "retiredness" to Paul's letter to the Galatians, he awakens the Pauline potential of "subjection." In Galatians, Paul writes, "but God forbid that I should glory, save in the cross of our Lord Jesus Christ, by whom the world is crucified unto me, and I unto the world" (6:14). In Walton's account, Donne's removal from the world results in crucifixion to it. That has a monastic ring to it. Walton does provide a way to understand this removal as not necessarily physical: it is mental and spiritual death to "vanities" and "imaginary pleasures." Nonetheless, a sense of real physical displacement informs his observation that Donne "was often from the sight of his dearest friends." Donne is not, of course, removing himself to a monastery, but "solitary" and "retirement" are two words redolent of the monastic life.

William Perkins's exegesis of the same scriptural passage reveals its potential for legitimizing monasticism, a potential that Walton does not entirely avoid. Perkins identifies the directive of Galatians 6:14 as the following: "To be crucified to the world, is to be dead unto it, to despise and contemne it, to count all the glorie of it to be no better then dongue, in respect of Christ and his righteousnes, as Paul did, Phil. 3. 8." He cautions, though, as to the interpretive license one should give this passage: "Thirdly, that to be crucified to the world, is not to professe monasticall life, and to be shut up in a Monastery: but to renounce the world, and the corruptions that are therein, both in affection of hart, and practise of life."[50] Perkins carefully eschews the potential of Galatians to redound to the credit of monasticism. While the phrase "practise of life" countenances some of the physical removal Walton mentions, Perkins emphasizes a spiritual and emotional crucifixion, one that is primarily located in an "affection of hart." This crucifixion "wean[s] our affections from the love of this world"; it mortifies "our own wicked wils" and "carnall reason"; and it is resident in those who "*feele* the power of the spirit of Christ crucifying the flesh in them, with the affections and lusts" (my emphasis).[51] Perkins orients Galatians 6:14 inwards and towards the spirit.

Walton partly shares that orientation (i.e., "vanities" and "imaginary pleasures"). What he does not share, though, is Perkins's explicit disavowal of how this scriptural passage might be used to support characteristic features of the monastic life (solitude and retirement). Where Perkins limits the physical ascetic implications of Galatians, Walton does not. This means that solitude, retirement, and a refusal to marry lead to the advanced spiritual state of Galatians. On the issue of spiritual and/or physical monasticism, the variance between Walton and Perkins is, admittedly, slight. But it nonetheless indicates that a member of Donne's congregation of St. Dunstan-in-the-West, his first biographer, and a good friend (close enough that some conjecture he was at

Donne's bedside when he died) conceived of his widowhood in terms that credit monasticism (*ODNB*).

The monastic connotations of Donne's widowhood raise one final issue, and it is especially provoked by the Washington sermon's tolerance of vowed virginity. Does the "voluntary assurance" suggest a vowed commitment to the unmarried life? In *Synopsis papismi*, Willet discusses the psychology of votarists, and some of his observations apply to Donne:

> This is meant onely of those that have the gift of continencie, who, if they be sure they have received it, may vow and purpose single life: but without such assurance no man can vow continencie lawfully. Secondly, but as for meriting, it commeth neither by being maried or unmaried, but is the free gift of God through Christ.[52]

Willet's admonition that "without such assurance no man can vow continencie" recalls Donne's "voluntary assurance," but with one major difference. For Willet, that assurance originates with God, since continence is the "free gift of God through Christ." In Walton, it is Donne who assures. Of course, that assurance might be the product of rigorous soul-searching in which Donne found continence to be God's will, but no such explanation appears. The fact that many authors go out of their ways to identify the divine source of such an assurance makes the omission conspicuous. Moreover, the subjection and monastic withdrawal in Walton's account suggest the exertion of strenuous effort that could tilt the scale in favour of personal resolution. Arduous striving obtains single chastity; it is not just a gift from God. In this reading, the assuredness of Donne's "voluntary assurance" smacks of a vow (Walton does call it a "promise"), and "voluntary" strikes both a volitional and confident note. These constitute a pair of presumptions – that chastity lies in our power and that we can be so sure of ourselves – Protestants often accused votaries of making. Donne exhibits those presumptions in both his personal life and tolerance of vowed virginity in the sermons.

A clue as to why Donne risks the assuredness of such votive presumptions lies in the sonnet he wrote in response to his wife's death. "Since She Whom I Loved" (ca. 1617–1619) displays an admiration for the holiness of the unmarried life that is apparent as the poem considers the relation between matrimony and devotion to God. It ultimately concludes that marriage affords less of an opportunity to serve God in prayer.

> Since she whom I loved hath paid her last debt
> To nature, and to hers and my good is dead,
> And her soul early into Heaven ravishèd,

Wholly in heav'nly things my mind is set.
Here, the admiring her my mind did whet
To seek thee, God: so streams do show the head.
But though I've found thee, and thou my thirst hath fed,
A holy thirsty dropsy melts me yet.
But why should I beg more love, whenas thou
Dost woo my soul, for hers off'ring all thine?
And dost not only fear lest I allow
My love to saints and angels, things divine,
But in thy (tender) jealousy dost doubt
Lest the world, flesh, yea, Devil, put thee out? (1–14)

A coldness chills the line "to hers and my good is dead." As Robbins notes, with a trace of disbelief, "this phrase must signify that her death profits both of them: she is in bliss, he is freed from earthly love."[53] The speaker may be trying to put a positive spin on things, but the preternatural effort devolves into the merely unnatural: it verges on unfeeling. Yes, nothing compares to God's love; and yes, she is in heaven. But is the speaker not a bit too easily consoled by these perfunctory rehearsals of Christian consolation? Is not a *de rigueur* recognition of their inability to console part of the affective power of their consolation? Paradoxically, comfort derives from the consolations' inefficacy: it highlights the specialness of the individual lost. Instead of indicating irreparable loss, the forcefulness and clarity of line four – "Wholly in heav'nly things my mind is set" – comes as a sigh of relief. It makes whole the sinuous dependent clauses that begin the poem, freeing the speaker from the contingencies (grammatical and personal) that lines 1–3 contain. Liberation from a typological system of mere approximation also informs this sense of relief. Donne acknowledges embracing the conventional typology, in which earthly marriage between spouses serves as a type for Christ's eventual betrothal to the soul: "Here, the admiring her my mind did whet/To seek thee, God" (5–6). Through typology, the speaker finds God. After the death of his wife, however, the level of intimacy that the typological understanding of earthly marriage afforded now strikes him as inadequate: "But though I've found thee, and thou my thirst hath fed,/A holy thirsty dropsy melts me yet" (7–8). Marriage enabled God to find Donne; the conclusion of his earthly marriage enables God to woo him: "But why should I beg more love, whenas thou/Dost woo my soul, for hers off'ring all thine?" (9–10). Really, what hope does earthly love have when one becomes the object of a wooing (and jealous) deity? The hopelessness underscores how feeble the typological interpretation of earthly love now seems for Donne and what a distant relationship with God it provided.

As the poem turns from octave to sestet, formal and thematic features further emphasize its devaluation of earthly love.[54] The transition from the octave to the sestet seems less like a turn and more like more of the same. The coordinating conjunction that inaugurates the volta ("But") also occurs in the last two lines of the octave: "But though I've found thee, and thou my thirst hath fed,/A holy thirsty dropsy melts me yet" (7–8). An insignificant volta structurally affirms the patent obviousness of lines nine and ten: anti-climax represents a structural form of presupposition. To present the proposition that divine love brooks no competitors – and that it has no substitutes, typological or otherwise – might be daft at best, blasphemous at worst. A volta that fails to turn also suggests the poem has a coherence of meaning, one traceable from the bloodless "to hers and my good is dead" to its conclusion. Indeed, the poem concludes by expressing not just a competition between earthly and divine love, but a kind of antagonism: "Lest the world, flesh, yea, Devil, put thee out."[55] Earthly love – and, more specifically, remarriage – becomes a conduit through which these sinful phenomena can enter into Donne's life. God fears that Donne's begging more love might lead to the world, flesh, and devil gaining a foothold. That does not offer an especially flattering view of marriage, but it does hold the single life in special esteem. The esteem offers evidence for Donne's "voluntary assurance," and why he risks the assuredness of votive presumptions.

Other writers do not share Donne's belief in marriage impeding devotion. William Perkins resists the notion that the unmarried life has a greater potential for prayer during his interpretation of 1 Corinthians 7:34 ("The unmarried woman careth for the things of the Lord"):

> Obiect. 2. 1. Cor. 7. 32. He that is unmarried careth for the things of the Lord, how he may please the Lord; but the married person careth for the things of the world. Answ. The place is not generally to be understood of all, but indefinitely of those married persons that are carnall and fleshly. And he that is married, is to bee so carefull for the things of the world, as that he ought, and may have also a special regard of those things that concerne God and his kingdome.[56]

From the perspective of Perkins, the notion that the married are less equipped for a life of prayerful piety relates only to those "married persons that are carnall and fleshly." Paul's observation is not meant to be applied generally but particularly. This is a method Protestants often use to contest what they regard as the Roman Catholic extrapolation from the particular to the general. Without that limitation in place, this passage could support the superiority of virginity to marriage or even a universal Christian directive to the single life. With remarkable ingenuity, Perkins turns Corinthians inside out. Because the married "ought" to be "so carefull for the things of the world," they might end up having "a special regard" of that which relates to God. In pure Pauline fashion, weakness becomes strength. Solicitude about the potential for the married life to lead away from God results in it leading back towards Him. While some writers assert that marriage is not inimical to holiness and heavenly cares, Perkins goes – subtly – beyond that, implying that marriage is especially well-suited to godly concerns.[57] It certainly does not provide an opportunity for the world, flesh, and devil to gain entry into one's life.

So far, this section has sought to show the asceticism of Donne's widowhood by examining the monastic connotations of his "voluntary assurance" and the holiness of unmarried life in "Since She Whom I Loved." While some traces of austere sentiment are visible throughout Donne's work in how he configures body and soul relations, his ascetic views intensify after ordination and especially after the death of his wife. That intensification can be glimpsed by contrasting those ascetic views with how Donne treats monastic virginity in an earlier work. In a stanza on the virgins in "A Litany" (1608), the poem ostensibly offers praise of the virgins. It is highly ambivalent praise at best.

> Thy cold, white, snowy nunnery,
> Which, as thy mother, their high abbess, sent
> Their bodies back again to thee
> As thou hadst lent them, clean and innocent:
> Though they have not obtained of thee
> That or thy Church or I
> Should keep as they our first integrity,
> Divorce thou sin in us, or bid it die,
> And call chaste widowhood virginity. (100–108)

In *The femall glory* (1635), Anthony Stafford takes Donne's image of a "cold, white, snowy nunnery" and runs with it towards uncomplicated praise of monasticism: "You who have vow'd virginity mentall, and corporall, you shall not onely have ingresse here, but welcome. Approach with Comfort, and kneele downe before the Grand white Immaculate Abbesse of your snowy Nunneries, and present the all-saving Babe in her Armes with due veneration."[58] Stafford's praise is exuberant; Donne's nuns are frigid. In their chill, they are quite close to Donne's description of monks in "To the Honourable Lady the Lady Carey" (1612):

> So cloist'ral men, who in pretence of fear
> All contributions to this life forbear,
> Have virtue in melàncholy, and only there. (25–28)

The virtue of these monks derives from an excess of melancholy or black bile. Black bile is a humor often described as cold.[59] The nuns' frigidity, which some might mistake for sexual purity, is a consequence of humoral excess. This is not virtue but physiology. The nuns take credit of conscience for biological determinism.[60] "A Litany" does not go quite so far in confronting the virgins, but the poem treats them with suspicion.

Skepticism of the virgins explains the phrase "Though they have not obtained of thee"; this is a curiously negative way to put an intended compliment. "Obtain" means, of course, "procure." It can also mean to "attain," to "prevail upon," or to "win" some kind of victory.[61] These senses all seem latent, and they deflate the line at its moment of potential praise. Not to prevail upon God sounds quite alienating, almost like estrangement. A.J. Smith glosses these lines as "they have not obtained from Christ the grace that would have preserved either his Church or the poet in their native singleness, or purity."[62] Under any circumstances, can we imagine *not* receiving grace in 17th-century England being a good thing, and as not exposing a profound inefficacy in the devotional activity that seeks it? That question points to the lines' deeply ambivalent attitude towards vowed virginity.

The discomfort with physical virginity reaches its peak when "A Litany" redefines it: "Divorce thou sin in us, or bid it die,/And call chaste widowhead virginity." The lines refer to the idea that every faithful believer is married to Christ. As part of that marriage, Christ divorces the believer from his/her previous betrothal to the world, lust, and sin. Thus, Donne envisions a version of virginity within marriage. Moreover in calling something that is patently not virginity "virginity," he further advances a conception of the single life that is spiritual rather than physical.[63] By arrogating to spiritual purity the name of virginity, the attitude displays a marked indifference towards the condition's anatomical reality. In a stanza on virgins who understand their virginity as both a spiritual and physical condition, to redefine virginity as spiritual has an air of presumption and betrays a certain irreverence towards sexual abstinence. The redefinition shows the desirability of virginity while at the same time cheapening it. As the stanza broadens access to what makes the virgins uniquely holy, virginity loses some of its luster. "A Litany" coarsens its own praise of virginity.

The same self-defeating booby traps – and the negative attitude towards austerity they indicate – are not evident in Walton's statement about Donne's "voluntary assurance" or in "Since She Whom I Loved." Walton depicts Donne the widower in monastic terms, and Donne's celebration of the single life's aptitude for devotion employs an argument to which proponents of virginity frequently resorted. Due to tragic circumstances, but also due to the increasing openness towards asceticism those circumstances produced, Donne would do more than *call* chaste widowhood virginity in 1617. But it is not only tragic circumstances that force Donne's hand. As the next section proposes, ordination means both something transformative and difficult. The role of being God's ambassador entails duties of austere self-regulation. A full consideration of that austerity challenges conventional ways in which scholars coordinate Donne's amorous and religious poetry.

## III Jack Donne, John Donne, and Asceticism

In an article on the relationship between Donne's erotic poetry and religious verse, Paul R. Sellin urges "bridging the troublesome cleft between the profane verse of Jack the rake and the sacred vein of John the divine that has haunted Donne studies from the days of Walton to the present."[64] Also seeking to bridge that cleft, Achsah Guibbory employs Donne's Arminian theology to demarcate a "fine, if unexpected, symmetry" between the erotic verse and sermons.[65] Why, I wonder, does this cleft require bridging? Why does Donne scholarship need to exorcize the ghost of a broken subjectivity that has haunted its inquiries since Walton? Asceticism documents a body in revolt against its soul, a self in need of extirpation. Broken subjectivities are its métier. The following pages do not seek to mend the Jack Donne and Dr. Donne divide. In fact, they endeavour to widen it through an interpretation of Donne's 1618 poem "To Mr Tilman after he had Taken Orders." In many ways, this poem serves as a companion piece to the 1617 sonnet; both recount ascetic imperatives that issue from personal and professional change. Whereas "Since She Whom I Loved" recounted the ascetic intensity accompanying the personal loss of his wife, the poem to Tilman depicts the demanding austerity ordination entails. Ordination results in spiritual transformation of the kind that can accommodate the dichotomy between Jack Donne and Dr. Donne. In outlining the asceticism of the ordained life, "To Mr Tilman after he had Taken Orders" alludes to "The Canonization." The consequence of that allusion is not an unexpected symmetry or a bridged cleft, but a revision and superseding of the earlier poem by the sober and grave divinity of the clerical life.

"To Mr Tilman after he had Taken Orders" is intensely interested in how ordination has changed Tilman. Lines 5–22 propose several models for that change. Does Tilman feel "New thoughts" and "new motions" (7–8)? Has he, like a cargo ship, exchanged one set of goods for another (9–12)? Is he the same materials, but a new coin minted out of them (13–18)? And, finally, has he become like a newly embellished painting

(19–22)? None of these changes represents a full transformation. Indeed, the poem articulates some unease with this lack of total change during the coinage analogy: "Art thou the same materials as before,/Only the stamp is changèd, but no more,/And, as new-crownèd kings alter the face/But not the money's substance, so hath grace/Changed only God's old image by creatïon/To Christ's new stamp at this thy coronatïon?" (13–18). The phrase "but no more" registers potential dissatisfaction with the transformation; *only* the stamp has changed, as if that were not enough. Donne wants evidence of a renewal that surpasses the merely superficial. As the speaker becomes increasingly desperate and insistent, the inability of the proposed models to express Tilman's conversion experience is apparent: "Dear, tell me where thy purchase lies, and show/What thy advantage is, above, below" (23–24). Donne asks for evidence of a commitment and change in devotional life greater than the proffered examples can supply. It is one that exceeds the expressive capacity of speech: "But if thy gaining do surmount expressïon,/Why doth the foolish world scorn that professïon/Whose joys pass speech?" (25–27). *This* is what the speaker wants: an attestation beyond speech, evidence impossible to give, change so big language cannot quantify it. The rehearsal of various models for Tilman's change seems, in retrospect, perfunctory: those were not the questions (or the answers) the speaker was interested in. Not only do those models of transformation represent a lack of total alteration, but, should Tilman have answered in the affirmative (yes, it is like the ship metaphor), that would not adequately rebuke the "lay scornings" (3) of the priestly life.

During the question "Dear, tell me where thy purchase lies," "purchase" hints at the intensity of the commitment and conversion experience the speaker longs to attribute to Tilman. "Purchase" is a striking choice. It recalls the mercantile and coinage metaphors of lines 11–16, but it also conjures visions of indulgences, venality, and the worst excesses of Roman Catholicism. Donne must have a reason more pressing than metaphorical symmetry to play with such fire. What the poem means, and wishes to mean, by "purchase" are indicated by Thomas Becon in *A new postil* (1566): "But there is not so great vertue in a cowle, apparell, eating and faste. &c. death is not slayne herby, syn is not put asyde by this. For both they remayne under a cowle as well, as under other garmentes. But this thing is here gone about, that the heart it self may purchase a new light."[66] Becon associates "purchase" with the Roman Catholic presumption that ascetic acts such as the votive life are so exceedingly laborious and meritorious that they obtain heaven through effort. Becon repudiates the way in which an author such as Girolamo Piatti, in *The happines of a religious state* (1632), configures the relationship between ascetic works and heavenly reward. Piatti quotes

John Damascene as saying that religious people "powred forth teares, and continued in sorrow night and day to purchasse eternall comfort; they voluntarily debased themselves, that in heaven they might be exalted."[67] In contrast with Piatti, Becon denies that ascetic debasement can buy eternal comfort, contending that faith – not exertion – obtains divine favour. Donne, of course, sides with Becon over Piatti. Or does he? The inadequacy of the models proposed for Tilman's transformation yearns for the kind of strenuous exertion and supererogatory commitment Piatti's "purchase" signifies. The vainglorious presumptions of the Roman Catholic purchase, in so far as they presume merit based on arduous toil, represent a confidence and a commitment that the passivity of lines 5–22 do not. In those metaphors, Tilman remains the passive recipient of God's grace. He is a vessel who has things done to him: steel touched by a lodestone; a ship carrying new cargo; a coin stamped by a new impression; an angel painted with wings. In these examples, grace does the touching, the exchange of goods, the stamping, and the painting. "Purchase," on the other hand, longs to *do*: to participate in a process rather than observe it. "Purchase" – with its connotation of willfulness, effort, and expense – suggests a soteriology consistent with supererogatory acts, a soteriology amenable to asceticism.

Ascetic implications are also evident in the poem's attitude towards the body and sexual promiscuity:

> Would they think it well if the day were spent
> In dressing, mistressing, and compliment?
> Alas! Poor joys! But poorer men whose trust
> Seems richly placèd in refinèd dust!
> For such are clothes and beauties, which, though gay
> Are, at the best, but as sublimèd clay. (29–34)

While the poem defines "refinèd dust" and "sublimèd clay" as "clothes and beauties," a suggestion of the body is implicit. Gardner, for example, reads "beauties" as referring back to "mistressing."[68] In the stanza on the Holy Ghost in "A Litany," Donne refers to the body as "mud walls and condensèd dust" (20). In a verse epistle "To the Countess of Bedford" ("Honour is so sublime perfection"), the poem compliments the countess with the observation that, for her body, "God made better clay" (22). "Satyre I" imagines bodies as clothing for the soul – "And till our souls be unapparellèd/Of bodies, they from bliss are banishèd" (43–44) – indicating how clothing in "clothes and beauties" has a corporal association. The result of implicit reference to the body as dust, clay, and clothing is an indifference towards materiality that licenses a punitive (viz. ascetic) approach. Animosity towards those who revel in the perishability of the body and its transitory pleasures is proved, finally, by the discovery of the nugatory things in which worldly dandies expensively misplace their trust. Some irony results, perhaps even cynicism, in that these "poorer men" spend their money on trifles ("spent"). Tilman, who is not wholly liberated from a model of economic exchange, nonetheless *purchases* holiness. For him, exchange does not constitute mere wasteful expenditure. There are materialisms – such as sacred versus secular ones – that are beneficial.

An aggrieved sense of the indignities suffered by the clergy at the hands of the laity motivates the poem's exposure of the rich men's poverty. To remedy these indignities, the poem articulates a clericalism in which asceticism makes ever greater sense. The "lay scornings" of the clerical estate are first mentioned in line three, and the poem returns to the topic, often with a certain wounded bitterness: "Why do they think unfit/That gentry should join families with it?" (27–28). The "foolish world" scorns the priestly profession, and it disrespects Tilman's calling (26, 35). In response, the speaker emphasizes the nobility and dignity of the priestly life (37, 40). The noble dignity of priests even vies with that of the sovereign: "What function is so noble, as to be/Ambassador to God and Destiny;/To open life, and give kingdoms to more/Than kings give dignities: to keep Heaven's door?" (37–40).

Donne's view of the priesthood accords with the unique intercessory capacity a High Church Anglican such as Henry Hammond claims for consecrated persons. For public prayer to prevail upon God, Hammond outlines the following optimal conditions:

> For the prevailing with God, (the union of so many hearts being most likely to prevaile, and the presence of some godly, to bring downe mercies on those others, whose prayers have no promise to be heard; especially if performed by a consecrated person, whose office it is to draw nigh unto God, i. e. to offer up prayers, &c. to him, and to be the Embassadour and Messenger betweene God and Man; Gods Embassadour to the people, in Gods stead beseeching them to be reconciled; and the peoples Embassadour to God to offer up our requests for grace, pardon, mercies, to him.[69]

The union of many hearts might prevail upon God, but the chances are much better should a consecrated person be involved. Hammond's direction magnifies the consequentiality of the clergy; they serve as the ambassadors between God and humanity. By contrast, the godly writer Richard Younge widely disperses ambassadorial duties, placing them in the power of each individual believer: "Yet, because thine owne Prayer is most proper; and seeing it is the mindes Embassadour to God, and never faileth of successe, if it be fervent."[70] This is truly a priesthood of all believers. For Younge, every individual can serve as his or her own ambassador to God. That is not the case for Hammond and Donne. In order to counteract the devaluing of the clergy, "To Mr Tilman after he had Taken Orders" outlines the unique role clerics perform as intermediaries between humanity and divinity. The holiness and dignity of priests, along with the crucial soteriological functions they perform, have a clear relation to asceticism. "The paramount argument for priestly celibacy," Peter Marshall maintains, "was that it demonstrated more clearly than almost anything else the unique and superior status which belonged naturally to the consecrated person of the priest."[71] As this poem asserts the unique holiness, power, and salvific importance of priests over and against the hostile belittling of a secular world, it creates a context conducive to the link between clericalism and asceticism. Asceticism forms a bulwark against the world's depredations.

Ascetic interests – evident in the poem's clericalism, its devaluing of the body, and the connotations of "purchase" – receive their fullest expression in a startling image at the conclusion. To assert the special holiness of the clerical estate, Donne assures Tilman of his identity as a "bless'd hermaphrodite":

These are thy titles and pre-em'nences,
In whom must meet God's graces, men's offences,
And so the heavens, which beget all things here,
And th'earth our mother, which doth those things bear,
Both these in thee are in thy calling knit,
And make thee now a bless'd hermaphrodite. (49–54)

Much work has been done to explain the striking image of the hermaphrodite, with explanations as various as Renaissance love poetry, the Trinity, and the *Poetria Nova* of Geoffrey of Vinsauf.[72] While these interpretations testify to the theological, literary, and intellectual richness of "bless'd hermaphrodite," a sense of the phrase's ascetic connotation seems to have been lost in the mix. The ascetic connotation of "bless'd hermaphrodite" derives from its depiction of Tilman as another Adam. Thomas Browne, in *Pseudodoxia Epidemica* (1646), explains the scriptural interpretation of Genesis that casts Adam as hermaphroditic: "That God created man in his own Image, in the Image of God created he him, male and female created he them: applying the singular and plural unto Adam, it might denote, that in one substance, and in himself he included both sexes, which was after divided, and the female called Woman."[73] This interpretation of Genesis leads some commentators to conclude that the Fall occasioned the division of sexes and, with it, procreation. In *On the Making of Man*, the fourth-century Church Father Gregory of Nyssa writes, "for it was not when He made that which was in His own image that He bestowed on man the power of increasing and multiplying; but when He divided it by sexual distinctions, then He said, 'Increase and multiply, and replenish the earth.'"[74] In other words, as Peter Brown succinctly notes, for Gregory the division of the sexes "made sexuality possible."[75] Were it not for the Fall, "we should not have needed this form of generation by which the brutes are generated."[76] Instead, as Gregory explains, humanity would have reproduced in the manner of the angels:

> So, in the same way, if there had not come upon us as the result of sin a change for the worse, and removal from equality with the angels, neither should we have needed marriage that we might multiply; but whatever the mode of increase in the angelic nature (unspeakable and inconceivable by human conjectures, except that it assuredly exists), it would have operated also in the case of men, who were "made a little lower than the angels," to increase mankind to the measure determined by its Maker.[77]

Various Neoplatonic and Renaissance sources offer a hermaphroditic interpretation of Genesis 1:27.[78] Donne could also have encountered hermaphroditic asexuality through his vast knowledge of alchemy.[79] Cynthea Masson argues that the philosopher's stone in medieval alchemical texts "is the hermaphrodite (or 'asexual neutrality') representing human nature before the Fall."[80] Wherever Donne encountered hermaphroditic Adam, or if he arrived at it independently based on exegesis of Genesis, his image of Tilman as a hermaphrodite envisions a return to a primordial wholeness, a world before sexuality.[81] Hermaphroditism obviates the coming together of the sexes for reproductive purposes. What would the gallants who spend their time mistressing say to *this*? What, for that matter, might Jack say to Dr. Donne's discovery of reproduction without sex and without eroticism? It would surely constitute a Pyrrhic victory for scholars who wish to assert the unity of Jack and Dr. Donne to claim the relevance of Jack to this sexless, antierotic procreation. Asexual reproduction represents a fitting culmination for the clericalism that runs throughout the poem; it celebrates Tilman as another Adam. And the "bless'd hermaphrodite" constitutes, finally, another indication of the poem's investment in the ascetic responsibilities of – and the rewards attendant upon – the ordained.

The asceticism of "To Mr Tilman after he Had Taken Orders" is finally evident in its allusions to, and ultimate supersession of, the amorous poem "The Canonization" (ca. 1604). Minor argumentative and metaphoric details connect the poems. They both begin with defensive responses to the world's devaluation of the activities they describe, and they employ similar coinage metaphors.[82] On a larger, thematic level, the poems are also connected in their examination of sanctifying processes. One of Donne's interests in the poem to Tilman, we have seen, is to assert the unique holiness of the priestly profession. For Donne, that might form a natural corollary with the concept of canonization, especially considering its meaning beyond the merely hagiographical. For example, one of the sermons in the anonymous *Threnoikos* (1640) encourages imitating the sanctity of martyrs and holy men. That imitation "saints us, so that we need not be at that extreame expence and charge, which wee reade some have beene at in the Court of Rome to procure Canonization."[83] John Florio, while defining apotheosis, treats canonization and consecration as synonyms.[84] By establishing a connection with "The Canonization" through the concept of canonizing, Donne means for the mock canonization of the love poem to give place to the serious consecration of Tilman.

A sober revision of the earlier poem is also apparent in the strongest parallel between the two works. The "bless'd hermaphrodite" recalls the phoenix image in "The Canonization." In the third stanza, the speaker declares, "The phoenix riddle hath more wit/By us: we two, being one, are it./So to one neutral thing both sexes fit,/We die and rise the same, and prove/Mysterious by this love" (23–27). Neutrality in the phoenix derives from its ability to fit both sexes. Tilman's hermaphroditism resides in knitting together the masculine heavens and the feminine earth in the duties of his calling. The phoenix is also inexhaustibly prolific: "We die and rise the same," with a heavy pun on orgasm, retraction, and erection. Tilman's duties as a cleric are far from sterile: "Mary's prerog'tive was to bear Christ, so,/'Tis preachers' to convey him" (41–42). One of the meanings of "convey" is "bear," suggesting that Donne employs near-synonyms to impute some fecundity to the ministerial function.[85] Similar to the hermaphrodite, the Virgin Mary offers a sexless method of reproduction. The final way in which the hermaphrodite and phoenix are joined together revolves around the conjunction of unlikely things. In "The Canonization," it is the lovers' capacity to unite the eagle and the dove (22) that prompts the phoenix comparison. Tilman combines disparate things by forcing "God's graces, men's offences" (50) into close proximity. In Donne's "Epithalamium Made at Lincoln's Inn" (1594–1595), the other poem in his oeuvre that contains a reference to a hermaphrodite, the combination of study and play constitutes hermaphroditism: "(Of study and play made strange hermaphrodites)" (30). In sum, then, a connection between "bless'd hermaphrodite" and the phoenix proceeds from androgyny, gravidity, and the merging of dissimilarity over and above gender difference. Donne coordinates this connection precisely, so that Tilman's hermaphroditism answers – in every way – the phoenix-like lovers.

As a result of this methodical coordination, asceticism supersedes eroticism. In "The Canonization," the lovers achieve hermaphroditic status through sex; in "To Mr Tilman after he had Taken Orders," hermaphroditism obviates sex. Tilman – on his own, in the performance of his ministerial duties, and through procreation without sex – claims all the fecund mystery that, in the earlier poem, only two lovers could achieve through insatiable copulation. A continuity exists between the erotic verse and the poem to Tilman. But it is a continuity that uncovers a profound disparity between the two poems. It is disparity on the far side of continuity. Asceticism drives a wedge between Jack and Dr. Donne.

More broadly, the momentous change ordination produces, the rebuke of procreative sexuality, and the denigration of the body in "To Mr Tilman after he had Taken Orders" correspond to the ascetic implications of Donne's "voluntary assurance" and the asceticism of the marriage sermons. The intensification of asceticism that coincides with the assurance represents the kind of change in post-ordination life that the poem to Tilman envisions. The "voluntary assurance" and the supererogatory potential of "purchase" are allied in the considerable ascetic effort they expend. As the marriage sermons counsel more extreme efforts to maintain chastity, they reflect the rebuke of procreative sexuality and bodily temptations that "To Mr Tilman after he had Taken Orders" contains; they treat the body as "refinèd dust" and "sublimèd clay." Taken together, Donne's widowhood, the marriage sermons, and the poem to Tilman reflect the intensity of his ascetic feeling; they challenge his reputation as the patron saint of heterosexual love; and they complicate attempts to assert the symmetry between the libertine poems and Donne's late austerity.

# 2 *A Mask*, Asceticism, and Caroline Culture

The next two chapters focus on asceticism in the early work of John Milton. In several ways, Milton's asceticism represents a counterpoint to Donne's. Donne's personal severity intensifies following ordination; some have speculated that Milton offered his virginity as compensation for not taking orders.[1] While Donne's commitment to austerity increases after the death of his wife, the young Milton abandons an ascetic interpretation of Revelation 14:4 shortly before his first marriage.[2] For each author, compositions that celebrate sexuality and marriage have the potential to obscure each poet's interest in asceticism. Donne's erotic poetry could render an intensity of ascetic feeling (e.g., his "voluntary assurance") implausible. In the case of Milton, how could the author of *Paradise Lost* – that epic to companionate marriage – entertain any kind of virginity but the strictly pre-marital (i.e., limited and temporary)? And yet, as these chapters contend, Milton's *A MASK Presented At LUDLOW-Castle* (1634; hereafter, *A Mask*) and *Lycidas* (1637) deliberate the comparative value of physical and spiritual virginity. Rather than uniformly privileging spiritual over physical asceticism, an emphasis one might expect from Milton's reputation as a puritan, these works celebrate virginity as soteriologically significant and they conceive of asceticism in terms similar to Laudians. As a result of this similarity, the following chapters do not claim Milton as a Laudian. Nor do they try to disprove his puritanism. These chapters emphasize, instead, an uncertainty that could comprehend – at different times and to different extents – both affiliations. Miltonic asceticism often vacillates between possible conformist sympathies and contrasting reformist impulses. Scholars often make conclusions about the young Milton's religious affiliation on the basis of literary and biographical evidence, with particular attention paid to statements regarding clerical corruption, ceremonial worship, church polity, and Roman Catholicism. While asceticism by no means supplants these indices of religious affiliation, it does offer the opportunity to determine that affiliation with increasing precision, for it introduces a new metric by which to measure it.

Several previous accounts miss the opportunity for increasing precision because the confessional terms in which they discuss the topic of Miltonic asceticism are simply too large. Often, scholars treat ascetic views in Milton's work as exemplifying conflict between Roman Catholics and Protestants. The broader Reformation context is no doubt important, but the significance of Milton's ascetic attitudes is not always visible at that scale. His asceticism engages more consistently the skirmishes of *intra*-confessional conflict as opposed to the pitched battles of *inter*-confessional war. By examining these contexts, the present chapter responds to Brooke Conti's call for more attention to "the literary or intellectual origins" of asceticism in Milton's works.[3] The psychological origins of Milton's austerity,[4] the personal reasons for his ascetic predilections,[5] and even the scriptural passages influencing his approach to virginity have all been amply demonstrated by other scholars.[6] What is lacking in these accounts, though, is a sense of how the psychological origins, personal reasons, and particular exegeses engage the Laudian and puritan debate over asceticism.

The tendency to outsource Miltonic asceticism to Roman Catholic and continental sources has existed since the advent of modern interest in the topic. In a 1925 essay, James Holly Hanford considers the conclusions of *Lycidas* and "Epitaphium Damonis" and determines that the "religious rapture [of the poems] allies [Milton] for the moment with the tradition of Catholic Christianity. It does so, to be sure, only outwardly, for there is fundamental disparity between his essentially humanistic attitude and the devout asceticism of the Middle Ages. He belongs by temper and inheritance to the Renaissance."[7] The conclusions about virginity to which his own analysis leads him discomfit Hanford: "for the moment"; "it does so, to be sure, only outwardly." The discomfort derives from two sources. Hanford, and E.M.W. Tillyard after him, assume that asceticism consists only of negation; that is, it has no positive content: "What *Comus* did not do was to end the mood of youthful excitement by giving full imaginative expression to Milton's emotional life. Such an expression demanded not the exaltation of a negative virtue, but some more fervid celebration of the mystery of love."[8] For Hanford, a negative virtue such as chastity cannot fully express Milton's emotional life; it is tepid when measured against the healthy heat of mysterious love (viz. "mysterious law" [4.750]).[9] And secondly, a sense of the Middle Ages as barbarous and benighted when compared with the enlightened humanism of the Renaissance pervades Hanford's account of asceticism. He regards Milton's ecstatic virginity as Roman Catholic and medieval. To soften the blow, the medieval Catholicism is at least temporary and superficial.

Throughout Hanford's analysis, a contemporary context, both temporally (non-medieval) and geographically (non-continental) closer to Milton, clamors for attention. Hanford, as distinct from other scholars, *knows* about Laudian asceticism. To explain why Milton embraces polygamy in *De Doctrina Christiana*, Hanford reasons thusly:

> I am not disposed to take this strain [polygamy] in Milton's thought too seriously. It is for him a kind of *a fortiori* directed against the lingering tendency of men like Laud to return to an attitude regarding marriage which did violence at once to Milton's instinct and to his reason, and which he felt to be unscriptural and unprotestant. For him the married state was divinely instituted and without the shadow of a stain.[10]

Polygamy, though, surely does violence to marriage. Hanford does not consider that Milton's medieval and Roman Catholic asceticism might, even if only for the moment, ally him with someone like Laud. Such a proposition is a nonstarter for Hanford, and its dismissal (or its lack of consideration) is traceable back to the following: "The Puritanism, or more properly the liberalism, of Milton was evidently of very early growth."[11] It makes more sense to back-date Miltonic asceticism to the Middle Ages than to question his precocious puritanism.[12]

Disassociating Milton's ascetic thought from more contemporary, proximate, and exigent English sources receives its strongest expression in a 1961 article by Ernest Sirluck. He associates the young Milton's asceticism with the most flagrantly Roman Catholic of practices: vowing virginity and clerical celibacy. In the article, Sirluck maintains that Milton's decision not to take orders required sacrifice of another kind:

> The celibacy which had until recently been imposed upon the priesthood was wrong, of course. But it had nevertheless been for many ages the sacrifice demanded of those who would be God's priests. Had [Milton] taken orders as intended, he would not have been called upon to make this sacrifice. But what if he now made it voluntarily, as the symbol of his poet-priesthood?[13]

No documentary or poetic evidence exists for this vow: it amounts to an unfortunate distraction. The idea of a vow has let scholarship off too easily by framing the issue of the young Milton's asceticism in terms handily dispatched, as if the only conclusion one could draw from austerity were vowed celibacy. For example, Barbara Lewalski writes, "Milton's exaltation of virginity in 1637 does not imply that this staunch Protestant made a temporary vow of celibacy – a gesture he would surely see as popish."[14] The elision of "exaltation of virginity" with "vow of celibacy" illustrates that Miltonic asceticism has become shorthand for vowed virginity and its blatant Roman Catholicism. Sirluck's extreme claim shuts down inquiry into that "exaltation of virginity" before it even begins. As Lewalski rightly notes, that vow would have the effect of calling into doubt Milton's Protestantism, an issue that, to my knowledge, has never been seriously questioned. The prospect of a vow casts a long shadow over Milton scholarship, and chapter 3 will consider recent responses to it in the work of John Leonard and Nicholas McDowell.

The idea of Milton taking a vow of celibacy and, more largely, the Roman Catholic connotations of Miltonic asceticism have seemed implausible to many scholars. Another scholarly tradition has emerged of interpreting asceticism in both *A Mask* and Milton's early work in ways inoffensive to the author's puritanism or, even more paradoxically, as expressive of it.[15] Instead of denoting Roman Catholicism and vowed virginity, asceticism represents Milton's trenchant rebuke of the permissive court culture of Charles I and Henrietta Maria. To this end, many scholars regard the relationship between *A Mask* and Caroline masquing culture as oppositional.[16] They contend that Milton arraigns Caroline libertinism and Laudian carnality via asceticism. As Marina Leslie writes, "it was the chaste, companionate marriage rather than an austere, unyielding virginity that governed the themes of court masques and poetry prior to the civil war."[17] Milton, in choosing such a thoroughly ascetic theme for his masque, implicitly censures court culture; he "sets the Lady's chaste virginity over against the Queen's Neoplatonic mystifications of chaste marital love."[18] Milton plays one (true) chastity against an impoverished one. But that claim not only ignores the ascetic investments of both church and court, it also fails to consider that puritans would have had little sympathy for the corporal virginity Milton often celebrates in *A Mask*.[19] As with Hanford et al, the attribution of virginity to a puritan source pretermits the consideration of conformist ones.

The following pages resist ascribing asceticism in *A Mask* to either puritan opposition to the Caroline Court or a Roman Catholic practice such as vowed virginity. As the first three sections demonstrate, *A Mask* reflects intra-confessional Protestant debates about the physical and/or spiritual nature of asceticism in its depiction of virginity; it engages (with some hostility) the Reformed defense of sex and marriage; and the work refuses to grant marriage's inevitability, a concession some have found the masque's epilogue to make. These issues are, as this book argues, the unique problems of asceticism facing post-Reformation Protestantism. But while all Protestants might have faced these problems, they did not all respond alike. As section four of this chapter argues, the expression of asceticism in *A Mask* has many descriptive and mythographic similarities with Robert Crofts's *The Lover* (1638). This work fuses Neoplatonic chastity and Laudian austerity into a vision of privation and its heavenly rewards that *A Mask* also imagines.

## I Physical and Spiritual Asceticism

First performed on 29 September 1634, *A Mask* commemorates the Earl of Bridgewater's elevation to the post of Lord President of Wales.[20] The work follows the journey of three children – the Lady, the Elder Brother, and the Second Brother – as they pass through a "drear Wood" to "attend their Fathers state,/And new-entrusted Scepter" (36–37). The children's parts were played by the Earl of Bridgewater's daughter, the 15-year-old Lady Alice, and her two brothers, aged 11 and 9. While traveling through the wood, the children become separated and the Lady falls prey to the sorcerer Comus, "Of Bacchus, and of Circe born" (522). Comus immobilizes the Lady, tempting her with a "cordial Julep" (672). The two brothers, upon the instruction of an Attendant Spirit, disrupt Comus's temptation. To free the Lady from Comus's sorcery, the Attendant Spirit calls on Sabrina, a nymph and "Virgin pure" (826). The masque concludes with the presentation of the children to their father, and an epilogue that draws on the myths of Venus and Adonis and Cupid and Psyche. The structure of the masque consists of the following: an opening exposition, in which the Attendant Spirit explains the plight of the three children and the masque introduces Comus and the Lady; two central debates; the intervention of Sabrina; a rustic dance, the counterpart to an earlier anti-masque danced by Comus and his revelers; and the epilogue. In the first of the debates, the two brothers consider the power of virginity to protect their sister. A confrontation between Comus and the Lady comprises the second debate. The opening introduction of the Lady and the first debate scene illustrate how *A Mask* negotiates spiritual and physical ascetic modes.

In the Lady's first speech in the masque, she describes what reassures her when faced with the "drear Wood": "O welcom pure-ey'd Faith, white-handed Hope,/Thou hovering Angel girt with golden wings,/And thou unblemish't form of Chastity" (213–215). The address alludes to 1 Corinthians 13:13 ("And now abideth faith, hope, charity, these three; but the greatest of these is charity") with one important exception: chastity replaces charity.[21] That replacement is as much a recollection, for the word chastity visually recalls charity; the absence of the latter is mitigated by its tacit presence. A strong connection obtains between chastity and charity in *A Mask*. The connection is significant, for proponents of virginity often stress a greater capacity for charity as one of its chief commendations.

In *The pilgrime of Loreto* (1629), the Jesuit Louis Richeome describes the marriage of Joseph and Mary as "an excellent band of Fayth, Charity, and inviolable Virginity." He continues to exhort Christian women to profess the single life, "to marry your selves to God, to give him your body and soule." As a consolation for not having children, Richeome contends that the virgins will accrue "a thousand goodly workes that shall accompany you above, as an honourable and immortall posterity."[22] The "goodly workes" demonstrate virginity's potential for charitable deeds. While it may not produce children, it does propagate charity. As Richeome illustrates, the maintenance of physical virginity and the performance of good works both belong to a theology that emphasizes an individual's ability to contribute to salvation. Not surprisingly, Laudians, many of them Arminians, also emphasize the conjunction between virginity and charity. In *The femall glory* (1635), Anthony Stafford celebrates the Virgin Mary as a "union of superlatives. Charity, obedience, pietie, virginity, all were in her at height."[23] During his discussion of "Acts of virginal chastity" in *The rule and exercises of holy living* (1650), Jeremy Taylor contends, "virgins have a peculiar obligation to charity: for this is the virginity of the soul; as puritie, integrity, and separation is of the body."[24] As these examples indicate, the greater opportunity for charity is a benefit those advancing a *physical* conception of virginity often cite. Those advancing this view are Roman Catholic and Laudian. Previous scholarship might note the resonance with Richeome and regard the chastity and charity link as evidence of Roman Catholic influence or even a vow of virginity. But a supervening Laudianism represents an equally plausible intellectual and theological context and source of influence. Roman Catholicism is relevant but not dominant. Most importantly, the Lady's substitution of chastity for charity, and the intimate connection between the two that such substitution denotes, illustrate the masque's sympathy with corporal asceticism.[25]

The frequency of approving references to corporal austerity also indicates that sympathy. While attempting to convince his younger brother that the "single want of light and noise" will not "stir the constant mood of [the Lady's] calm thoughts" (369–371), the Elder Brother offers the following example:

And Wisdoms self
Oft seeks to sweet retired Solitude,
Where with her best nurse Contemplation

She plumes her feathers, and lets grow her wings
That in the various bussle of resort
Were all to ruffl'd, and somtimes impair'd. (375–380)

The Second Brother's response clarifies the lines' hermitic connotations: "Tis most true/That musing meditation most affects/The Pensive secrecy of desert cell ... / For who would rob a Hermit of his Weeds,/ His few Books, or his Beads, or Maple Dish" (386–391). Together, these speeches invoke the monastic life. "Desert cell" recalls the earliest forms of monasticism practiced by the desert fathers. In addition to removal from society, the ascetic practices include the simplest of clothing and, presumably, a very sparing diet. The attitude of the two brothers is largely approving towards this manner of asceticism. The Elder Brother quite simply refers to a retired, solitary life as "sweet." In "Pensive secrecy," the Second Brother channels the delight "Il Penseroso" takes in retirement: "Com pensive Nun, devout and pure,/Sober, stedfast, and demure ... /Come, but keep thy wonted state,/With eev'n step, and musing gate,/And looks commercing with the skies,/Thy rapt soul sitting in thine eyes" (31–40). In the brothers' speeches, the potential for contemplation and meditation accords with the nun's commerce with the skies. As the Elder Brother maintains, chastity enables virgins to "oft convers with heav'nly habitants" (459). Revard glosses "commercing" as "communicating," illustrating the symmetry in the conversation both virgins and the nun hold with divinity.[26] And so, on the one hand, *A Mask* contains a positive depiction of the solitary life.

On the other hand, a tension exists between the basic logic of monasticism and how the Elder Brother consoles himself about the Lady's unknown whereabouts: "He that has light within his own cleer brest/ May sit i'th center, and enjoy bright day,/But he that hides a dark soul, and foul thoughts/Benighted walks under the mid-day Sun" (381–384). In other words, you take yourself with you regardless of where that is. This sentiment exhibits a complete indifference to physical location. Monasticism, though, is based on sequestration, isolation, and physical removal having a spiritually edifying effect. Girolamo Piatti, writing in *The happines of a religious state* (1632), commends monasticism because "it taketh away and keepeth from us al occasions and allurements of sinne, removing us out of the world, and wordlie traffick, into a most calme and quiet haven, or rather into a strong fortifyed Castle."[27] The calm and quiet haven, the fortified castle, are only accessible through displacement. The monastic life requires removal. The insistence on actual physical dislocation contrasts with the new, internal otherworldliness Protestants emphasized. Richard Baxter writes, "its one thing to creep into a Monks Cell, or an Anchorets Cave, or an Hermits Wilderness, or Diogenes Tub; and another thing truly to be Crucified to the world; and in the midst of the creatures to live above them unto God."[28] The crucifixion to the world that monks, anchorites, hermits, and even cynics claim to achieve through removal from it is still very much possible *in the midst* of it. As monasticism becomes a mental attitude rather than a physical reality, it no longer necessitates segregation from the world. The Elder Brother's contention that an internal light overwhelms an external darkness places him on a logical continuum that extends into and intersects with Baxter's interior monasticism. And yet, in its escape from the "various bussle" into a "Desert cell," its hermit weeds and beads, monastic life in *A Mask* has striking characteristics of traditional monasticism. Asceticism in *A Mask* often requires holding two viewpoints – in this case, spiritually isolated versus physically sequestered monasticism – in an irresolvable tension.

## II A "LATITUDE OF JUST PLEASURE"

This tension places *A Mask* in a rather precarious position in relation to Protestant attitudes towards modest pleasure and holy matrimony. This is apparent in the Lady's confrontation with Comus (lines 659–813). In particular, it appears in similarities between Comus's arguments in favour of profligacy and defenses offered by Heinrich Bullinger, Richard Ward, Thomas Beard, and Joseph Hall of sex and marriage. These defenses belong to a Protestant tradition of reversing a history – Pauline, patristic, medieval, and Roman Catholic – of elevating virginity above marriage and regarding the latter as an unfortunate necessity. When the Lady responds to Comus, not only does she *not* take the opportunity to rescue these defenses from Comus's rhetorical prostitution of them, but her response champions virginity in such exalted terms that she denies the value they place on pleasure, sex, and marriage.

While Comus's longest and most vehement temptation occurs later, his sinister intentions appear even during his first exchange with the Lady. His extravagant praise of her song leads to her peremptory response: "Nay gentle Shepherd ill is lost that praise/That is addrest to unattending Ears" (271–272). The temptation at this moment is to egotism. While the Lady easily dismisses the prospect of narcissism, the exchange that begins at line 659 exposes her to more various and sophisticated threats, as Comus uses a combination of flattery, physical menacing, enchantment, and specious logic in his seduction. Employing many *carpe diem* themes, Comus importunes the Lady,

> Why should you be so cruel to your self,
> And to those dainty limms which nature lent

For gentle usage, and soft delicacy?
But you invert the cov'nants of her trust,
And harshly deal like an ill borrower
With that which you receiv'd on other terms,
Scorning the unexempt condition
By which all mortal frailty must subsist,
Refreshment after toil, ease after pain,
That have been tir'd all day without repast,
And timely rest have wanted, but fair Virgin
This will restore all soon. (679–690)

Comus's speech contains *carpe diem*'s usual suspects: the appeal to nature and charges of ingratitude towards it, an imputation of self-violence or peevish selfishness, and accusations of unnatural austerity or an overvaluation of self-restraint; finally, the speech articulates a seemingly irresistible logic wherein ease follows pain. Comus's importuning of the Lady expands on many of these themes. His claims about procreation, desire, and what rejecting them means correspond to arguments Protestants offer to defend the dignity of holy matrimony.

Comus develops the claim that the Lady's restraint makes her "deal like an ill borrower" with generous nature. He argues that adopting an ascetic existence means that "Th'all-giver would be unthank't, would be unprais'd,/Nor half his riches known, and yet despis'd" (723–724). By stressing the ingratitude of the ascetic life, Comus borrows a page from Heinrich Bullinger's discussion of the reasons for marriage's institution. In *Fiftie godlie and learned sermons* (1577), Bullinger offers this exegesis of Genesis 9:7 ("And you, be ye fruitful, and multiply"):

> The second cause why matrimonie was ordeyned, is the begetting of children for the preservation of mankinde by increase, and the bringing of them uppe in the feare of the Lord … The glorie also and worship of God, is greatly augmented, when as by wedlocke there doth spring up a great number of men y[t] acknowledge cal upon, & worship god as they ought to do.[29]

When Comus argues that "Th' all-giver would be unthank't, would be unprais'd" (723), he echoes Bullinger's logic. The glory and worship of God "is greatly augmented" by increasing and multiplying. As a result of wedlock – that is, the begetting and raising of children "in the feare of the Lord" – men "acknowledge cal upon, & worship god as they ought to do." Bullinger's "acknowledge" has a sense of recognize and, potentially, express gratitude towards. Both of Comus's warnings to the Lady about austerity – that God would be "unthank't" and "unprais'd" – are expressed in Bullinger's interpretation of Genesis.

Comus appropriates another pillar of the Protestant defense of holy matrimony in his appeal to "the unexempt condition/By which all mortal frailty must subsist." In *Theologicall questions, dogmaticall observations, and evangelicall essays, vpon the Gospel of Jesus Christ, according to St. Matthew* (1640), Richard Ward discusses Matthew 19:10–12, where Jesus remarks to his disciples about virginity, "He that is able to receive it, let him receive it." Ward interprets Christ's response as demonstrating "our Saviour, First, opposeth the necessity of marriage, which is such, that but few are exempted from it."[30] Ward's exempt few and Comus's unexempt condition make similar claims about the ubiquity and intensity of human desire. Of course, Ward offers holy matrimony as an answer to the problem of desire, Comus illicit sex. Nonetheless, it is not difficult to imagine Comus's attribution of mortal frailty to all humanity being found in Protestant dissuasives from universal, vowed virginity. To exempt oneself from that condition is unnatural. In *A retractiue from the Romish religion* (1616), Thomas Beard regards clerical celibacy as a doctrine that "crosseth not onely the ordinance of God, who was the first ordainer of Marriage, but also the instinct of nature; for this was naturally instilled into all living Creatures, especially Man, at the first creation, that he should encrease and multiply." To deny this instinct is to "offer iniury to nature, and tyrannize over the bodies and soules of men." The instinct to propagate betokens another, baleful necessity for single life: "For, whence ariseth this necessary conclusion, that the vow of single life is repugnant to nature."[31] Embracing that repugnance, as the Lady does, truly convicts one of self-cruelty.

Bullinger, Ward, and Beard offer different reasons to impress upon their audiences the solemnity and necessity of marriage. For Ward, few exceptions exist from desire, while Beard contends that resisting such desire is unnatural. Finally, Bullinger stresses the ingratitude that accompanies an unwillingness to procreate. Comus pillages these arguments and makes liberal use of them in his temptation of the Lady, illustrating how Milton puts into the disreputable mouth of Comus the seemingly reputable Protestant defense of matrimony.

As part of that defense, Protestant writers urged a different attitude towards pleasure and sex. There need not be, some contend, an inverse relationship between the pleasure an activity affords and its capacity for moral edification. This is an argument ripe for Comus's taking. He employs it while appealing to nature's bounty as evidence that it should be enjoyed: "Wherefore did Nature powre her bounties forth,/With such a full and unwithdrawing hand,/Covering the earth with odours, fruits, and flocks,/Thronging the Seas with spawn innumerable,/But all to please, and sate the curious taste?" (710–714). Comus's argument, meant to be specious and casuistical, corresponds to one

Joseph Hall makes in *Christian moderation* (1640), not meant to be either. During a chapter discussing "The liberty that God hath given us in the use of his creatures," Hall delineates "a lawfull and allowed latitude of just pleasure."[32] That latitude includes the following celebration of God's bounty:

> But now, Since our liberall Creator hath thought good to furnish our Tables, vvith forty kindes at the least of beasts, and Foules; vvith two hundred (as they are computed) of fishes, besides the rich, and dainty provenues of our gardens, and orchards, and the sweet juice of our Canes, and the Cells of our hives, what should this argue, but that he (vvho made nothing in vaine, and all for man) intended to provide, not for our necessity only, but for our just delight?[33]

The catalog of dainties helps prove Hall's point that God has not used "asparing [sic] hand" (cf. with "a full and unwithdrawing hand") in satisfying man's appetite.[34] In an argument that Comus would surely admire, Hall contends that *not* taking just delight in all this bounty accuses God of vainly making it. The "odours, fruits, and flocks" in which Comus delights compare with the beasts, fowls, gardens, and orchards that Hall suggests as the unique provision of man. Though Hall does not furnish the seas with a "spawn innumerable," his parenthetical – "(as they are computed)" – expresses some incredulity at limiting the number to two-hundred.

*Christian moderation* does not restrict moderated pleasures to those of food and drink. Hall encourages married couples to "enjoy each other in a mutuall, and holy communion, and to enjoy themselves in their single and personall contentments."[35] Latitudes of pleasure also encompass sex, as the several ways of saying "private" ("single and personall") indicate. This is indeed a Gospel of prosperity and pleasure, and its wealth is further evidenced by the parsimony and austerity it indicts. Hall condemns the "hard usages" that "zealous self-enemies put upon their bodies," including lying on hard mats, wearing hair shirts, self-flagellation, the austerities of the desert fathers (especially those practiced by Hilarion and Simeon), and an "over-valuation of the merit of virginity."[36] Comus too finds recourse in all the prosperity and pleasure he recommends to reject ascetic severity. He derides the "foolishness of men" that results in "Praising the lean and sallow Abstinence." In particular, he criticizes the hermitic life, observing "if all the world/Should in a pet of temperance feed on Pulse,/Drink the clear stream, and nothing wear but Frieze,/Th'all-giver would be unthank't" (720–723). Similar to Hall's claim, if enjoyable things are not made to be enjoyed, then they have been made in vain. Finally, of course, Comus enjoins the

Lady, "be not cosen'd/With that same vaunted name Virginity,/Beauty is nature's coyn, must not be hoorded" (737–739). With the image of a miserly virginity – jealously hoarding what nature intended for sharing – we return to Beard's singular definition: "the vow of single life is repugnant to nature."

Comus's hedonistic arguments echo Protestant defenses of pleasure, sexual and otherwise. The sorcerer distorts those arguments, "pranckt" as they are in "reasons garb" (759). One might expect *A Mask* to set the record straight: for the Lady to rise to the defense of these defenses, rescuing them from the indignity of expression within Comus's salacious speech.[37] That does not happen, and this is clear when we consider how the Lady might respond to the claims of Bullinger, Ward, Beard, and Hall. She does mention moderation (769), but her conception of it differs sharply from Hall's. Her moderation consists of "sober laws," "spare Temperance," "unsuperfluous eeven proportion," and the "sage/And serious doctrine of Virginity" (766–787). In comparison with Hall, the Lady's sobriety and sparseness give precious little latitude to the superfluities and personal contentments of "just pleasure." Based on her celebration of virginity, exemptions must exist from the universality of desire (Ward). Single life is not repugnant to nature, for her laws are a model of sobriety and temperance (Beard).

While the Lady would scarcely disagree with Bullinger that God deserves gratitude, she does outline different conditions that lead to gratefulness. For Bullinger, procreation and an adherence to Genesis 9:7 exhibit gratitude. In the Lady's estimation, every "just man" enjoying a "moderate and beseeming share/Of that which lewdly-pamper'd Luxury/Now heaps upon som few with vast excess" would mean "the giver would be better thank't" (768–775). The "just man" and his "moderate and beseeming share" allude to the Second Brother's praise of the hermit who lives in "The Pensive secrecy of desert cell" (387). An allusion to the hermit makes sense because Comus's accusation of ingratitude targeted the solitary life the hermit represents: "if all the world/Should in a pet of temperance feed on Pulse,/Drink the clear stream, and nothing wear but Frieze,/Th' all-giver would be unthank't" (720–723). Comus's "Frieze" puts us in mind of the hermit's "Weeds," possibly including a hair shirt, and the "Pulse" recalls his "Maple Dish" (390–391). Moreover, the Lady's vision of egalitarian distribution complements the thrift of the "desert cell": "For who would rob a Hermit of his Weeds" (388–390). Frugal living obviates the disparity in wealth that serves as a provocation for theft. The Lady's conception of gratefulness towards the giver includes a leveling of such disparities. In this way, her gratitude points us back towards the hermit and primitive asceticism, forming a natural contrast with Bullinger's godly proliferation. God must be thanked, but fertile sex and frugal eremitism imagine different ways of thanking Him.

The Lady's panegyric to virginity also illustrates how her response to Comus is incompatible with the defense of pleasure and matrimony. It no doubt risks overvaluing the virginal life in ways Hall would feel excessive. Were the Lady to unfold the "sage/And serious doctrine of Virginity,"

> The uncontrouled worth
> Of this pure cause would kindle my rap't spirits
> To such a flame of sacred vehemence,
> That dumb things would be mov'd to sympathize,
> And the brute Earth would lend her nerves, and shake,
> Till all thy magick structures rear'd so high,
> Were shatter'd into heaps o're thy false head. (793–799)

The Lady threatens Comus with the untapped power of her "pure cause," of virginity. Something superhuman informs that threat, as Comus later confirms (801). Correspondence between the Lady's warning and an earlier depiction of Comus's sorcery also confirms its paranormal power. At the beginning of their exchange, as the Lady attempts to escape her "inchanted Chair," Comus admonishes, "Nay Lady sit; if I but wave this wand,/Your nervs are all chain'd up in Alabaster,/ And you a statue; or as Daphne was/Root-bound, that fled Apollo" (659–662). The power of Comus's wand places the Lady's "nervs" in danger; the Lady harnessing the "nerves" of the "brute Earth" would bring Comus to ruin. A narrative symmetry, whereby the threat Comus earlier made stands poised to fall on his false head, organizes the scene. While the Lady does not act on her threat, neither does Comus make alabaster statuary of her. The Lady's promise of causing Comus's "magick structures" to fall into "shatter'd heaps" has a potential not unlike that which the Attendant Spirit earlier attributed to Comus's wand: "He with his bare wand can unthred thy joynts,/And crumble all thy sinews" (614–615). Crumbling sinews, shattering magic structures; both are capable of dreadful demolition. At the moment when the Lady proclaims a power that can overpower Comus's sorcery, the means of overpowering bear striking resemblance to it. The Lady's threats are not totally devoid of magical connotations, as their reciprocity with Comus's enchantments makes clear.

Those connotations channel a long tradition of virgins being thought to possess extraordinary powers. Ambrose, in his treatise *Concerning Virgins*, details how Thecla "changed even the disposition of wild beasts by their reverence for virginity."[38] In *A very frutefull and pleasant boke called the Instructio[n] of a Christen woma[n]* (1529), Juan Luis Vives discusses Ambrose's observation: "Saynt Tecla/as saynt Ambrose sayth/altered the nature of wylde beastes with the reverence of virginite. Virginite hath so moche marveylons honoure in hit/that wylde lyons regarde hit."[39] Patristic writings are not the only source to explain the Lady's sway over dumb things and the earth. Thomas Heywood's *Londini artium & scientiarum scaturigo* (1632), one of his seven Lord Mayor's pageants written for the Haberdashers Company, includes a speech from the company's patroness, St. Katherine. The speech begins with the question, "DOth [sic] any wonder, why St. Katherine, shee/The Patronesse of this faire Companie/Is mounted on a Lyon?" The lion's subjection is partly explained by her virgin state: "Besides I come/Both with Virginity and Martyrdome,/Sainted moreover, and (of these) the least/Able to tame the most insulting Beast."[40] The examples of Ambrose and Heywood suggest the applicability of extraordinary virginity to the Lady, of the ability to tame a beast like Comus. The line from virginity to controlling beasts and the natural world is not as direct in *A Mask*; it passes through "sacred vehemence." Even Heywood, whose High Church predilections are much less contested than Milton's, dilutes that link, using martyrdom as an additional and less controversial witness to the saint's extraordinary powers. This is not a refutation of extraordinary virginity so much as a slight modification. As the retaining of virginity's extraordinariness in *A Mask* demonstrates, it is highly and, probably to Hall, over-valued.

The ascetic morality of *A Mask* is largely incompatible with the arguments of Bullinger, Ward, Beard, and Hall. To put that another way, a compatibility emerges between Comus's *carpe diem* arguments and a Protestant impulse towards anti-asceticism, especially as it overlaps with a defense of holy matrimony. Just because Comus ventriloquizes the Protestant defense of moderate pleasure and holy matrimony does not invalidate those defenses. Neither, though, does *A Mask* rush to defend these seemingly uncontroversial and widely accepted doctrines. We would imagine the Son in *Paradise Regained* (in all his animadverting exactitude) vigorously protesting this kind of misappropriation as a way of cleansing the Protestant defense of moderate pleasure from the least blot of impurity and readying it for use. The Lady does not, the preceding paragraphs have shown, defend moderate pleasure. Instead, she articulates a version of moderation and temperance in which the pleasurable latitudes and procreative emphases of Bullinger, Ward, Beard, and Hall make little sense. Their champion is Comus. *A Mask* never takes the time to disentangle the association of something good with someone bad. Its energies are put into the Lady's full-throated defense of virginity. And so while no inevitable harm comes to these doctrines through Comus's usage of them, they are either not in need of defense or not of sufficient moment to command it. If *A Mask* had not confused, or had taken care to *un*-confuse, Comus's temptation and the Protestant reclamation of sex and marriage, then Milton's positive attitude towards that reclamation would not be in doubt.

## III Eternal Brides and Unspotted Sides

In *A Mask*, Protestant anti-asceticism waits for a defense that never comes. It has been thought to come in the epilogue, but even there asceticism and a discomfort with sexuality linger. *A Mask* concludes with a vision of Elysium and the marriage of Cupid and Psyche. One way to interpret this marriage is as a kind of counterbalance to the depiction of Sabrina, the Goddess of the Severn whose intercession frees the Lady from Comus's ensorcellment. Fleeing her "enraged stepdam Guendolen," Sabrina commends "her fair innocence" to the Severn River (830–831). Harriett Hawkins contends that Sabrina's commendation occurs because she tries "to escape some form of violation with broadly sexual connotations."[41] As the Attendant Spirit explains, "maid'nhood she loves, and will be swift/To aid a Virgin, such as was her self" (855–856). And so while it is easy to debate the physical or spiritual nature of the Lady's virginity – is it meant to be perpetually physical? – that is more difficult with Sabrina. Her virginity possesses a strongly physical connotation. It is not just an internal condition, for she has achieved the "sublimation of flesh" that the Elder Brother offers as one possible result of chastity (453–469). "Her perfect chastity," William Kerrigan writes, "has prevented the orifices that admit the external world, whether as substance or as sensation, from becoming 'clotted.'"[42]

A minor detail about Sabrina also points in the direction of physical virginity. The Attendant Spirit recounts the aid she provides local inhabitants, "For which the Shepherds at their festivals/Carrol her goodnes lowd in rustick layes,/And throw sweet garland wreaths into her stream/Of pancies, pinks, and gaudy Daffadils" (848–851). Crowning the Severn with garland wreaths is a provocative detail, especially in light of English Protestantism's changing attitude towards holy wells, sacred springs, and their apotropaic function. In the 1630s, "the climate of theological opinion," Alexandra Walsham writes, "was altering in favour of a qualified reassertion of the sacred. Both perambulation and the decoration and blessing of springs surely benefited from these tendencies."[43] Though it may seem innocuous, crowning waters with garlands detracted from the omnipotence, from the sole-mediatory authority, of Christ. It acknowledged an intermediary, tutelary world that smacked to many of paganism and popery. Such crowning recalled the Roman Feast of the Fountains, described in a 1654 travel guidebook as "Crowning the Wells with flowers, and casting Garlands into the Fountains."[44] Thomas Manton expresses the offense the godly felt at the theology behind the ceremony: "Is it that you are inabled in this Estate to do any thing that concerneth the Glory of God? The Romans were wont to cast Garlands into their Fountains: So we must ascribe all to God."[45] The introduction mentioned how some Protestants rejected extreme forms of Roman Catholic asceticism because they detracted from the sufficiency of Christ's sacrifice. Thomas Lupton writes in *The Christian against the Iesuite* (1582), "you that thus whippe your selves for your owne offences, you make your selves your owne Christes: And they that are their owne Christes, shall never dwell in heaven with Christ."[46] Crowning wells with garlands, what Walsham calls the Laudian reassertion of the sacred, lapses into the same theological error as rigorous forms of corporal discipline. The shepherds' celebration of Sabrina reinforces the physical connotations of her virginity.

Sabrina's bodily virginity places greater pressure on the masque's conclusion to come out in decided favour of chaste conjugality and sexuality. And indeed the epilogue (976–1023) has been interpreted as doing just that. William Kerrigan views the epilogue as affirming the inevitability of sexuality: "The return of erotic imagery concedes that sexuality is, if not in the end, in the end of this work at least, the protean lord of our desire."[47] William Shullenberger notices a similar concession. He regards the conclusion as accomplishing the "socialization, stabilization, and sanctification of erotic delight and fecundity in marriage."[48] Even if we acknowledge the masque's praise of virginity, this marriage settles the matter, moving the Lady away from a jejune virginity towards mature fecundity. Or does it?

As the Attendant Spirit describes "those happy climes" (976), his description has several virginal connotations:

> But farr above in spangled sheen
> Celestial Cupid her fam'd son advanc't,
> Holds his dear Psyche sweet intranc't
> After her wandring labours long,
> Till free consent the gods among
> Make her his eternal Bride,
> And from her fair unspotted side
> Two blissful twins are to be born,
> Youth and Joy; so Jove hath sworn. (1003–1011)

The Attendant Spirit calls Psyche's side "unspotted": "And from her fair unspotted side/Two blissful twins are to be born." Psyche's "unspotted side" represents a fortification of the Lady's previous and precarious condition. As Comus earlier asks, had her brothers "left your fair side all unguarded, Lady?" (283). "Unspotted" renders "unguarded" inviolable. As the inviolability signals, "unspotted" is a word that has a close association with virginity. Heinrich Bullinger quotes Chrysostom as saying "the first degree of chastitie is unspotted virginitie, the 2. is faithful wedlock."[49] William Kerrigan, who ultimately finds the epilogue to affirm chaste conjugality, nonetheless notes about the use of "unspotted" that Psyche's "vagina will not be 'used' for birth, a displacement that continues the *noli me tangere* of virginity"[50] In *A Mask*, marital fecundity has virginal implications. How can we account for this? Milton may be thinking of Hebrews 13:4 ("the bed undefiled"), a passage he will return to in *An Apology for Smectymnuus*. Another exemplar looms large.

In addition to its general application to virgins, "unspotted" also applies to the Virgin Mary.[51] John Stoughton's *XI. choice sermons* (1640) states that "Iesus was borne of Mary an unspotted virgin."[52] *Eniautos* (1664) regards her unspottedness as a point worth catechizing: "Do you think that Mary was an unspotted Virgin?"[53] Mary's womb is also depicted as uniquely unspotted. Cardinal Bellarmine refers to "the unspotted wombe of the B. Virgin MARIE" in *An ample declaration of the Christian doctrine* (1604).[54] Milton uses "side" not womb, but the word has obstetric implications. The *Oxford English Dictionary*, in fact, adduces Psyche's "unspotted side" in *A Mask* as an example of "side" meaning "the womb."[55] In *Paradise Regained*, Satan wonders about Christ, "If he be Man by Mothers side at least" (2.136). The primary meaning of "side" here is, of course, side of the family. But the manner of birth could also evidence the Son's humanity. Moreover, Comus's earlier reference to the Lady's unguarded side also possesses a possible sexual meaning, an implicit suggestion of the pudendum. He references her "fair side all unguarded" during a stichomythic exchange (277–291), a verbal context that heightens the possibility for double entendre and sexualized meaning. Stichomythia causes a penetration of the Lady and Comus's dialogue that David N. Dickey describes as "textual intercourse."[56]

Psyche's designation as an "eternal Bride" also intimates a possible Marian reading. A panegyric to Mary in Anthony Stafford's *The femall glory* (1635) proclaims, "Mary must Bride to thy Creatour be,/And clad in flesh part of the Trinity."[57] Cupid might be read, as in Joseph Beaumont's *Psyche, or, Loves mysterie in XX canto's, displaying the intercourse betwixt Christ and the soule* (1648), as a type of Christ. Revelation 19 foretells the marriage of Christ and the Church. Mary's identification with the church represents both a historical reality as well as a typological one. As John Donne explains, many Roman Catholic theologians contend that "during the time that Christ lay in the Grave, there was no faith, and consequently no Church, but onely in One, in the person of the Virgin Mary."[58] Her designation as the church could reinforce Mary's status as a bride eternal.

Finally, if this seems a bit too Marian for Milton's tastes, Juan Luis Vives offers another possibility. Vives contends that "virgins and all holy soules/engendre Christe spiritually." As a result, *every* professed virgin can occupy the seemingly contradictory roles of mother, maid, and spouse: "O thou mayde/thynkest thou this but a small thing that thou art bothe mother/spouse/and daughter to that god/in whom nothynge can be/but hit be thyn: and thou mayst with good ryght challenge for thyn? For bothe thou gettest and art gottē and maryed unto hym."[59] Whether the conclusion alludes to all virgins or the Virgin Mary, virginity is not superseded. Psyche returns the reader to the Lady and not in such a way that cancels virginal connotations and replaces them with nuptial inevitability. At the moment of triumphant matrimony, when fecund motherhood looms, virginity persists.

It also persists in how the epilogue deploys the myth of Cupid and Psyche. Cupid and Psyche in *A Mask* delineate, some believe, a procreative future for the Lady's barren virginity. Stewart Baker concludes that Milton's use of the myth leaves the Lady's chastity behind: "The embrace of Cupid and Psyche is an immediate transfiguration of the Lady's state of chastity."[60] Ann Baynes Coiro makes a similar claim when she writes, "nevertheless, the Attendant Spirit's lushly mythological epilogue makes clear that sanctioned sexual union must be the Lady's promised end."[61] In explaining Milton's usage of the myth, scholars point to Book III of *The Faerie Queene* and Spenser's depiction of the Garden of Adonis. While heavily indebted to Spenser, Milton's rendering of the myth also departs from him. Gordon Teskey notes that Milton suppresses the "sexual explicitness of Spenser's account."[62] Also, as Maggie Kilgour explains, Spenser's Cupid and Psyche "appear *in* the Garden of Adonis with Venus and Adonis" (original emphasis).[63] Spenser, following the *Metamorphoses* of Apuleius, portrays Pleasure as the child of Cupid and Psyche. Milton elevates Cupid and Psyche above the sensual lovers Venus and Adonis, and he avoids any suggestion of mere sexual gratification by describing their issue as youth and joy instead of pleasure. Despite these differences, for Kilgour, Milton's alterations of Spenser still predict marital fecundity: "The description of the happy couple anticipates the much more extended examination of married love in *Paradise Lost*."[64] In the account that follows, alterations of Spenser preserve (rather than transfigure) chastity and do not simply reinforce conjugal eroticism. Performing an inventory of Spenser's

Garden of Adonis in *A Mask* turns up some striking omissions. What Milton leaves out, and where a concomitant sentiment can be found, exemplify Spenser's and Milton's different attitudes towards sex and procreation.

In the epilogue, several allusions restate Spenser with minor alterations. For example, in the "middest of that Paradise" in *The Faerie Queene* stands a "gloomy groue of mirtle trees": "And from their fruitfull sides sweet gum did drop,/That all the ground with precious deaw bedight,/Threw forth most dainty odours, and most sweet delight" (3.6.43).[65] Milton recalls these lines when the Attendant Spirit describes the Hesperian Garden as where "eternal Summer dwels,/And West winds, with musky wing/About the cedar'n alleys fling/Nard, and Cassia's balmy smels" (988–991). Flinging balmy smells corresponds to the trees that "Threw forth most dainty odours." Milton's "eternal Summer" recalls that in Spenser's Garden of Adonis "There is continuall spring" (3.6.42).

Allusions to Spenser also work in a less straightforwardly affirmative way. Spenser's Adonis is "Lapped in flowres and pretious spycery," always available for Venus to enjoy: "and of his sweetnesse takes her fill" (3.6.46). The epilogue to *A Mask* imagines a less erotic configuration of the two lovers: "and on the ground/Sadly sits th'Assyrian Queen" (1001–1002). The sadness throws cold water on Spenser's Venus, who is always ready to "reape sweet pleasure of the wanton boy" (3.6.46). A small detail also points to the change in erotic tone. The flowers sensuously lap Spenser's Adonis; Milton's Adonis "reposes" on them (999). The reposition is both more dignified and more self-contained. Milton's Adonis is not the passive recipient of all kinds of erotic attention, Venereal and horticultural. Venus sitting on the ground, moreover, connects her to the terrestrial love that Cupid and Psyche transcend. As *A Mask* proclaims, they are "But farr above" Venus and Adonis (1003).

Milton's vision of the Garden of Adonis does not contain the overt, pullulating sexuality of Spenser's depiction. This is particularly clear in what Milton omits from Spenser's account. In Spenser's Garden of Adonis, "All things, as they created were, doe grow,/And yet remember well the mightie word,/Which first was spoken by th'Almightie lord,/That bad them to increase and multiply" (3.6.34). A reference to Genesis 9:7 ("And you, be ye fruitful, and multiply") is not found in the epilogue to *A Mask*. Instead, an indirect reference is found in an earlier speech by Comus. We have seen how Comus's claim that "Th'all-giver would be unthank't, would be unprais'd,/Nor half his riches known, and yet despis'd" (723–724) echoes Heinrich Bullinger's exegesis of Genesis 9:7 in *Fiftie godlie and learned sermons*. In Spenser's Garden of Adonis, that scriptural passage licenses generativity. Not only does

Milton's epilogue *not* contain a similar scriptural reference, but in order to find that sentiment *A Mask* takes the reader back to its arch-villain.

*A Mask* also omits Spenser's depiction of how prolific the garden is. After Spenser explains the garden's fecundity through Genesis 9:7, he offers a marine example of that fertility: "And all the fruitfull spawne of fishes hew/In endlesse rancks along enraunged were,/That seem'd the Ocean could not containe them there" (3.6.35). Milton's epilogue does not offer a comparable example of explosive fecundity. But Comus does. In his attempt to persuade the Lady to throw over her peevish virginity, he asks

> Wherefore did Nature powre her bounties forth,
> With such a full and unwithdrawing hand,
> Covering the earth with odours, fruits, and flocks,
> Thronging the Seas with spawn innumerable,
> But all to please, and sate the curious taste? (710–714)

The "spawn innumerable" that throng the sea recall Spenser's description of a sea bursting with "fruitful spawne" of fishes. In Milton, the "endlesse rancks" become innumerable. Spenser offers this example of nearly fissiparous fish after invoking Genesis 9:7. *A Mask* relegates a similar example to Comus persuading the Lady to engage in illicit sex. In general, scholars contend that Milton rejects illicit sex but embraces licit sex within marriage. The problem with such a formulation is that Milton puts two of Spenser's licit examples (Genesis 9:7, via Bullinger and those randy fish) in the dirty mind of Comus. A discomfort with sexuality, and the procreative rationale justifying it, complicates the triumphant movement towards matrimony many apprehend at the conclusion of *A Mask*.

Critics often see the Spirit's epilogue lurching (albeit complicatedly) towards *Paradise Lost*, or, at the very least, conceiving of a sexual future that contains it.[66] As John Guillory writes, the epilogue "has both puzzled critics and reassured them that Milton was not so fixated, after all, on the subject of chastity."[67] The epilogue, the preceding pages argue, provides no such reassurance. Trying to locate Spenser's eroticism and sexuality in the epilogue of *A Mask* takes the reader back to Comus and not forward to the Garden of Eden. Milton has misgivings about procreative sexuality that Psyche's "unspotted side" and his changes to, and particularly omissions from, Spenser's Garden of Adonis illustrate.

## IV *A Mask* and Caroline Culture

The preceding sections have identified the kind of asceticism *A Mask* advocates and showed its complexly disapproving relation to

Reformed debates about sex and marriage. As the introduction to this chapter suggested, contexts in addition to large-scale Reformed ones explain the religious affiliation of asceticism in *A Mask*. It remains to be considered, therefore, how this asceticism relates to a much more immediate cultural arena: the royal court. For some commentators, the answer about this relation has seemed obvious. Milton upbraids the libertinism of Caroline culture and the indulgences of Laudian ceremonialism with the forbidding virginity of the Lady. This conclusion fails to account for the asceticism that thrived at both church and court. When taken into account, similarities emerge between asceticism in *A Mask* and its courtly thriving, particularly as those similarities involve Caroline Neoplatonism.

Caroline Neoplatonism – imported from French salons, the writings of Honoré d'Urfé, and the devotional spirituality of St. Francis de Sales – emphasized a chaste conjugality in which lovers mingled minds and souls, not bodies.[68] The notion of Caroline Neoplatonism as pervasively erotic, or the claim that its investment in conjugality renders it inhospitable to virginity, oversimplifies an ascetic strain that runs throughout it.[69] James Holly Hanford performs this oversimplification by describing Caroline Neoplatonism as "more than ever a mask of triviality and corruption."[70] Bonnie Lander Johnson, by contrast, acknowledges Caroline masques' interest in "monastic piety, ritualised devotion, ornament, wonder, and chaste female fertility."[71] Caroline culture's interest in ascetic themes presages a broader link between church and court, Laudian asceticism and Caroline Neoplatonism.[72] It is not surprising that a philosophic discourse seeking to transcend the body and a church seeking its constraint found common ground.[73] That common ground further complicates presenting the asceticism of *A Mask* as evidence of anti-court sentiment rooted in puritan strictness. Does *A Mask* articulate a rival version of asceticism, one intended to criticize and replace the moral bankruptcy of its Caroline and Laudian version? Robert Crofts's *The Lover; or, Nuptiall love* provides an answer to this question. *The Lover* combines Caroline Neoplatonism and asceticism while evincing several descriptive and mythographic parallels with *A Mask*.

No entry for Crofts appears in the *Oxford Dictionary of National Biography*. He published three other works (of which I am aware) in addition to *The Lover*, including *The terrestriall paradise, or, Happinesse on earth* (1639), *Paradise within us; or, The happie mind* (1640), and *The way to happinesse on earth concerning riches, honour, conjugall love, eating, drinking* (1641). As the titles suggest, the works are largely derivative of each other and quite repetitive. In *The Tragic Muse of John Ford*, G. F. Sensabaugh speculates that Crofts may have been a puritan. Grouping *The Lover* with tracts impugning licentious court culture, Sensabaugh argues that Crofts connects the puritan "attack upon worship of beauty in woman with devotees of the Queen's cult of love."[74] In contrast with Sensabaugh, Reid Barbour finds a rebuke of puritan stoicism in *The terrestriall paradise*.[75] As the following pages document, Crofts's views of marriage, virginity, and mystical union with God are not suggestive of puritanism. A clue to Crofts's courtly connections may also be supplied by William Marshall (fl. 1617–1649), the engraver of *The Lover*. Marshall benefitted greatly from the patronage of Charles I and engraved the famous frontispiece to the *Eikon basilike* (1649). Peter M. Daly and Mary V. Silcox have analyzed the royalism of Marshall's work and his association with royalists.[76]

The royalist connotations of *The Lover* appear in Crofts's opening description of his subject, nuptial love: "the bravest, the most noble, generous, and gallant spirits, are commonly most and best taken and possest with this Love: wherefore it is called Heroicall Love."[77] In the phrase "Heroicall Love," Crofts alludes to the frequent labeling of Charles and Henrietta Maria's relationship – and the Neoplatonic chastity it symbolized – with a similar term. For instance, in *Loues triumph through Callipolis* (1631), Ben Jonson admiringly references "the dignity of that heroique love, and regall respect borne by [Charles] to his unmatchable Lady, and Spouse, the Queenes Maiesty."[78] In a similar phrase, Aurelian Townshend's *Tempe restord* (1632) celebrates "Heroicke Vertue," or "that kind/Of Beautie, that attracts the mind,/ And men should most implore."[79] This virtue is, in other words, preparative for Platonic love. For Crofts, the heroism of Caroline Neoplatonism derives from its privileging non-corporeal love at a time of rampant sensuality, when "the land is full of adulterers."[80] Neoplatonism is not symptomatic of promiscuity: it serves as a corrective to it. Crofts's adoption of the trope of Neoplatonism as "heroic" and his connection to William Marshall indicate *The Lover*'s place within – not alienation from – Caroline Court culture. A comparison of *The Lover* and *A Mask* also illustrates the coherence between Miltonic asceticism and Crofts's Caroline Neoplatonism. Both *The Lover* and *A Mask* contain an ambivalent attitude towards matrimony, link Neoplatonism and asceticism, and depict the unique access and proximity virginity affords its practitioners to divinity.

In a tract on nuptial love, it may seem peculiar to devote much attention to virginity. It is passing strange, then, that Crofts privileges the single life above marriage while emphasizing virginity's potential for greater holiness. The discussion of virginity begins about two-thirds of the way through *The Lover*, when Crofts turns to the topic "Remedies, against the Losse of Love."[81] Of course, the ultimate remedy against losing love is abstinence, as Crofts implies by quoting Paul's teachings on virginity (1 Corinthians 7): "Saint Paul, preferres a Single life before marriage, and I hope you will beleeve him."[82] There is no temporizing in this assertion: that is, attributing (as puritans were wont) Paul's preference to a particular historical context or avoiding an interpretation of the preference as a maxim. Such an interpretation coheres with a Church of England culture in which Laud may have (or was thought to have) advocated priestly celibacy. As we have seen, in his defense of Laud's unguarded statement in *Cyprianus anglicus*, Peter Heylyn presents the very same Pauline precedent as possible justification.[83] Crofts's interpretation of Paul also corresponds to the ambivalent attitude towards matrimony in *A Mask*. Crofts is more forward in that ambivalence: "I hope you will beleeve him." Psyche's "unspotted side" and allusions to (and omissions from) Spenser's Garden of Adonis complicate the straightforward and affirmative relation critics find between *A Mask* and matrimony.

Similar to Milton's masque, *The Lover* outlines the contemplative ascent and divine proximity available to virgins. Crofts describes virginal contemplatives as "raysed to the knowledge of divine things"; they "are elevated above all the pleasures of the earth."[84] *A Mask* depicts the unique divine knowledge to which practitioners of virginity have access. As the Elder Brother explains, virgins can apprehend "things that no gross ear can hear" (458). In *The Lover*, the Neoplatonic mingling of souls is also possible for virginal contemplatives who, instead of communing with their beloved's soul, are actually joined to God. *The Lover* urges divine contemplators, "let us powre forth our soules into God, and In-soule our selves into him."[85] In *A Mask*, Milton does not contend that asceticism joins the virgin to God. But he does make the corollary claim that lust causes the licentious to lose "The divine property of her first being" (469). For Crofts, contemplative ascent and proximity to God culminate in the experience of divine love, as the last section of his work documents. Though Crofts presents this experience as available to both virgins and Platonic lovers, divine lovers "shall have a new being, and a new Name."[86] This renaming echoes what Isaiah 56:5 describes as one of the rewards for eunuchs: "and I will give them an everlasting name, that shall not be cut off." To depict the inexpressible beauty divine lovers glimpse, *The Lover* employs the Garden of Adonis: "What sweet Ioy and pleasure, hath the Heart of man imagined of the Orchards of Adonis; The Gardens of Hesperides; The Delights of the fortunate Islands. Of the Elizian Fields, and Turkes Paradise." And yet these all constitute shadows, chimeras, vain ideas in comparison with the beauty of God.[87] That beauty lies, to borrow a phrase from Milton, "farr above" the mundane example of the Garden of Adonis and all the delights it encloses.

Finally, both *The Lover* and *A Mask* adopt attitudes towards the body and materiality that license ascetic practices. For Crofts, remaining virginal and loving Platonically require subordination of the body. When virginal contemplatives "are in these divine Extasies, their Spirits are so strong, as they doe overcome their bodies, so heavenly, as they doe then esteeme the chiefest pleasures of the body (as this of carnall desire and love) but as dung and drosse in comparison of those more heavenly pleasures which they enjoy in their soules." Crofts enjoins a similar boycotting of bodily pleasures on Platonic lovers: "Then, though their Beauty and Bodies should decay and become infirme, yet their very Soules may bee in Love with one another, which is farre more excellent then bodily love."[88] Those in love with their beloved's soul also practice the subjection of the body that a life of divine contemplation entails. In each example, the body does not come out favourably. The pleasures of the body being "dung and drosse" and soul-love being "farre more excellent then bodily love" even denote a certain disgust for the body. They are reminiscent of the Neoplatonic derogation of materiality evident when the Attendant Spirit bemoans the "smoak and stirr of this dim spot," he deplores the feverish frailty of humanity, and he compares human existence to the indignity of beasts (5–8). The Attendant Spirit would not deign to "soil these pure Ambrosial weeds,/With the rank vapours of this Sin-worn mould" if he did not have a *very* good reason (16–17). Those attitudes comprehend a disgust for the body that is symptomatic of asceticism.

Most importantly, *The Lover* illustrates how a work deeply enmeshed in Caroline culture approaches asceticism in ways similar to *A Mask*. Instead of impugning Caroline culture, Milton's asceticism shares key points of emphasis with a work partly representative of it. This chapter has also sought to illustrate the extent of Milton's ascetic commitments. They are so extensive that they place him in oppositional relation to Protestant theories of pleasurable moderation and the Reformed exaltation of holy matrimony. Perhaps most surprisingly, the sage and serious doctrine of virginity in *A Mask* registers differences with Milton's sage and serious original.

# 3 The Virgin's Body and the Natural World in *Lycidas*

This chapter continues the investigation of John Milton's early ascetic views, and the religious affiliation they suggest, by taking into account *Lycidas*, perhaps the most well-known of all the young Milton's poetic compositions. Scholars continue to read the poem in terms such as those suggested by Christopher Hill, who calls *Lycidas* "a tremendous denunciation of the dominant clique in the Church of England, the Laudians."[1] Recent appraisals of *Lycidas* by Anna Beer, Nicholas McDowell, Jeffrey Alan Miller, and John Leonard also stress the poem's radicalism and its inherent hostility to Laud.[2] For example, Miller notes that "scholars have often identified 1637 as a watershed year in terms of Milton's relation to the English Church, the most compelling reason being that the autumn of that year was when Milton composed 'Lycidas.'"[3] A tendency to read *Lycidas* as such a watershed moment is deeply ingrained in criticism. Writing in the early part of this century, James Holly Hanford anticipates many later readings of the poem by describing "the outburst against the clergy in *Lycidas*" as "the first great passage in which [Milton] voices his convictions on an issue of the day."[4] My interest here is not to deny the intensity of that passage or its possible criticism of Laudianism. Rather, this chapter employs asceticism to uncover rival intensities and pressures in *Lycidas*, ones that do not point uniformly (or even directly) towards the champion of anti-episcopacy Milton would become in the 1640s. The picture of the poem that emerges is consistent with what Colin Burrow sees throughout *Poems* 1645: "What the collection offers, that is, is not a manifesto or a self-portrait of a rising bard but a group of poems which explore the many past impulses, half-formed ideas, personal connections and ties which make up the life of a poet, and on which he attempts to impose a retrospective structure."[5] *Lycidas* proffers such half-formations, and the headnote Milton later appends to the poem represents a structural imposition. It is a poem poised between the hateful contraries of anti-clerical outburst and the possibility of Laudian sympathies.

As the following pages argue, those sympathies appear in a connection *Lycidas* establishes between consecration of the natural world and the virgin's body. The poem contains an unacknowledged instance of religious ceremony – rogation, or the tracing of parish boundaries on foot – that hallows nature in a way similar to how virginity purifies Edward King. While virginity sanctifies the body, rogation is a ritual of perambulation and ascent that sanctifies the shore.[6] Through this parallel, *Lycidas* illustrates the close relationship between the reformation of the landscape and asceticism.[7] The relationship had a particular relevance for the Laudian Church. As Laudians rediscovered a sanctified natural world, they reemphasized the sanctity of bodily virginity.

Early reformers, in fact, had used similar logic to an opposite theological end as a way of discrediting a sanctified natural world and physical asceticism. In the same way that shrines, wells, and sacred springs have no unique claims to holiness, they argued, neither does the ascetic body. To make God respect these external spaces – whether somatic or natural – is both idolatrous and presumptuous. In *An exposition of the Epistle of St Paule to the Colossians deliuered in sundry sermons* (1615), Edward Elton concludes "that no outward want or meanes whatsoever, doth in it selfe hinder men in respect of holinesse." To illustrate the folly of an over-reliance on the circumstantial, Elton adduces the single life:

> Now then first this meets with an error of the Papists, who teach that some outward callings and actions commend men to God, as single life, fasting, and voluntary poverty, yea, they say, that virginity and single life is a state of perfection farre excelling marriage, and in it selfe of such dignity as it commends the person before the iudgement seat of God, and deserves Gods grace, full remission of sins, the kingdome of God, and life eternall, a doctrine not only blasphemous and full of contumely, and derogation from the bloud of Christ, but such as doth directly crosse that often repeated (and therfore most infallible) sentence of Scripture: that God is no accepter of persons, that he regards no outward state, condition, or dignity in the world for what else is single life, but an outward state, or manner of life, and therefore admit it to be most excellent, yet of it selfe it cannot commend, or make any one more pleasing to God.[8]

As Elton contests any "derogation from the bloud of Christ" that perfect virginity implies, his theology of corporal externality has a ready applicability to the external world. An indifference towards externals is a major component of what Walsham describes as the Protestant reappraisal of sacred space and the natural world: "Building on the conviction that God had 'abolished all distinction of places' and emphasizing the transcendental omnipresence of the divine, Protestants vehemently denied that space had any kind of inherent sanctity and that particular tracts of it provided unique points of access to the Almighty."[9] Elton transposes this argument into an ascetic key. The denial of space's inherent sanctity articulates as the single life not being "of it selfe ... more pleasing to God." As Elton illustrates, Protestant attempts to debunk myths about the inherent sanctity of virginity relied on a rejection of externals that also de-sanctified the natural world.[10] More largely, this approach to virginity and the natural world tracks with a Protestant emphasis on human sinfulness and divine supremacy. The inherent sanctity of a place detracts from God's ubiquity; it makes Him subject to, and capable of summons from, a location. The idea of virginity's inherent sanctity accruing some heavenly reward renders God's will subject to human action. The one is an affront to his omnipresence, and the other to his omnipotence. Elton's Calvinist sympathies would have made him especially sensitive to the idea of human limitations placed on divine power as a result of meritorious action.

In *Lycidas*, as the subsequent pages elaborate, both virginity and a natural world sanctified through rogation impose such limitations. To understand how they do so, it is first necessary to consider how, following the Reformation, rogation becomes a flashpoint for the various theological tensions involving a sanctified natural world. Milton's depiction of the sacralizing power of rogation enters this controversy in earnest.

## I Rogation: Days of Devotion or Fish-Days?

Rogation is the perambulation and demarcation of parish boundaries that was also intended to exorcize agricultural lands from malfeasant spirits and protect against natural disaster. Edward Muir offers this description of the ritual:

> The week of Ascension, called the Rogation Days or in Germany *Kreuzwoche*, attracted a wide range of supplicatory appeals, designed to protect the crops and community from natural misfortunes. In much of Europe these rites appeared at a critical agricultural moment when the spring buds were still vulnerable to freezes and tempests. The typical procedure after the celebration of a morning mass was for the priest to lead a procession out to the fields to beat the bounds, invoking divine protection for the crops and livestock.[11]

In addition to Muir's broad outline of the ritual, several features of rogation will be particularly relevant to *Lycidas*. On the liturgical calendar,

Rogationtide was the Monday, Tuesday, and Wednesday preceding Ascension Thursday. Since it took place during Lent, the colour associated with rogation was purple. As with many liturgical festivities, the ritual was based on the Roman festival of Ambarvalia, a celebration in honour of Bacchus. The Christianization of Ambarvalia, one tradition holds, occurred to strengthen boundaries besieged by beasts such as wolves.[12] In addition to a lupine threat, rogation protected against disease, intemperate weather, or even, as we shall see, foreign invasion. It also offered aid against unseen spiritual menaces. During Roman Catholic rogation, participants processed behind the priest holding a consecrated host or even behind saints' bones. These sacred objects imbued rogation with the power to purify and hallow the bounds, exorcizing not only disease, but also demonic spirits, often represented in the form of dragons. The Reformation introduced other changes to the ritual, and they can best be glimpsed by considering how Laudians attempted to reverse some of them.

Laudians and their detractors differed over whether rogation had a primarily secular or ecclesiastical function. Did the ritual have any sanctifying power, or was it merely a secular means of establishing clear boundaries between parishes? To reinvigorate a fully sacralized rogation, Laudians abandoned many of the anti-Catholic caveats associated with the ritual's post-Reformation practice. It is telling that, because of its Roman Catholic connotations, rogation was largely discontinued under the Protectorate of Somerset.[13] When allowed again, defensive anti-popery informed Elizabethan and Jacobean visitation articles about it. John Jewel's *Iniunctions* (1569) for the see of Salisbury stipulate that rogation should be performed by a minister without surplice and "without carying of banners, staying at crosses, or using anye other superstitious ceremonies in any of your perambulations."[14] Richard Bancroft's 1604 visitation articles for London advise that ministers conduct rogation "without addition of any superstitious ceremonie heretofore used."[15] Bishop Miles Smith, who as Dean of Gloucester famously clashed with Laud, clarifies what these superstitious ceremonies are in Gloucester visitation articles (1622). Perambulation should proceed "without wearing any surplesse, or carrying of banners, or handbels, or making any stay at crosses, or such like popish observations."[16]

Laud's articles for London and Canterbury rarely evince any defensive anti-popery. Admonitions to avoid superstitious ceremonies or to perform perambulation without banners, surplices, handbells, crosses, and other popish devices are absent from them.[17] More generally, Laudian visitation articles are often silent when it comes to warning against the popish connotations of rogation.[18] While clergy in the Laudian era were not disciplined for including "Romish" practices during rogation, they could be for omitting them.[19] As Margaret Stieg documents, William Clifford's parishioners at Yarlington presented him for not perambulating in 1629. Clifford's "parishioners had refused to consent to no prayers and no psalms on the occasion and Mr. Clifford had claimed that it was superstitious and papistical to use prayers or sing psalms in the fields."[20]

Indeed, we can further gauge the conflict over rogation by observing the different treatment of its fasts in the Laudian Henry Mason's *The epicures fast* (1626) and the puritan William Prynne's *A briefe suruay and censure of Mr Cozens his couzening deuotions* (1628). Mason's and Prynne's approaches to these fasts serve as an index of their attitude towards the ritual's holiness. In *The epicures fast*, Mason urges a more robust conception of the austerity of rogation fasts. He bemoans the fact that the Roman Church has become "very liberal of their Dispensations … even in the holy and strict time of Lent." In particular, Mason criticizes the Roman Church because it "hath abrogated the Fast of the Rogation weeke, which was commanded by the Canon Law: as also the Wednesday and Fryday Fast, which, as they say, was enioyned by Precept ever since the Apostles time."[21] The apostolic institution of rogation offers further reason to take the ritual, and the fasts accompanying it, seriously; its holiness is primitive. Moreover, instead of retreating from the Roman Catholic connotations of rogation fasts, Mason seeks to intensify the Roman position, rescuing it from laxity. This corresponds to how Laudians unapologetically recovered many of the pre-Reformation practices performed during rogation processions. By contrast, William Prynne's *A briefe suruay and censure of Mr Cozens his couzening deuotions* approaches rogation with less reverence for its sanctifying function. In the work, Prynne responds to Cosin's claim that "Rogation dayes" are "Apostolicall Praecepts and Constitutions" by arguing for their "Politicall" significance. These days are

> prescribed and enioyned by the State for Politique endes: As the increase of Cattell, the maintaining of Ships, and Marriners, and the incouragement of Fishermen: (in which respect our Church doth principally observe these dayes: not as Fasting dayes, or dayes of Devotion to be spent in Prayer and Fasting: but rather, yea chiefly, as Fish-dayes, for the advancement of Fishing, and sparing of young Cattle: not as dayes enioyned by the Churches but designed by the States Authority.[22]

Where Mason sacralizes, Prynne secularizes. He finds that the Laudian interpretation of rogation has too much abstinence and devotion in it; Mason argues that Roman rogation is not nearly abstinent and devoted enough. The discrepancy derives from opposite conclusions regarding rogation's holiness and ability to confer holiness.

As that discrepancy reveals, while both Laudians and puritans might perform rogation, disagreement remained about the manner of its performance. The godly balked at rogation's Roman Catholic connotation; they favoured a minimal use of ceremony during the ritual; and many wanted to see rogation divested of any religious and sanctifying power whatsoever. What resulted from these godly objections, as Nathan J. Ristuccia notes, "was a liturgy of surveying, an opportunity for the parish to define itself as a geographical unit and even to repair parish markers along the way."[23] The effect of this approach on traditional rogation could be thoroughly vitiating. A telling moment occurs in a sermon John Rawlinson preached on Rogation Sunday in 1605. He refers to three spiritual benefits provided by his scriptural source text, The Song of Solomon 6:13 ("Return, return, O Shulamite").[24] About these benefits he remarks, "these are the lists and land-marks, wherewith at this time I must bound the procession of my discourse."[25] This is the sermon's most explicit commentary on rogation. Without its ceremonial accoutrements, its capacity to sanctify, and, indeed, with questions arising about the ritual's basic legitimacy, rogation was reduced to the merely metaphorical.

No mere metaphor, *Lycidas* envisions a rogation with the full power of sanctification, apotropaic function and all. Milton's engagement with rogation is thorough to the point of being exhaustive. No major component of the ritual, from its historical institution (guarding against beasts, pestilence, and intemperate air; Ambarvalia) to its habitual practice (purple, handbells, saints' bones, placement before Ascension on the liturgical calendar), goes unaccounted for. Were a puritan revision of rogation intended, the fidelity of Milton's depiction to details of its historical origin and practical implementation would be much more in question. There are peculiarities, no doubt, about rogation in the poem. Still, while some alterations to the ritual do occur, Milton's re-imagining does not exact such drastic revisions as to meet the puritan threshold of completely secularizing the ritual or simply rejecting it out-of-hand as too popish to handle. Rogation in *Lycidas* is neither bloodlessly secular nor frantically anti-Catholic.

## II Rogation and *Lycidas*

Only two other commentators (to my knowledge) suggest the relevance of rogation to Milton's elegy: the eighteenth-century antiquarian John Brand (examined below), and the Victorian naturalist Anne Pratt. In *The Flowering Plants of Great Britain* (1855), Pratt discusses Milkwort, the official rogation flower that can come in a purple colour. To describe the flower, Pratt quotes (somewhat inaccurately) a famous imperative from the flower catalog in *Lycidas*. She writes, "our milkwort is little heeded now by any but the lovers of wild flowers; but few of these would pass it without a thought of praise for its beauty, as they see it among the short grass of the hill-side, where it 'Purples [sic] all the ground with vernal flowers.'"[26] Pratt makes no explicit argument about the poem, only correlating Milkwort with the vernal flowers' purpling. There remains, though, evidence to support her intimation and reading rogation into *Lycidas*. The poem contains an implicit depiction of the ceremony in these lines of the ninth verse paragraph:

> Ay me! Whilst thee the shores, and sounding Seas
> Wash far away, where ere thy bones are hurld,
> Whether beyond the stormy Hebrides,
> Where thou perhaps under the whelming tide
> Visit'st the bottom of the monstrous world;
> Or whether thou to our moist vows deny'd,
> Sleep'st by the fable of Bellerus old,
> Where the great vision of the guarded Mount
> Looks toward Namancos and Bayona's hold;
> Look homeward Angel now, and melt with ruth.
> And, O ye Dolphins, waft the haples youth.[27] (154–164)

About the geographic expansiveness of these lines, Joad Raymond notes, "Michael's boundaries in 'Lycidas' include the shores of Britain, extending into the Irish Sea."[28] The circuit that the bones travel – from the extreme Hebrides in the north to land's end in the south – is reminiscent of rogation's perambulation of parochial borders. Milton's cartography also demarcates confessional boundaries. St. Michael maintains a vigilant watch over Catholic Spain. In its preoccupation with local borders, rogation could inspire reflection on larger ones. For example, George Wither uses his poem on rogation in *The hymnes and songs of the Church* (1623) to ask God for the following: "Domesticke Brawles expell thou farre,/And be thou pleasd our Coast to guard,/The dreadfull sounds of in-brought Warre,/Within our Confines be not heard:/ Continue also here thy word,/And make us thankefull (we thee pray)/ The Pestilence, Dearth, and the Sword/Have beene so long with-held away."[29] Rogation's capacity to prevent "in-brought Warre" by guarding the coast is similar to the function of the "guarded Mount" that Milton envisions.

The ritual's presence is also proved through a complex web of classical allusion and historical fact that concludes verse paragraph nine.

The paragraph's final line contains this classical reference: "And, O ye Dolphins, waft the haples youth" (164). Here, Milton alludes to the poet Arion of Methmyna. In *The Histories*, Herodotus relates that, in addition to being carried safely to Taenarum by dolphins, Arion invented the dithyramb at Corinth.[30] The dithyramb was a hymn in honour of Bacchus. Structurally and tonally, this allusion to Bacchus is an important moment in the poem: it (along with a petition for God's blessing) initiates the celebratory consolation of the penultimate verse paragraph. The wafting of Lycidas repairs the damage done by the maenads (the "rout that made the hideous roar" [61]) in the fifth verse paragraph. Whereas previously Bacchus's worshippers were a destructive and dismembering force, here the dolphins sacred to the god provide aid, collecting King and/or his remains.[31] Additionally, a composed dithyrambic hymn supplants the Bacchantes' frenzied ululations.

Like the dithyramb, the Roman festival of Ambarvalia was also in honour of Bacchus. The ritual took place each year on 29 May, and both Tibullus and (possibly) Virgil attest to Bacchus's role in the ceremony.[32] For rogation, the importance of Ambarvalia and, by extension, an allusion to Bacchus is amply explained in Lancelot Andrewes's *A learned discourse of ceremonies retained and used in Christian churches* (1653): "And as for the bounding of the Meares of Parishes, our Clergy-Priests on their Rogation week go on Procession. So likewise did the Heathen, their perambulations for this purpose were called Ambarvalia."[33] The German theologian David Pareus makes the connection among Bacchus, Ambarvalia, and rogation even clearer: "And as the heathens had their feasts of Baccus, Ceres, Pan: so these [Catholics] keep shrovetide, Rogation weeke, & such like festivities, having altered onely the names thereof."[34] While depicting a series of events with connotations of Rogationtide *Lycidas* alludes, via Arion, to the god who was honoured during the pagan festival upon which rogation was based. We might call that coincidence were it not for the consummately gifted classicist behind it.

We might also call it coincidence were it not for important details preceding lines 154–164 that create a context predisposed towards the ritual's portrayal. Rogation maintains parochial distinctions and guards against the kind of creeping intrusiveness St. Peter decries in the eighth verse paragraph (115). It may be significant that St. Peter himself draws attention to this threat, since one tradition attributes the ritual's founding to him.[35] The most dramatic expression of invasiveness comes at the hands of the "grim Woolf": "Besides what the grim Woolf with privy paw/Daily devours apace" (128–129). The rapacity of the "Blind mouthes!" (119) is matched only by the hunger of a ravening wolf. The grim wolf evokes rogation not only because of the trespass the image symbolizes, but also because it is a wolf that trespasses. Rogation was originally instituted to ask for God's protection against wolves. Alexander Ross explains in *Pansebeia* (1655) that the rogation litany was "invented by Mamertus Bishop of Vienna [A.D. 452],[36] in a time when Wolves and other wild Beasts had broke out of the woods, and killed divers people."[37] The wolves are not only a physical reality, but can also represent a spiritual menace. Arthur Hopton's *A concordancy of yeares* (1612) describes rogation as offering "praiers as well against the bodily Woolves, such as late were in France, as also against the spirituall Woolves."[38]

In the eighth verse paragraph, menace also comes in the form of disease: "The hungry Sheep look up, and are not fed,/But swoln with wind, and the rank mist they draw,/Rot inwardly, and foul contagion spread" (125–127). One of the functions of rogation was to beseech God to protect individuals, but especially the flocks and fields, from disease and intemperate weather. The spreading contagion that *Lycidas* depicts recurs in discussions of rogation. Like Hopton, Richard Taverner, the great English translator of Erasmus, defines the menace spiritually, projecting the natural world onto the interior, spiritual landscape of each individual believer. According to Taverner, rogation is a time to pray that "God woll vouchsave to blesse hys creatures not only (as before is sayd) for the cōmoditie of oure bodyes, but also for our soules helth, lest our miserable soules do herby catche unto themselves pestiferous infection and damnable contagion."[39] In Wither's poem on rogation in *The hymnes and songs of the Church*, he asks, "Let not the Seasons of this yeare … / Engender those Contagions here … / Let not the Summer wormes impaire/Those bloomings of the Earth we see;/Nor Blastings, or distemper'd Ayre/Destroy those Fruites that hopefull be."[40] *Lycidas* also worries about contagion. In the fourth verse paragraph, the speaker bemoans the effect of Lycid's death on the natural world as being "As killing as the Canker to the Rose,/Or Taint-worm to the weanling Herds that graze,/Or Frost to Flowers" (45–47).

The final ways in which the poem anticipates rogation are found at the beginning of the ninth verse paragraph, when the speaker importunes, "… call the Vales, and bid them hither cast/Their Bels, and Flourets of a thousand hues" (134–135). Small handbells were a common feature in rogation rituals, though following the Reformation most Protestants rejected them as popish.[41] Hereford visitation articles from 1592 define the carrying of handbells as "such like popish ceremonies" that must be avoided; similarly, Jacobean articles from 1621 prohibit the use of handbells during rogation and "such like Popish observations."[42] Translating the handbell into the image of a flower with a bell-shaped blossom (possibly a bluebell) ingeniously rethinks rogation ritual. Nature is responsive to Rogationtide, supplying the bells that were previously carried, and synchronous with the rhythms of the liturgical calendar. The bell-flowers also revise rogation in the direction of less ceremony (popish ceremony at least) by pointing to the redundancy of ceremonies that duplicate what nature already provides. Nature's assuming – almost reabsorbing – some of rogation's ritual is apparent when the speaker directs the valleys, "And purple all the ground with vernal flowres" (141). The traditional colour associated with rogation is purple. Celebrants would wear purple vestments during masses in Rogationtide, and the colour was also used because of the general Lenten, penitential theme. The threats of trespass upon parochial boundaries and of blight in the natural world, along with details about handbells and the colour purple, create a context conducive to rogation's depiction. The ritual included, or was intended to prevent, all of the above.

The following details, however, may seem very unlike rogation rituals: Edward King's bones are performing a circuit of these boundaries, with some uncertainty as to their whereabouts and lack of human agency; pain and monstrosity are prevalent parts of the ritual; and finally, perhaps most pressingly, rogation occurs at sea. Rather than signaling the inapplicability of the ritual to *Lycidas*, these variations attest to some fairly detailed knowledge of the practice. Rogation could, and did, take place at sea. The famous Venetian ritual, the Marriage of the Sea, described in Samuel Purchas's *Purchas his pilgrimes* (1625), was preceded by perambulating boats.[43] (Milton would later travel to Venice during Easter-time in April of 1639.) Rogation was also a ritual with strong associations of pain and the monstrous. In *Lycidas*, a sensation of pain is the unavoidable consequence of depicting bones washed far away, tossed about in stormy seas, overwhelmed by whelming tides, and "hurld." Edward King's bones are, to a large degree, *pulverized*. In his study of rogation and the formation of community, Steve Hindle writes about the ritual's connection to pain: "the recollections of old men about the precise locations of mere-stones, boundary streams, or decisive trees are replete with references to being bumped, ducked, or beaten at the appropriate point."[44] The old men were once young children who participated in rogation, and whose memories of parish landmarks had been beaten into them. Pain has always been an unfortunately reliable mnemonic aid.

The frightfulness associated with rogation might also aid in remembrance of geographic and ritualistic particulars. *Lycidas* invokes the ritual's depiction of monstrosity in these lines: "Where thou perhaps under the whelming tide / Visit'st the bottom of the monstrous world." Rogation's exorcizing function may inspire the reference to monsters. The practice was often believed to purge demonic spirits and to purify the fields. Additionally, "monsters," in the form of dragons, were a part of rogation processions: "as a visual symbol, the dragon seems first to have been used during Rogation processions at Vienne, under bishop Mamertus, and to have spread from there … Yet by the twelfth century practically every major town in Gaul could boast a dragon-taming saint, and mounted Rogation Festivals with processional dragons."[45] The practice of exhibiting dragons on banners during Rogationtide was also common in England. As Eamon Duffy observes, the dragon would have "a long cloth tail before the procession on the first two of these 'Cross-days' or 'gang-days,' and carried, shorn of its tail, after the procession on the last day, as a symbol of the Devil's overthrow."[46] There may be something reassuring, and predictive of the poem's consolatory end, about Edward King's bones traveling this terrifying circuit: they hallow the monstrous ends of the earth. They help to shear that frightful dragon's tail.

Bones could have this sanctifying power in rogation rituals because saints' bones were often employed during them and, as we shall see, King is described as a saint through scriptural allusion in the next verse paragraph. Again, Hindle: "the Rogationtide festivities in St Newlyn (Cornwall) in the 1520s involved the parishioners of four adjacent parishes processing behind the bones of four local saints."[47] Ronald Hutton elaborates that it was probably during the Henrician reforms of 1538 that these "four villages besides the dunes and cliffs of north Cornwall lost the major part of their Rogation week rites, which had consisted of exhibiting the bones and crosses of their patron saints upon four raised stones in the chapel yard at St Newlyn East."[48] Though Milton may not have known of this Cornish practice, a reference to Cornwall (i.e., Michael's Mount) coinciding with a depiction of King's perambulating bones seems especially appropriate and redolent with the potential for local meaning.[49]

It is true, however, that the lines seem uncertain about the exact location of King's bones. In a modification of rogation related to this uncertainty, human agency does not drive the ritual. To some degree, beating the bounds is *about* the uncertainty of human agency. The word comes from the Latin verb "rogare," meaning "to ask" and "to entreat."[50] One pleadingly asks a question, of course, when uncertainty prevails. Rogation was a time to ask for God's blessing. The etymology provides evidence for how the ritual serves as a fitting culmination of the poem's incessant interrogatives: "Where were ye nymphs" (50); "He ask'd the Waves, and ask'd the Fellon winds,/What hard mishap hath doom'd this gentle swain?" (91–92); "Ah! Who hath reft (quoth he) my dearest pledge?" (107); "How well could I have spar'd for thee young swain./ Anow of such as for their bellies sake,/Creep and intrude, and climb into the fold?" (113–115); "What recks it them? What need they?" (122). All the poem's inquisitorial energy, interrogating nymphs and waves and winds, is collected here and redirected towards the only interlocutor who really matters. Up to this point, the poem has only asked questions that sought to blame. Instead of questions that are explicitly loaded with blame and accusation, the implicit question in the poem's depiction of rogation seeks God's blessing; it relies on a store of mercy that has been described as infinite. In that transformation, from explicitly accusatory to implicitly pleading, a certain acceptance of fate, unfortunateness, and God's will is evident. Implicitly suing for God's blessing represents some reconciliation with the reality of King's hard mishap. The finger-pointing interrogatives have stopped, and a more meditative and prayerful internalization of questioning signals a greater acceptance of the tragedy the poem narrates. That acceptance is a prerequisite for the consolations of "Weep no more." While the lack of human agency is not characteristic of rogation, it is also not wholly inconsistent with its supplicatory narrative. More importantly, it is the poem's raison d'être, the consolatory function of elegy, that supersedes it. And console it does, as the poem explodes into a brilliant vision of Lycid triumphant.

## III Ascent and the "Genius of the Shore"

The ascension of Lycidas comprises a powerful tie to rogation and its place on the church calendar. The poem imagines that ascent when, following the depiction of rogation in lines 154–164, Milton writes, "So Lycidas sunk low, but mounted high" (172). Rogationtide was the Monday, Tuesday, and Wednesday immediately preceding Ascension Thursday. Though rogation prepares for the ascension of Christ (Acts 1:1–14), participants are also affected by ascendancy. Godfrey Goodman describes this relationship between rogation and ascension: "Thus we continue to the Ascension of Christ, before which we have a Rogation-week, that so our prayers, and we our selves in heart and affection, may together ascend with Christ." Rogation enables this ascension; it is when the individual believer "might rise together with him [Christ]."[51] The ascendance that rogation initiates is, in many ways, the perfect counterpoint to Edward King's perambulating bones. The ponderous weight and density of "the whelming tide"[52] and "the bottom of the monstrous world" dissipate in Lycid's buoyant ascent.

Accompanying this ascent is King's institution as a local saint, the "Genius of the shore" who "shalt be good/To all that wander in that perilous flood" (183–185). King's investiture with this sanctifying, prophylactic power accords with the belief that rogation "conferred some benediction upon the community"[53] and would "protect the crops and community from natural misfortunes."[54] Sanctification – in the protective presence of King's genius – is precisely what occurs in *Lycidas*, and precisely what puritans rejected in the ritual.

The element of King's protective genius is the basis on which the eighteenth-century antiquarian John Brand seems to have intuited rogation in the poem. The 1813 edition of *Observations on Popular Antiquities*, revised by Henry Ellis, contains the following description of rogation:

> On Ascension Day, the Magistrates, Rivery-Jury, &c. of the Corporation of the above town [Newcastle-upon-Tyne], according to an ancient custom, make their annual procession by water in their barges, visiting the bounds of their jurisdiction on the river, to prevent encroachments. Chearful libations are offered on the occasion to the Genius of our wealthy Flood, which Milton calls the "coaly Tyne."[55]

The "coaly Tyne" is a reference to Milton's "At a Vacation Exercise in the College" (line 98). The "Genius of our Wealthy Flood" seems to splice together these lines from *Lycidas*: "Hence forth thou art the Genius of the shore,/In thy large recompense, and shalt be good/To all that wander in that perilous flood" (183–185). "Genius of the shore" and "perilous flood" become "Genius of our wealthy Flood." It is suggestive that perambulation, *Lycidas*, and genius all occur together in Brand's description. Perhaps he did, on some level at least, sub-consciously associate them. Of course, this work tends to be more folklore than fact, but it does coordinate rogation and the celebration of a local genius. It is applicable to *Lycidas* as King becomes a kind of tutelary deity, providing the "succour of God and of his Saints" that rogation could supply.[56] Saintliness is clear, for just as the saints in Revelation 7:17 have the tears wiped away from their eyes, so too are the tears wiped from King's eyes in line 181.[57] He is also associated with the 144,000 of Revelation 14:4; it is an exegetical commonplace to interpret those not defiled with women as saints.[58] This connection among saints, genius, and protective aid does not have a puritan connotation.

Alison A. Chapman observes that "in 'Lycidas,' Milton seems to be experimenting with how much he can imagine Edward King as continuing to protect the living after his own death, an idea that by its very nature curves dangerously close to the Catholic idea of sainthood."[59] To Chapman's point, the Roman Catholic controversialist John Sergeant urges believers to apply to and invoke a saint so that they "shall at length be wrought up (an endeavour to imitate him going along) into the very genius of that Saint."[60] Puritans rejected the kind of specificity in person (those wandering the flood) and need (safe passage) that Milton represents King as responsive to. George Downame argues, "it may well be supposed that the Saints departed do pray in common for the faithfull upon the earth, as fellow-members of the same bodie. But they are not acquainted with particular persons, or their particular wants or desires."[61] Downame asserts that the saints cannot offer aid "nor have promised to heare and help us, as having no such power, yea are so farre from hearing and helping that they neither know us nor our desires."[62] Downame and other puritans dispute the capacity of saints to hear prayers and provide aid because it detracts from the omnipotence of Christ. In *Canterburies doome* (1646), William Prynne objects to Laudians censoring the following argument against saintly intercession: namely, that such interceding is a "horrible sacriledge"; it "rob[s] Christ of his right; he is our Intercessor; if not, yet blasphemy to disable him, he belike is unsufficient, they put into his office the Saints, as Coadjutors."[63] Lycid and his largesse have the potential to accomplish this theft.

Arguments such as those found in Prynne, as this chapter stated earlier, relate closely to arguments against the sanctification of natural environments. Those environments – and the numinous figures associated with them – could detract from the omnipotence of Christ. In describing the shift in pre- and post-Reformation attitudes towards rogation, Walsham writes, "the aim of these measures [post-Reformation] was to shift the emphasis away from the apotropaic function of rogation towards the utilitarian purpose of fixing and maintaining contestable boundaries."[64] That Lycidas is now susceptible to the objections against intercession quoted by Prynne – that he performs this "apotropaic function" – provides evidence for the sanctifying rogation that has taken place. There is, no doubt, a utility in demarcating confessional boundaries; St. Michael's Mount keeps a vigilant watch on the Roman Catholic menace. But the overwhelming effect of rogation is the institution of Lycidas in tutelary benignity. Rogation's ability to perform that institution and sanctify the natural world makes the strongest case for its Laudian connotations.

The following pages contend that virginity confers a similar sanctification in the poem. Indeed, it represents an extension of the theological rationale by which rogation operates. In their capacity to consecrate, both virginity and rogation possess the ability to bestow holiness as a result of ascetic or ceremonial effort. "For 'beating the bounds,'" Sarah Beckwith writes, "conventionally signified at once a ritualization of space and a consecration of property."[65] The virgin's body underwent a similar consecration. Cyprian describes virgins as those who have "consecrated themselves to Christ."[66] For virgins to violate their vows was considered sacrilege; they consecrated their bodies to God.[67] While

Edward King took no vow of virginity, the poem imbues his virginal state with holiness.

## IV "The Unexpressive Nuptiall Song"

As the previous chapter discussed, a number of influential scholarly accounts examine the presence of asceticism in Milton's early work in general and *Lycidas* in particular. This chapter follows Hanford, Sirluck, and J. Martin Evans by reading virginity in "Epitaphium Damonis" as an intensification of its presence in *Lycidas*.[68] It departs from attempts by Nicholas McDowell and John Leonard to disassociate these poems from ascetic meanings. The contribution that this section makes to the existing scholarship on the subject is two-fold. It reads the ascetic interests of *Lycidas* and "Epitaphium Damonis" alongside the lively debate between Laudians and godly writers about these issues. The argument particularizes and contextualizes Miltonic asceticism in the hopes of remedying one of the problems Brooke Conti identifies in scholarly treatment of the topic: "The assumption seems to be that Milton's interest in virginity was a private eccentricity: one that might have received inspiration from sources such as Spenser, Plato, or the Bible, but that otherwise had no precise precedent and that vanished upon Milton's maturation as easily as it had come."[69] As the following pages contend, Miltonic asceticism does not represent a private eccentricity but a head-on engagement with a major source of contemporary religious division. That engagement reveals Milton's uncertainties about the Laudian Church, the uncovering of which constitutes the second contribution this section makes to critical discussion of the poem. An analysis of asceticism in *Lycidas* leaves Milton on the fence about Laudianism.

The ascetic connotations of *Lycidas* derive from the poem's depiction of the heavenly rewards of virginity, as outlined in Revelation 14. Since some disagreement exists about whether Milton alludes to this chapter, I wish first to establish the allusion before considering how it participates in contemporary debates regarding virginity. In the penultimate verse paragraph, the heavenly joys that Edward King experiences include admittance into a very select group. As he laves his locks "With Nectar pure," Lycidas "hears the unexpressive nuptiall Song,/In the blest Kingdoms meek of joy and love" (175–177). The lines allude to Revelation 14:3–4: "And they sung as it were a new song before the throne, and before the four beasts, and the elders: and no man could learn that song but the hundred and forty and four thousand, which were redeemed from the earth. These are they which were not defiled with women; for they are virgins." The allusion to Revelation 14 seems to me clear in "unexpressive," which corresponds to the ineffability of a song that "no man could learn."

Both John Leonard and Nicholas McDowell, however, contest the allusion to Revelation 14. Leonard cogently observes that the passage also alludes to Revelation 19, a point to which I will turn shortly and one that does not disqualify simultaneous allusion to Revelation 14. For his part, McDowell questions the allusion (in a note) with the following reasoning:

> As John Leonard argues, there is no need to equate King's apotheosis with celibacy rather than chastity: the "unexpressive nuptial song" more likely refers to Rev. 19, in which St John hears the voice of "all [God's] servants ... saying 'Alleluia,'" than 14:1–4, in which 144,000 men "who were not defiled with women" are "redeemed from the earth" ("Milton's Vow of Celibacy," 191–3). Milton anyway emphasizes in the *Apology* that defilement in Rev. 14 "doubtlesse means fornication: for marriage must not be called a defilement." (i.893)[70]

For McDowell, King's hearing the song connects him to Revelation 19 as opposed to Revelation 14. Leonard, too, seems to employ a similar rationale when he writes, "the fact that Lycidas hears a 'nuptial Song' also points towards Revelation 19 (not 14) as the dominant source text."[71] The implicit argument, I take it, is that the 144,000 "*learn* that song"; they do not *hear* it. Thus, this salient detail increases the strain of associating King with those "not defiled with women." E.M.W. Tillyard, no friend to Miltonic chastity, argues that in Milton's early poems "we get a hint of the doctrine that chastity is the means of hearing the celestial music."[72] For Tillyard, "That undisturbed Song of pure concent" (6) in "At a solemn Musick," and "the heavenly tune, which none can hear/Of human mould with grosse unpurged ear" (72–73) in *Arcades* describe the unique listening abilities of the chaste. In Tillyard's analysis, King hearing the nuptial song in *Lycidas* constitutes another iteration of a common theme found throughout Milton's early poems.

The clearest answer as to why King hears, and does not learn, the "unexpressive nuptiall Song" lies in the original language of Revelation 14:3: "καὶ οὐδεὶς ἐδύνατο μαθεῖν τὴν ᾠδὴν εἰ μὴ αἱ ἑκατὸν τεσσεράκοντα τέσσαρες χιλιάδες, οἱ ἠγορασμένοι ἀπὸ τῆς γῆς."[73] The English "learn" derives from the Greek "μαθεῖν," a variant of "μανθάνω." Both classical and biblical usages of the word support Milton's translating it as "hears." Definition three of "μανθάνω" in Liddell and Scott's Greek lexicon lists the following: "to perceive by the senses, remark, notice."[74] In Euripides's *Electra*, the Chorus (and a disguised Orestes) urges Electra to relate her current misfortune: "νῦν δὲ βούλομαι κἀγὼ μαθεῖν" (299).[75] A recent translation renders this line by "sad Electra's poet" (Sonnet VIII, 13) as "I wish to hear."[76] Finally, Gerhard Kittel's *Theological Dictionary of the New Testament* discusses the usage of "μαθεῖν" in Revelation 14:3: "The question is whether μαθεῖν simply means 'to learn' in the ordinary sense or whether it is to be taken in a more technical sense for hearing of a higher kind. A clear-cut decision is hardly possible, but there are certain passages which seem to favour the second view." Discussion of 2 Corinthians 12:4 and the *Corpus Hermeticum* follows, ultimately leading to this conclusion: "In this light the μαθεῖν of Rev. 14:3 might be understood as a deepened hearing."[77] As these examples demonstrate, Milton's "hears" comprehends an inflection of the Greek "μαθεῖν," thereby confirming his allusion to Revelation 14.

Through this allusion, Milton engages the debate concerning exegesis of the chapter and what its interpretation means for the value of physical virginity. Revelation 14:4 often fuels debate over asceticism, especially because its literal interpretation would seem to support the exclusivity of bodily virginity. In *Staffords Niobe* (1611), Anthony Stafford employs a quotation from Jerome's *Adversus Jovinianum* to prove that the Church Fathers "thought the same difference to bee between matrimonie, and virginity, that is betwixt to sin, and not to sinne, good, and better."[78] While on the one hand, Stafford tries to balance praise of virginity with respect towards marriage; on the other, he equates marriage with sin. Moreover, "good, and better" is most certainly *not* descriptive of the difference between sinning and not sinning. It also does not describe what Jerome says. Stafford is harsher even than Jerome, who is often thought to be harshest of all the Fathers towards marriage.[79] Jerome contends that the difference between marriage and virginity is similar to the difference between "*not* sinning and doing well" ("non peccare, et bene facere").[80] Stafford translates this as "betwixt to sin, and not to sinne," thereby making a muddle of the qualitative evaluations of the two as "good, and better." As a result of Stafford's mistranslation, virginity comes out far more exalted than matrimony in a comparison that sought to be charitable to both. Stafford's mistranslation anticipates the praise he would lavish on virginity in *The femall glory* (1635), a work that became a lightning rod for anti-Laudianism. To prove that virginity is better in *Staffords Niobe*, Stafford presents various scriptural passages (e.g., 1 Corinthians 7:1, 1 Kings 2, etc.), but he emphasizes "amongst all these places, this one in the Revelatiō is most of all to be noted." A quotation of Revelation 14:3–4 follows with Stafford concluding, "these are words that would inforce any sober soule to imbrace that single, simple, and sincere kinde of life."[81] Jeremy Taylor also uses Revelation 14 in *The rule and exercises of holy living* (1650) to account for the holiness of "chosen and voluntary" virginity. Virgins should "expect that little coronet or special reward which God hath prepared (extraordinary and besides the great Crown of all faithful souls) for those who have not defiled themselves with women."[82] Taylor's careful distinction between those who receive the reward and "all faithful souls" avoids dispersing virginity's rewards to all the Elect.

In contrast to these literal interpretations, godly writers de-emphasize the exalted view Revelation 14 takes of corporal virginity. To do so, they employ two main methods: they make virginity mean something else, especially something spiritual and metaphorical; and/or they widely disperse the rewards its maintenance promises. In *The image of bothe churches after reulacion of saynt Iohan the euangelyst* (1545), John Bale writes, "And they that ded synge them to the prayse of the lorde/ were not defyled with women. Wyth no straunge doctrynes/nor yet Prophane worshyppynges ys their faythe contamynate/that unfaynedlye have done on Iesus Christ." Not being defiled with women means resisting strange doctrines and profane worship; it does not stand for bodily virginity but "the maydenhede of the sowle."[83] Idolatry is often considered the spiritual equivalent of adultery, and thus the passage's frequent interpretation as denouncing idolaters. Arthur Dent, in *The ruine of Rome: or An exposition vpon the whole Reuelation* (1603), observes, "this holy cōpany are not defiled with women, that is, with grosse & divers sins, or rather with idolatrous pollutions."[84] And finally, in order to refute the idea that an act of supererogation such as virginity might entitle one to heavenly recompense, some make it more broadly accessible. Contesting how "papistes by this place would confirme the single life of the popish clergie," William Fulke writes, "neither doth it make any thing for their purpose yᵗ they are called virgins. For this doth perteyne to the whole companie of the elect, & not to the ministers of the worde only, much lesse to the popish priestes."[85] This is most decidedly *not* a distinction "extraordinary and besides the great Crown of all faithful souls [cf. 'the whole companie of the elect']."

*Lycidas* allows for a literal interpretation of Revelation 14:4. The reason for a literal understanding of Edward King's participation in the "unexpressive nuptiall song" is simple, and it lies in an important fact of King's biography: he died unmarried. In light of this fact, how can bodily virginity not be one possible meaning for his being undefiled with women? Soteriologically, the allowance for a literal interpretation of Revelation 14:4 is significant. It means that something Edward King has done, a physical state he has maintained, has accrued some kind of merit. To guard against this possibility in his exegesis of Revelation, David Pareus attributes the lack of defilement to the imputation of Christ's merit: "For they that are washed from their filthines are not defiled: And they are virgines: because they are made white in the blood of Christ, that is, justified and sanctified by the merit and spirit of Christ."[86] The presence of physical virginity makes these lines about something King does rather than what Christ imputes. Milton does not put it as bluntly as Jeremy Taylor; namely, that King should "expect that little coronet or special reward which God hath prepared (extraordinary and besides the great Crown of all faithful souls) for those who have not defiled themselves with women."[87] But by connecting the dots between King's unmarried state and Revelation 14:4, a similar logic obtains. To David Pareus's strenuous assertion that Revelation 14:4 does not "establish the merit of corporal virginity," *Lycidas* cannot assent.[88]

Other poems in *Justa Edouardo King naufrago* (1638) allude to King's virginity and, at the same time, Revelation 14:4.[89] For instance, the prefatory poem in the *Justa* states, "Virgin-killing Thetis (the sea), there had fallen slain by your betraying hand that head dear to Apollo and the Muses."[90] The virgin that Thetis/the sea kills is Edward King. The original Latin poem gives Thetis the epithet "virgin-killing" through the Greek adjective "παρθενοκτόνος."[91] The use of a Greek word in a Latin poem, and the root of the Greek adjective itself, "παρθένος" ("virgin/maiden"), are both important. "Παρθένος" most often means a "maiden," and one cannot make sense of its application to Edward King without recourse to Revelation and King's unmarried state.[92] Out of the fourteen usages of "παρθένος" in the Greek New Testament, the only time the word refers exclusively to male virgins is in Revelation 14:4: "παρθένοι γάρ εἰσιν" ("for they are virgins").[93] Revelation mediates the meaning of "παρθενοκτόνος" in the *Justa*; it supplies the most significant precedent for applying "παρθένος" to a male virgin.

"Παρθενοκτόνος" would have been of particular interest to Milton if, as some have conjectured, contributors to the *Justa* read each other's poems before publication.[94] Describing Thetis as "παρθενοκτόνος" alludes to the *Alexandra* of Lycophron (b. ca. 330–325 B.C.E.), where this epithet occurs: "παρθενοκτόνον Θέτιν" ("virgin-killing Thetis").[95] In 1634, Milton purchased his own edition of the *Alexandra*. In the copy of Milton's Lycophron found in the University of Illinois Urbana-Champaign Rare Books Library, Milton stars a word at line 21 and includes a marginal note next to it, referencing Tztetzes's scholia: "παρθενοκτόνον Θέτιν" occurs at line 22 (see figure 3.1).[96]

The use of "παρθένος" in the *Justa*, and in such a form that would have piqued Milton's intellectual interest, indicates that *Lycidas* is not alone in coordinating King's unmarried state with Revelation 14:4. That coordination privileges a literal interpretation of the scriptural text. What's more, the two poems accomplish this coordination through similar means. In an intertextual enactment of what the process of

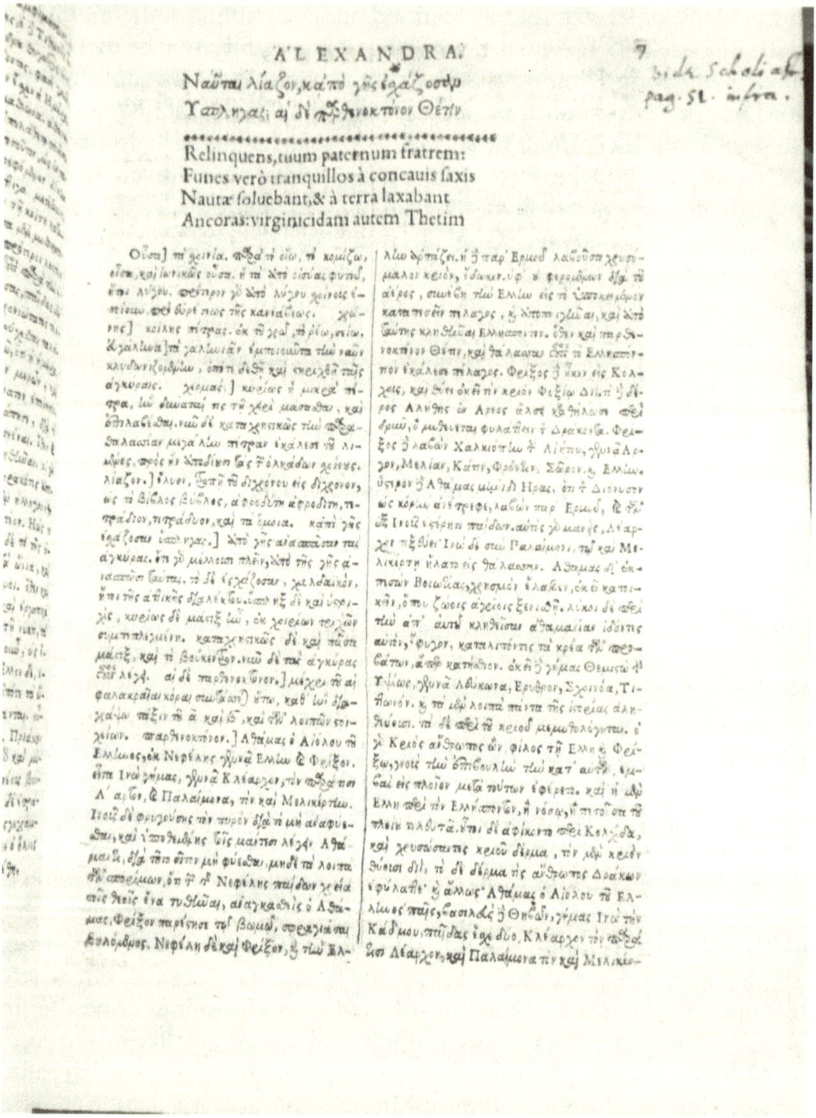

ALEXANDRA.

Relinquens, tuum paternum fratrem:
Funes verò tranquillos à concauis saxis
Nautæ soluebant, & à terra laxabant
Ancoras: virginicidam autem Thetim

Figure 3.1. Isaac Tzetzes, *Lycophronos tou Chalkideōs Alexandra* (Geneva, 1601).

coterie reading and manuscript circulation entails, both poems coordinate through a process of extra-textual supplementation. In *Lycidas*, to make sense of allusion to Revelation, the reader supplies the biographical fact of King's unmarried state. In the *Justa*, to make sense of allusion to Lycophron, the reader supplies that biographical fact and Revelation 14's use of "παρθένος." That another poem in the *Justa* connects King's virginity with Revelation 14:4, and that it uses a similar methodology to do so, provides corroboration for Milton's own literal exposition of the passage. Regardless of whether or not Milton saw the *Justa*, or whether he read poems from other contributors in advance, these similarities at least point to a similar way of thinking about King's virginity.

But as we have seen consistently in this study, even a seeming emphasis on corporal asceticism exists alongside its spiritual compeer. Accordingly, the literalism of Milton's allusion to Revelation is not without qualification. The "unexpressive nuptiall song" alludes, as various commentators record, to Revelation 19.[97] Conflation of the passages is not unique, and their combination means that "nuptiall" refers to the marriage supper of the Lamb in Revelation 19:7–9.[98] That reference provides the poem with an alternative to a literal interpretation of "not defiled with women." In Revelation 14, the condition of one's admittance to heavenly joys is physical virginity; in Revelation 19, no such condition is a prerequisite for being "called unto the marriage supper of the Lamb" (19:9). The "song" in "nuptiall song" must still reference Revelation 14 (the "new song," though also found at 5:9), since no mention is made of any song in chapter nineteen.[99] How can we make sense of these seemingly divergent allusions? Does physical or spiritual virginity prevail? Other scholars – such as James Holly Hanford, Ernest Sirluck, and J. Martin Evans – have long recognized that Milton's "Epitaphium Damonis" employs a similar set of allusions; like *Lycidas*, it is written to an unmarried young man and celebrates the rewards of the single life. This later poem provides important clues as to whether spiritual or physical virginity prevails in *Lycidas*. The insistence of "Epitaphium Damonis" on physical virginity throws into relief the absence of such pertinacity in *Lycidas*. Though Milton abandons a literal interpretation of Revelation 14:4 in *An Apology for Smectymnuus* (1642), "Epitaphium Damonis" (1639) embraces it.

Damon's epitaph was written to commemorate the death of Milton's closest friend, Charles Diodati, who died while Milton was abroad touring Europe. Similar to *Lycidas*, "Epitaphium Damonis" concludes with a vision of its hapless, prematurely deceased subject triumphant.

> Quòd tibi purpureus pudor, & sine labe Juventus
> Grata fuit, quòd nulla tori libata voluptas,

En etiam tibi virginei servantur honores;
Ipse caput nitidum cinctus rutilante corona,
Letáque frondentis gestans umbracula palmæ
Æternùm perages immortales hymenæos;
Cantus ubi, choreisque furit lyra mista beatis,
Festa Sionæo bacchantur & Orgia Thyrso. (213–220)

(Since blushing decency and youth without disgrace pleased you, and since you did not taste marriage's pleasures, virginal honours are still saved for you. Yourself ringed, radiant head with glittering crown, and bearing the joyful shading of the branching palm, you will forever act the timeless marriage out where song and the lyres mingled with the blessed dances rave, and under Sion's thyrsus the Orgies revel on.)

These lines allude to both Revelation 14 ("youth without disgrace," "did not taste marriage's pleasures," "virginal honours") and Revelation 19 ("forever act the timeless marriage out"). In "Epitaphium Damonis," allusion to Revelation 19 does not spiritually revise virginity the way it does in *Lycidas*. The reason is because the corporal connotations are so explicitly described that they are not subject to the same qualification. Whereas they are supplied in *Lycidas* by an extra-textual method of supplementation – that is, the biographical fact of King's virginity or the context of the *Justa* – they are prescribed in "Epitaphium Damonis." It is only because of the following that Damon experiences joyous revels: "since you did not taste marriage's pleasures" ("quòd nulla tori libata voluptas" [213]). In *Lycidas*, admittance to Revelation 19's marriage supper of the Lamb lowers the threshold of bodily virginity. In "Epitaphium Damonis," bodily virginity grants Damon admittance to the marriage supper. Damon's virginity primarily consists, not in some holiness of soul or not committing idolatry, but in not having had marital intercourse.

Some commentators, however, challenge an interpretation of "Epitaphium Damonis" that privileges physical virginity. For example, John Leonard focuses on these lines from the poem: "quòd nulla tori libata voluptas,/En etiam tibi virginei servantur honores" (214–215) ("and since you did not taste marriage's pleasures,/virginal honours are still saved for you"). Leonard argues that the equation of "tori" with "marriage" is inaccurate: "Hanford, Bush, Shawcross, and Carey all translate *torus* as 'marriage bed' or even 'marriage.' *Torus* actually means 'couch' and can refer to any bed of pleasure, licit or illicit."[100] Leonard adduces the use of "torus" in Ovid's *Amores* as evidence of the word's connotative flexibility. The notion that the poem celebrates Diodiati never having had illicit sex seems not only out of character for

Milton, but it also reduces the transcendent solemnity of the poem's final line to a crude joke: not having had earthly orgies, Diodati can get his fill of them in heaven. Separating "torus" from the marriage bed is also complicated by an important text: the Latin Vulgate Bible. In Coverdale's 1538 edition of the Vulgate, these famous lines from Paul's Epistle to the Hebrews occur: "Honorabile connubium in o[mn]ibus, & torus immaculatus" (13:4).[101] ("Marriage is honourable in all, and the bed undefiled.") Milton's later allusions to the Vulgate in *Paradise Lost* – documented by Thomas Newton – indicate the influence this text exerted on him.[102] At a time in his life when he was less ideologically restricted, that influence may have been even greater. That a text of the Vulgate's canonicity treats "torus" as a "marriage bed" renders dubious any attempt to disassociate the word from its marital connotation.

Patristic asceticism also corroborates bodily virginity in "Epitaphium Damonis" and provides further clues about how to interpret its religious affiliation. As we have seen, Laudians often enlisted patristics to validate their own ascetic predilections. Milton may similarly validate Damon's strange, orgiastic virginity by allusion to the *Symposium* of Methodius of Olympus (260–312 C.E.). The *Symposium*, probably written between 270–290 C.E., heavily borrows from Plato's work, except that the symposiasts are women who have devoted themselves to virginal lives, and their speeches consist of encomiums to virginity.[103] During the virgin Agathe's encomium, she exclaims, "these, my fair maidens, are the secret rites of our mysteries, the mystical rites of initiation into virginity; these are the rewards of undefiled conflicts of chastity."[104] The Greek word that Agathe uses for "secret rites" is "τὰ ὄργια" ("orgies").[105] The Latin equivalent of "τὰ ὄργια" is Milton's "orgia." Like Damon, Agathe experiences the orgies as a reward ("honores virginei") for her ascetic lifestyle. Christ's munificence in bestowing them prompts Agathe to refer to Him as "Christ my Rewarder."[106] As intertextuality with Methodius suggests, Damon's virginity is of soteriological significance.

Another patristic source may also be behind the verb Milton uses to describe Damon's experience of the orgies. In "bacchantur," Milton probably alludes to the *Historia Religiosa* (440 C.E.) of Theodoret of Cyrrhus (393–ca.460 C.E.). In the *Historia*, Theodoret states that two virgins' love of God "drove them into a Bacchic frenzy" ("ἐξεβάκχευσε").[107] In this verb, we find an antecedent for Milton's "bacchantur." The Greek verb, like its Latin counterpart in Damon's elegy, is rather conspicuously Bacchic. Also, the words' meanings are nearly the same. "βακχεύω" means to celebrate the mysteries of Bacchus, or to act like a frenzied Bacchic celebrant.[108] *The Oxford Latin Dictionary* defines "bacchor" as "to celebrate the rites of Bacchus" and "to rage."[109] In this way, the Bacchic frenzy that Theodoret's virgins experience as a result of their chastity informs Damon's Bacchic exultation. Intertextuality with the *Historia* and *Symposium* accords with the Laudian recovery of the Eastern Fathers, which culminated in Laud establishing a printing press for such works in London in 1631 (another was projected for Oxford).[110] An allusion to Theodoret and Methodius is particularly *au courant* considering the press's publication of Theophylactus (Lindsell), the *Catena* (Young),[111] and its projected edition of the *Codex Alexandrinus*.[112] In a 1633 doctoral disputation published posthumously in 1660, Eleazar Duncon alludes to the extreme austerity of Simeon Stylites in the *Historia Religiosa* while making a characteristically Laudian claim for the piety of reverencing the altar.[113] Placed within this context, Milton's allusion to Greek patristics in the "Epitaphium Damonis" – and the virginity that causes the allusion – is quite modishly Laudian. A literal interpretation of Revelation 14:4 prevails and erudite patristic allusion supports it.

The "Epitaphium Damonis" puts the corporal connotations of virginity in *Lycidas*, the literalism of Revelation 14:4, into perspective. "Nuptiall" provides an escape hatch for a purely literal interpretation of this unexpressive song, an escape from literalism that "Epitaphium Damonis" does not offer. One of the meanings we can derive from the "unexpressive nuptiall song" is expressly virginal and corporal; there is simply too much context – both historical and intertextual – for "nuptiall" to overwhelm this meaning and suggest an exclusively spiritual reading of virginity. Rogation, moreover, provides indirect evidence to support the presence of physical virginity in the poem. This was also the case in chapter 2, where the crowning of wells with garlands reinforced a theological attitude conducive to Sabrina's physical virginity. The sanctification of materiality, in both rogation and virginity, operate with a similar theological assumption: the performance of an action – whether beating the bounds or remaining virginal – impacts salvation. Actions have soteriological significance; they are not merely symptomatic of elect or reprobate status.

Nonetheless, the presence of "nuptiall" points to how both a bodily and spiritual conception of virginity persist in *Lycidas*. If we think of exegesis of Revelation 14 falling along a continuum, from a rejection of any connotation of bodily virginity to its celebration, Milton falls somewhere in-between. There is no way to find in the "nuptiall song" a meaning that redounds entirely to physical virginity's credit; nor is there a way wholly to disabuse the song of that meaning. And the way in which the poem stands poised between these different meanings of virginity, and the adherents who propound them, is significant for the common reading of *Lycidas* as a piece of puritan fulmination – or any claim that it is thoroughly Laudian. Rather, dissonance emerges between a Laudian rogation and the different treatments of virginity in *Lycidas* and "Epitaphium Damonis." The dissonance indicates cautious uncertainty on Milton's part. He had not yet made his mind up about Laud and his church. Asceticism, these last two chapters have argued, is one important reason why.

# 4 *Upon Appleton House* and the Impossibility of Asceticism

The last three chapters focused largely on uncovering surprising ascetic sympathies (often of the corporal kind) in Donne the amorist and Milton the puritan. This chapter, by contrast, examines a thoroughly more hostile response to asceticism in Andrew Marvell's *Upon Appleton House* (1651). Recent scholarship has offered significant insight into Marvell's complicated relationship to sexual desire. In *Andrew Marvell, Orphan of the Hurricane*, Derek Hirst and Steven N. Zwicker describe the sexuality of Marvell in the following way: "[he] seems almost programmatically to entertain varieties of asexual desire and reproduction."[1] This results from the "aversion [that] script[s] nearly every encounter with adult sexuality in Marvell's poetry."[2] John Michael Disanto advances a similar claim, contending that Marvell's poems evince "fantasies about the avoidance of adult sexuality."[3] Nigel Smith, too, sees in the verse "a brilliant sublimation of a set of social and sexual confusions and frustrations."[4] In George Klawitter's *Andrew Marvell, Sexual Orientation, and Seventeenth-Century Poetry*, he urges that we "seriously consider [Marvell] celibate"; that is, one who "choose[s] to refrain from active sexual practice."[5] Despite these claims about the austerity found to characterize Marvell's sexuality, this chapter uncovers a profound suspicion of asceticism and general antipathy towards it in *Upon Appleton House*. This is not because the poem favours sexual profligacy over strict restraint; rather, it finds asceticism to offer an insufficient escape from sexuality. Asceticism perpetuates, rather than escapes, the problematic relationship of the body to the soul: it does not provide what it claims to. And, in the other form Marvell's ascetic critique takes in the poem, if asceticism does access a reality beyond sexuality, it remains one impossible of imitation. As Paul Hammond writes, Marvell found "a language for the ambiguities of sexuality – including homoerotic desire, but including also the desire to be rid of desire and its complexities."[6] If Marvell desires to be rid of sexuality, one of the insights *Upon Appleton House* offers is that asceticism may not provide the path to such a reality.

A particular engagement with Laudian asceticism motivates the poem's more general assessment of the ascetic life. As the poem narrates the religious history of the Fairfax family against the backdrop of the Protestant Reformation, these events also hold relevance to more contemporary history. "In almost every element of this poem," Gary Hamilton writes, "we can detect a response to the clericalist arguments that the Civil War had served to defeat."[7] That response takes the form of criticizing the ascetic revival in the Laudian Church as a remnant of England's popish past. The poem exposes how contemporary religious history *re-litigates* settled arguments, *revives* outdated practices, and *returns* religion to a pre-Reformation benightedness. Laudian belatedness then leads Marvell to suppress the monasteries once and for all by disproving asceticism.

Sections 1–4 consider how *Upon Appleton House* rebukes Laudian austerity as sensual, pompous, and theologically unsound. The chapter then proceeds, in section 5, to examine how the poem extends that criticism to asceticism more generally. While *Upon Appleton House* offers its rebuke in satirical terms, that should not obscure how parody functions as a vehicle to effect weighty critique. What Leah Marcus calls the poem's "holiday topsy-turvydom" often conceals stinging "social criticism."[8] As Hugh Jenkins notes, what might begin as "playful comparison" in this poem quickly turns into "historical and admonitory elegy."[9] The following pages show how the serious and the satirical combine in *Upon Appleton House* to offer admonitions about, and celebrate the godly triumph over, the Laudian Church and the various corruptions (ceremonial, ascetic, theological) it represents.

## I Marvell, Fairfax, and Laudianism

*Upon Appleton House* allegorizes a godly struggle against Laudianism – a struggle both Fairfax and Marvell had experienced – as proto-Protestant resistance to Roman Catholicism. As the allegory suggests, the primary object of religious scorn is not Roman Catholicism but Laud and his church.[10] The victory of the godly faith that Fairfax epitomizes over Laudian irreligion provides exigent witness to the piety of Nun Appleton's inhabitants.[11] The biographies of Andrew Marvell and Thomas Fairfax supply evidence for interpreting the poem in relation to the policies of the Laudian Church. The poet's and the patron's religious lives intersected when it came to experiencing the divisiveness of those policies.[12]

The poet's father, Andrew Marvell Sr. (1584–1641), lecturer at Holy Trinity Church in Hull, was harried by Laudian authorities at the end of his career. On 14 August 1639, Marvell Sr. was ordered "to reade the later part of the prayers or divine service mencioned and expressed in the book of Common prayer in manner and forme as therein is prescribed, in his hood and surplize upon Wednesdays being lecture dayes and sundayes and at other tymes when he used to preach at the said Chappell."[13] The surplice was often especially objectionable to puritans, due in part to its association with priestly celibacy.[14] The coercive orders were repeated on 12 October 1639, and again on 14 December and 31 January 1640, identifying Marvell Sr. as a non-conformist.[15] The Reverend Marvell's godly leanings are also indicated by his marriage to Lucy Harries (née Alured) in 1638 after his first wife (the poet's mother) died. As Pauline Burdon has documented, the Alureds were long-committed Hull puritans and soon-to-be parliamentarians during the civil war.[16] In *The Rehearsall Transpros'd: The Second Part* (1673), however, Marvell contends that his father was "a Conformist to the established Rites of the Church of England, though I confess none of the most over-running or eager in them."[17] But many puritans defended their opposition to Laudianism by claiming conformity to the "established Rites of the Church of England." The question becomes to which rites one refers: those established in the Laudian/Caroline period, or the late Elizabethan/Jacobean? A rejection of Laudian ceremonial appurtenances, and neglecting the Book of Common Prayer by presumably focusing on preaching, suggest Andrew Marvell Sr.'s comfortable place within the Jacobean Church.

The Fairfax family had a similarly negative experience with Laudian pertinacity. Many of the old truisms about Thomas Fairfax – that he was politically disengaged and religiously a moderate puritan – are now being challenged. If we read backwards from Fairfax's 1663 labeling as a dissenting non-communicant, a consistent pattern of participating in and patronizing religious non-conformity emerges. Andrew Hopper identifies the Fairfaxes as leading supporters and defenders of West Riding puritans against the "Caroline church authorities."[18] In a 1633 letter to the first Lord Fairfax (Thomas's grandfather), the puritan Robert More complains of "some malignant spirits" who "till now very lately … have blown up some sparks of contention" into the church. More concludes by asking for Fairfax's "gracious assistance herein, for the glory of God and the peaceable state of the Church."[19] The Fairfaxes' defense of the godly led to an inevitable conflict with Richard Neile, the Archbishop of York (1632–1640), and scion of the Laudian movement. Ferdinando Fairfax (Thomas's father) took offense at Neile meddling in Otley grammar school appointments.[20] For Laudians, controlling appointments and suppressing lectureships were primary means of combating puritanism.

As a result of this combat, some of the puritan ministers the Fairfaxes patronized in Yorkshire suffered at the hands of the Laudian authorities.[21] For example, Richard Clarkson was called before the Chancery Court on 23 November 1638 for failure "to certify obedience to monition to Cs [chapels] Halifax to read prayers before their sermons."[22] Samuel Winter was brought before Chancery on 23 February 1637/8 for a panoply of offenses: he was "ordered to read service in Rowley church on Sundays and Holy Days, their Eves. and Weds. and Fris. according to B.C.P. without addition or diminution, wearing a surplice."[23] Like Andrew Marvell Sr., Winter was forced to read more of the prayer book and adhere to the requirements for ecclesiastical dress. Faced with the strictures of observing liturgical feasts, conforming to the Book of Common Prayer (B.C.P.), and doing all this while invested with a surplice, Winter chose to resign his curacy. To the Fairfaxes, the resignation must have symbolized the loss of another able and pious minister to the pettiness of Laudian policy. In addition to their love of poetry and scripture, Andrew Marvell and Thomas Fairfax shared an understanding of just how divisive Laudianism could be. In so far as *Upon Appleton House* relates the religious convictions of its patron and is informed by those of its poet, anti-Laudianism plays a role. This is one of the key ways in which the poet "interpellate[s] himself in a dynastic and providential history of the Fairfax family."[24]

## II Sacred Space and Nun Appleton

*Upon Appleton House* begins by celebrating the sobriety and humility of Fairfax's Nun Appleton House. In the course of this celebration, it satirizes architectural ostentation as prideful, vain, impious, and ridiculous. Those criticisms contain an implicit critique of the central tenet informing the building projects of the Laudian Church: the "beauty of holiness." While many commentators have documented how *Upon Appleton House* opposes the superstitious avoidance of sacrilege associated with the Laudian Church, how such opposition also refutes the "beauty of holiness" has not been as readily observed.[25] The "beauty of holiness," and the distinction it draws between sacred and profane spaces, subtends the Laudian resistance to spoliation. In a poem that will devote so much energy to dismantling asceticism, it is not coincidental that the first ten stanzas reject a view of space conducive to it. As chapter 3 argued, valorization of sacred space and virginal bodies operates by a similar logic: actions (consecration rituals or asceticism) imbue materiality with holiness. The idea of holiness residing in a particular space or a particular body could strike many as a kind of idolatry. When the poem rejects architectural ostentation, that places it in a position to question the "beauty of holiness" and with it the notion that internal holiness both manifests in – and is magnified by – externals, whether they take the form of consecrated spaces or bodies.

*Upon Appleton House* contrasts gaudy ornamentation and excessive space with the "sober frame" (1.1) of Appleton House in stanza three: "But he, superfluously spread,/Demands more room alive than dead./And in his hollow palace goes … / What need of all this marble crust/T'impark the wanton mote of dust,/That thinks by breadth the world t'unite/Though the first builders failed in height" (3.17–24).[26] The attribution of sentience ("thinks") to the "marble crust" satirizes the immodest ambition of the builders and palatial residents. Under the influence of their arrogance, they arrogate to the marble qualities that it does not – cannot – possess: rational decision-making and uniting all the world. Many of Laud's architectural improvements made use of marble. Richard Neile's Durham Cathedral – one of the models for Laudian innovations – included a marble altar. During his chancellorship of Oxford (1630–1641), Laud's renovations of ecclesiastical buildings often used marble.[27] Trinity College, Cambridge, which Marvell attended beginning in 1633, may even have prepared for Laud's projected 1636 visit by constructing a marble floor for its chancel.[28] More generally, Laud and Lambeth Palace – especially its chapel – were frequently criticized for the kind of fallalery that this "hollow palace" exhibits.[29]

A subtle allusion in the stanza's last two lines (23–24) identifies Laudianism as a possible referent of the dust's imparking. The lines describe those who ambitiously construct edifices like those "first builders" of the Tower of Babel who "failed in height." Some of the most vociferous and prominent critics of Laudianism denounced its innovations as Babylonian and an attempt to re-construct the Tower of Babel in England. Henry Burton, William Prynne, and John Lilburne all use the image of the Tower of Babel to describe the Laudian Church, though it also appears in the work of less outspoken critics of Laudianism such as William Jones.[30] Burton, the most frequent user of the image, criticizes the Laudian Church's Romish innovations in *For God, and the King* (1636): "And me thinkes I see the issue of their building in that of the Tower of Babell … Even so our new Babel-builders upon a strong combination and faction against Christ and his Kingdome, have begun to build a Tower reaching to heaven in their high imagination, as if they would (as the Giants of old) pull Christ out of his Throne."[31] These Babel-builders work not only in brick and stone, but they vault their imaginations with delusions of grandeur. To express their overreaching, Burton uses the ingenious image of the prelates deposing Christ as the Titans sought to oust the Olympians; or, in a meaning that Burton's syntax allows, as the giants sought to depose Christ. Mingling sacred and profane sources, Burton creates a confused miscellany that enacts the incoherence of babbling Babel.

Criticism of the Titanic aspirations of Babel-builders continues in stanza eight: "Height with a certain grace does bend,/But low things clownishly ascend" (8.59–60). Such clownish ascension by low things may satirically implicate Laud. Pamphlets frequently derided the archbishop with the sobriquet "Little Laud," a play on the cleric's short stature but rarely diminutive presence. In *Mercuries message, or, The coppy of a letter sent to William Laud, late Archbishop of Canterbury, now prisoner in the Tower* (1641), the author mocks Laud, declaring "but when such Pigmy Lords as you will cherish/Ambitious great desires, both lightly perish."[32] Here, "lightly" primarily means "with little weight," but a secondary connotation of "slightingly," or ridiculously, is implicit.[33] The two meanings draw further attention to Laud's littleness and the comedy that results when he strains towards greater, weightier things. Marvell's use of "clownishly" may also refer to Laud's quarrel with the court jester Archibald Armstrong. The jester infamously pronounced grace once (with Laud in attendance) by exclaiming, "great praise be to God, and little laud to the Devil."[34] Never able to take a joke (especially one at his own expense), Laud had Archie banished from the court. Armstrong, though, would have the last laugh. He published *Archys Dream, sometimes Jester to his Majeftie; but exiled the Court by Canterburies malice* (1641), in which he accused Laud of foolishness, pomposity (perhaps clownish ascension), and declared that "his litle Grace" now wore his jester's attire.[35] Criticism of clownish ascension, marble-crusted buildings, and an allusion to the Tower of Babel indicate that Marvell's valuation of humble designs in the opening stanzas of *Upon Appleton House* aims itself at the "beauty of holiness." That humility makes the pretensions and the pomp of architectural ostentation look ridiculous.

One of the aims of that ridicule is to reject distinctions between sacred and secular space and to argue that the internal piety of inhabitants, rather than the external and imputed piety of rituals, makes a space sacred. To put that another way, sanctity is not something you walk into but something you carry with you. Sanctity derives from belief, not the sacerdotal function of priests or the rituals they perform. In stanza nine, the speaker praises how at Nun Appleton "A stately frontispiece of poor/Adorns without the open door:/Nor less the rooms within commends/Daily new furniture of friends./The house was built upon the place/Only as for a mark of grace;/And for an inn to entertain/Its Lord a while, but not remain" (9.65–72). In these lines, the inhabitants, not any inherent quality in the physical space, invest it with meaning. In a bold affirmation of this idea, people comprise the space: the poor are a frontispiece, friends furniture. After the dissolution of the monastery in stanza thirty-five, the poem adopts a similar view, claiming "Though many a nun there made her vow,/'Twas no religious house till now" (35.279–280). The space contains no inherent holiness, and its designation as a religious house is not contingent upon any ritual of consecration. It is a religious house because godly people – Isabel and William Fairfax – live there. That resists the notion that any alteration to the consecrated bodies of the nuns (such as, in Isabel's case, marriage) or the consecrated space of the priory amounts to sacrilege. In a small detail, too, stanza nine identifies itself as reversing the basic principles of the nunnery. The "without"/"within" formulation of the stanza's first three lines changes to "within"/"without" in the first three lines of the monastery narrative: "'Within this holy leisure we/Live innocently as you see./These walls restrain the world without,/But hedge our liberty about" (13.97–100). This small detail gestures towards how stanza nine inverts the monastery narrative by deriving the sanctity of a place from inhabitants and not the space itself.

Stanza five, however, potentially undoes this inversion. In the stanza, the speaker comments on how Nun Appleton will be regarded by future generations: "And surely when the after age/Shall hither come in pilgrimage,/These sacred places to adore,/By Vere and Fairfax trod before,/Men will dispute how their extent/Within such dwarfish confines went:/And some will smile at this, as well/As Romulus his bee-like cell" (5.33–40). Those in this "after age" act like they are journeying to view the place of a martyr's death or where a relic is housed. In stanza thirty-three, the poem takes a dubious view of relics, relating how the "relics false" of the nunnery are exposed (33.261). "Pilgrimage," of course, has a definite Roman Catholic connotation; it also has a Laudian one. In *Canterburies doome* (1646), William Prynne offers selections of passages that Laud and his agents censored or removed from theological works in order to "usher the whole body of popery into our Church by degrees, without the least publike opposition."[36] Under the heading "Passages purged out against popish Purgations of sinne by other meanes then Christs blood, and against Purgatory," Prynne adduces the following removal from Richard Clerke's *Sermons* (1637): "A suppe of the Chalice, or a kisse of the Pax, offering to an Image, or creeping to a Crosse, Pilgrimage, Oyle, Holy-water, purgers of sinne; all, I thinke, all Popery is a purge."[37] To Prynne and Clerke, pilgrimage detracts from the sufficiency of Christ's sacrifice. That is enough to invalidate the practice, and precisely why Laudians balk at Clerke including this criticism: it is too good of an argument, one from which

Roman Catholic pilgrimages could not recover. Prynne cleverly chooses this passage. For him, it proves not only Laud's popish inclinations by a soft stance towards anti-Catholicism; it also arraigns the Arminian theology favoured by the Laudian Church. That church, too, could be accused of theological positions that similarly depreciate Christ's sacrifice. Other works use "pilgrimage" to decry the Laudian Church's popish leanings. An anti-Laudian tract from 1641 describes Laud's assembly of a popishly affected group around him, and the migration of the English church towards popery under his direction, with the title *Canterburies Pilgrimage*.[38] Richard Culmer, in his *Cathedrall newes from Canterbury* (1644), denigrates pilgrimage to holy shrines as a practice of "idolatrous people."[39] The adoration of the pilgrims in *Upon Appleton House* does border on the idolatrous.

Based on the overt idolatry and popery/Laudianism of the pilgrims in stanza five, it seems impossible to take this stanza seriously. In this instance, negotiating the porous boundary between satire and serious criticism, between when the poem is joking and when it is not (though, as we will see, the poem often pursues serious criticism by means of satire), requires the application of the following principle. When acceptance of a statement as un-ironic would result in a flagrant inconsistency within the poem (i.e., the attitude towards relics); or, indeed, would call into question Marvell's own well-established religious identity ca. 1651 as a godly Protestant, then an ironic interpretation is emphasized. To that end, the stanza satirizes the adoration and pilgrimage of this "after age." The stanza's description of the pilgrims' disputations also suggests this conclusion: "Men will dispute how their extent/Within such dwarfish confines went:/And some will smile at this, as well/As Romulus his bee-like cell." What and whom are these men smiling at? The men who dispute and those who smile are not the same. Instead, the some who smile are smiling at the pilgrims' adoration and idle, superstitious disputations just as they smile at pagan myths like Romulus's hut. The inclusion of Romulus's "bee-like cell" is something of a red-herring. The hut of Romulus was so loosely based in fact that the Romans could not even decide on one location for it. To cover all possibilities, the Romans built huts on the Palatine and Capitoline hills.[40] Catharine Edwards concludes that the hut and its literary representations signify a yearning for an idealized, perhaps fictive Roman past: "The hut of Romulus, many times rebuilt, was perhaps as much a fiction as the *mores maiorum* – customs of the ancestors – of which it was the physical symbol."[41] That the poem compares the idolizing and adoration of Vere and Fairfax in "sacred places" to the Roman veneration of their demi-god Romulus in his mythic hut is certainly fitting. But that *Upon Appleton House* expresses an approving attitude towards either custom is unlikely. Instead, the stanza satirizes the idolatrous sanctification of physical space that the pilgrims, venerators of Romulus's bee cell, and superstitious individuals such as Roman Catholics and Laudians, perform. In so doing, the poem combines the performance of an ascetic act (i.e., pilgrimage) with a certain adoring attitude towards sacred space. The type of people who undertake pilgrimages are the same people who idolatrously invest physical spaces with holiness. This argument prepares for a sustained critique of ascetic life in the monastery narrative. During that narrative, the poem brings these two viewpoints together – towards sacred space and asceticism – when Prioress Langton admonishes Isabel, "'Twere sacrilege a man t'admit/To holy things, for heaven fit" (18.139–140). By describing a violation of vowed virginity as sacrilege, the Prioress encourages the application of ideas about consecrated spaces to the virginal body.

## III The Monastery Narrative

As the previous section demonstrated, the approach to space in *Upon Appleton House* subtly lambastes the Laudian "beauty of holiness." The monastery narrative also censures Laudianism, though it has not often been interpreted as doing so. For example, in *Beyond the Cloister*, Jenna Lay makes the following claim about monasticism and *Upon Appleton House*:

> Yet in locating that alternative literary history [nuns controlling the materials and modes of representation] firmly in the past and transforming the female community from "nuns" into "gypsies," *Upon Appleton House* denies the possibility that such a path could still exist in seventeenth-century England: no longer central to their country's religious identity, nuns are pushed to the margins of history and associated with wandering, foreignness, and deceit.[42]

Pushing nuns and monasticism to these margins constitutes the "tenacious act of literary erasure" that Marvell performs in the poem.[43] Lay joins a body of scholarship on religion and *Upon Appleton House* that has illuminated the poem's engagement with anti-Catholic polemic and the Catholic history of the Fairfax family.[44] As the following pages argue, the monasticism the nuns represent is not only foreign, marginalized, erased, or Roman Catholic. A supervening Laudian asceticism renders the nuns' pre-Reformation monasticism exigent. At the same time, blurring the lines between Laudian asceticism and Roman Catholic monasticism emphasizes that the Reformation already superseded this asceticism. If it is exigent, then its contemporaneous appeal does not result from any new or valid arguments offered but the mere fact of their offering. Laudian asceticism emerges from the monastery narrative as at once very tired and, very surprisingly, in need of refutation.

This section begins by examining the arguments Anna Langton makes on behalf of virginity to persuade Isabel Thwaites to accept the votive life at the Cistercian Priory. As the Prioress explains the soteriology of virginity, her explanations broadly compare with Laudian opinion. After establishing this comparison, the section then proceeds to discuss the ways in which *Upon Appleton House* rebuts the nun's claims and how the rebuttal recalls anti-Laudian discourse.

To persuade Isabel to join the priory, Prioress Langton emphasizes the heavenly rewards accrued by virginity: "How should we grieve that must be seen / Each one a spouse, and each a queen; / And can in heaven hence behold / Our brighter robes and crowns of gold" (15.117–120). When describing the rewards that await virgins, Jeremy Taylor, who served as chaplain to Laud, writes that they should anticipate "that little coronet or special reward which God hath prepared (extraordinary and besides the great Crown of all faithful souls) for those who have not defiled themselves with women."[45] Part of the vow's happiness must arise from the reward reserved for it. The Laudian William Strode defines the reward of vowed virginity not as a crown but as an opportunity to do something for God.[46]

> Out of his great bounty, he hath left us an occasion to be bountifull towards Him; he hath not in plain terms challeng'd all our just debt, that we by a Voluntary Offer might more ingratiate our selves into his Favour; he hath left his Rule under a seeming imperfection, that we might appear before him the more perfect, and receive the reward of diligent servants, apt to understand his silent intimation, and doing things reducible to his Command, though not commanded.[47]

The idea of being "bountifull" towards an omnipotent deity would strike many as a horrifying, perhaps even a blasphemous, proposition. Strode somewhat qualifies this provocative remark by assuring that God has not forgotten "all our just debt" and that his rule exists in a state of "seeming imperfection." Nonetheless, the creature still establishes a relationship of some reciprocity – however putative – with the Creator. The opportunity to be bountiful towards God, to be diligent servants, to appear more perfect, and to understand God's "silent intimation" makes Strode present vowed virginity in terms similar to the Prioress: it would be an absolute shame *not* to enter into this life. The nuns look on those excluded from the happy vow with pity and grief (15.115–117).

The soteriological significance of the virginity the Prioress extolls leads to some unfavourable comparisons with matrimony. When the nun claims that Isabel would "disesteem" heaven by marrying, such a comment runs counter to Protestants who privilege marriage above virginity (19.150). It fits comfortably, though, with Anthony Stafford's exhortation to virgins to "never thinke more of the Faecunditie of Wedlocke, since you see here that God himselfe is the fruit of Virginity."[48] The alternative method of reproduction the nun identifies in stanza twenty-one – in which sanctity springs and increases – also corresponds to Stafford's location of generativity even in virginity (21.167). More generally, the monasticism Stafford praises in *The femall glory* (1635) resonates with monastic life at the priory: "You who ply your sacred Arithmeticke, and have thoughts cold, and cleare as the Christall beads you pray by: You who have vow'd virginity mentall, and corporall, you shall not onely have ingresse here, but welcome. Approach with Comfort, and kneele downe before the Grand white Immaculate Abbesse of your snowy Nunneries [the Virgin Mary]."[49] Similar to the votaries Stafford addresses, the nuns at Nun Appleton engage in constant and ritual prayer (cf. with *Upon Appleton House* 24.185); religious ceremonialism, particularly the use of rosary beads (32.255); and glorification of the Virgin (17.131). In sum, then, when Anna Langton persuades Isabel Thwaites to adopt a life of vowed virginity, she does so by stressing virginity's soteriological significance, its superiority to marriage, and she presents a vision of monastic life that could recall Laudian (i.e., Stafford's) idealizations of it.

Another of the idealizations Prioress Langton articulates centers on acts of supererogation and the obtainability of perfection. As we have seen, William Strode contends that a supererogatory vow such as virginity enables one to achieve perfection in this life. In stanza twenty-one, the nun offers Isabel a chance to attain to a nearer degree of perfection: "Your voice, the sweetest of the choir,/Shall draw heav'n nearer, raise us higher./And your example, if our head,/Will soon us to perfection lead" (21.161–164). Since Laudians viewed good works as salvifically consequential, they embraced the prospect of attaining perfection. For instance, in *Five Pious and Learned Discourses* (1635), Robert Shelford claims that not only is the law able to be fulfilled in this life, but its fulfillment endues man with "our first perfection and heavens felicities."[50] Perfection-via-virginity is also a recurrent theme in the many Laudian comparisons of virgins and angels.[51] In contrast, perfection and humanity becoming angelic were both inimical to the Calvinist emphasis on total depravity. This emphasis informs Robert Baillie's discussion of the Laudian view of supererogatory vows and perfection in *Ladensium Autokatakrisis* (1640). Baillie offers this summary of the

Laudian position: "That not onely many do fulfill the Law without all mortall sinne, but sundry also do supererogat by doing more then is commanded, by performing the counsels of perfection, of chastity, povertie, and obedience ... That our obeying the counsels of perfection do purchase a degree of glory above the ordinar [sic] happinesse."[52] The nun's belief in attaining perfection corresponds to Baillie's argument that monastic practitioners of chastity believe themselves to "purchase a degree of glory above the ordinar [sic] happinesse." Hers is, after all, a "happy vow" (15.16). More largely, Baillie's imputation to the Laudian Church of valuing works of supererogation recurs throughout anti-Laudian discourse and illustrates how the nun's claims of perfection can be situated within it.[53]

Up to this point, this section has mainly considered the type of virginity the poem presents and its soteriology. The following paragraphs turn now to how *Upon Appleton House* discredits (from within) the monastic practices of the nunnery and, indirectly, the claims of Laudian asceticism. More than anything else, insinuations of sexual immorality undo the asceticism of the priory.[54] To entice Isabel to adopt a votive life, Langton holds out the prospect of kinds of fulfillment other than spiritual: "'Each night among us to your side/Appoint a fresh and virgin bride;/Whom if Our Lord at midnight find,/Yet neither should be left behind./Where you may lie as chaste in bed,/As pearls together billeted" (24.185–190). Other commentators have usefully documented the same-sex eroticism that informs these lines, but little has been made of the relation between Fairfax family history and monastic sexual impropriety.[55] While the junior branch of the Fairfax family lived near Bolton Percy (and included the Lord General), the more senior Yorkshire Fairfaxes were based around Walton and Gilling Castle. The Walton Fairfaxes claimed a member who had succumbed to monastic life's unnatural temptations. Jane Fairfax, who lived at Nun Appleton Priory from 1536 until its dissolution in 1539, committed incest with Guy Fairfax.[56] On 10 May 1555, Jane not only confessed her incest in Chancery Court, but she also admitted that she had had a child with Guy. Adding to the ignominy of the affair, Jane was forced to do public penance for her crimes in Stonegrave parish. And yet, truly proving that *omnia vincit amor*, the couple remained obstinate, and Jane and Guy were hauled into court at least four more times for their continued offenses. The court would probably not have been so patient, as A.G. Dickens concludes, "had persons of less consequence than Fairfaxes been convicted."[57] The affair with Jane illustrates what anti-Catholic polemic always maintained: monastic asceticism results in sexual perversion.[58] There is even some question as to whether Isabel is seduced. Her seduction may account for the violence of William's actions against the nunnery and, possibly, for the detail of Isabel weeping at the altar when William rescues her (33.264).[59] If Isabel does resist the temptation, the poem would effectively disassociate the Bolton Percy Fairfaxes from the blot of sexual impropriety that stained their relatives at Walton. Since some ambiguity exists about the efficacy of the disassociation, it demonstrates the corrupting nature of asceticism. Sexual impropriety is an absurd defeat for the ascetic life.

Monasticism's sexual impropriety in *Upon Appleton House* should be partly understood as motivated by anti-Catholicism. The discourse of impropriety returns, though, and with especial force, in anti-Laudian polemic of the 1640s. William Prynne's *A Breviate* (1644) is the consummate example.[60] The *Breviate* was assembled while Prynne was prosecuting Laud for high treason in Parliament, and it consists of selections from Laud's diary that Prynne adduces to prove the Archbishop's treasonous popery. Among Prynne's accusations, he also suggests Laud's sexual immorality. That immorality indirectly references Laudian asceticism. From Prynne's other writings, it is clear he believed the Laudian Church to valorize monastic asceticism, and he refers to Laud as a "votary" in the *Breviate*.[61] In *Histrio-mastix*, "the frequent Sodomiticall wickednesses" of monasticism are "the unchast fruits of … vowed and much-admired chastity."[62] Thus, the *Breviate's* insinuations of sodomy may be the unchaste fruits of Laudian asceticism. A 1609 entry from Laud's diary supplies Prynne with fodder to make such an insinuation: "my next unfortunateness was with E.M."[63] He interprets the entry as proving Laud "fell into another greivious sinne (perchance uncleanesse) with E.M."[64] How "my next unfortunateness was with E.M." adds up to sodomy is never explained. Nonetheless, Prynne assuredly corroborates Laud's uncleanness by repeating the charge on the next page (though this time it is with E.B), and presenting a later event as divine retribution for it. Prynne writes, "September 16, 1617. He was very likely to have beene burnt by fier in St. Johns Colledge in Oxford, for his sinnes."[65] Few readers would fail to notice that Laud's death by fire after committing sodomy corresponds to the Levitical injunction (20:13) that all engaged in same-sex partnership should be put to death. In fact, in *Diotrephes catechized* (1646), Prynne lists "burning" as one of the possible punishments for sodomy.[66] Prynne depicts the fire as divine vengeance for Laud's heinous sexuality, even though the fire and unfortunateness are treated as unrelated by Laud, eight years separate them, and their relation occurs in separate places in the diary. Though perhaps entirely false, charges of sexual impropriety in the *Breviate* suggest the relevance of anti-Laudian polemic to the nuns' uncleanness in *Upon Appleton House*.

That relevance, the previous pages have argued, also manifests in the soteriology and theology of virginity in the priory. As the nun claims a heavenly reward for the votive life, or the possibility of achieving perfection in this one, she echoes claims that Laudians had already made about asceticism; or, rather, the Laudians echo claims already made by Roman Catholic monasticism. Pointing out the belatedness of Laudian asceticism – its rehashing of tired, corrupt, and patently false arguments – constitutes one of the poem's most effective methods of critique.

## IV Retreat and Parody

The next sections of the poem critiquing both Laudianism and asceticism occur in stanzas sixty-one to eighty-one. These stanzas function retrospectively and prospectively. They look backwards at the humble sobriety of Nun Appleton, comically applying many of its architectural recommendations in the wood. In so doing, the stanzas further disprove the Laudian view of sacred space by emphasizing the principles of sobriety and humility that impugn it. The stanzas also anticipate the ascetic severity of Maria Fairfax; the sensuality with which this section of the poem concludes creates a dynamic of parodic excess followed by withering restraint. As is the case so often, even these moments of parodic excess contain incisive criticism. While this section begins in a ludic manner, it soon criticizes Laudianism as carnal, pompous, and sexually corrupt. Beneath the comical and flowing robes of the "antic cope" lies a trenchant rebuke of the Laudian Church, as allegations of sexual impropriety return.

Stanzas sixty-one to sixty-five reprise and seemingly correct many of the wrong ideas about extravagantly beautified (i.e., Laudian) space in stanza three. Stanza sixty-one describes the speaker taking sanctuary in the wood: "And, while it lasts, myself embark/In this yet green, yet growing ark;/Where the first carpenter might best/Fit timber for his keel have pressed" (61.483–486). The arrogant and presumptive "first builders" of stanza three, those constructing the Tower of Babel, are replaced with a far more pious "first carpenter." What's more, the imparking of the "wanton mote of dust" to which the labours of the Babel builders are compared has progressed into the speaker's "embarking" (pun and all) in an ark of sorts. The poem's original spelling of "embarking" (i.e., "imbarking") makes the comparison visually clearer.[67]

Stanza sixty-four continues allusion to earlier statements by adopting the without/within construction the poem previously employs (e.g., in stanza one): "Dark all without it knits; within/It opens passable and thin" (64.505–506). The wood of the within/without construction contrasts with a similar phrase used to depict the nuns' living conditions. Within their holy leisure, "These walls restrain the world without,/But hedge our liberty about" (13.99–100). Instead of hedging liberty – a contradiction that undermines the Prioress's claims of personal freedom – the wood the speaker describes hedges night about: "And stretches still so closely wedged/As if the night within were hedged" (63.503–504). Echoing stanza four's praise of Appleton House where "all things are composèd here/Like Nature, orderly and near" (4.25–26), the hedging of night and containing of darkness result in the wood exhibiting a loose orderliness (64.507). A passage that opens "passable and thin" is also reminiscent of stanza four's entrance that can only be accessed through a narrow loop. The poem then juxtaposes the wood with the vaulting brain of the foreign architect in stanza one. The architect's arching brows homonymically transform into the wood's "arching boughs"; the columns that contend with height itself are now the "columns of the temple green" (64.509–510).

The arching boughs and columns represent correctives to the extravagant insobriety stanzas one through eleven criticize. In this way, the comic enactment furthers the poem's anti-Laudianism. The nightingale's inhabitation of the wood exemplifies the humility of design the poem earlier praises: "Low shrubs she sits in, and adorns/With music high the squatted thorns./But highest oaks stoop down to hear,/And list'ning elders prick the ear" (65.515–518). These lines recall the dimensions stanza four uses to define the sober age: "In which we the dimensions find/Of that more sober age and mind,/When larger-sizèd men did stoop/To enter at a narrow loop" (4.27–30). Similar to the men who are the avatars of the "more sober age and mind," the highest oak "stoop[s] down to hear."[68] Height does not disdain lowness. The nightingale's habitation of "low shrubs" while singing "music high" also recalls the humility of design that stanza six outlines, where "Things greater are in less contained" (6.44). Further, like the adornment of poor that signifies the "mark of grace" of the Fairfax estate (9.66–70), the nightingale's high song "adorns" this "temple green" (65.515). In a brilliantly inventive and subtly allusive way, the first six stanzas of the speaker's retreat put into practice – and thereby reinforce – some of the conclusions that the preceding parts of the poem have drawn about space and its disposition. They remediate the emptiness – both literal and moral/theological – of Laudian sacred space. This manner of sophisticated self-referentiality is consistent with the poetic ethos of a work in which a character comments on one of the poem's more outlandish, perhaps preciously metaphysical, comparisons ("'He called us Israelites'" [51.406]).[69]

The climax of this parodic episode occurs when a comic inversion takes place. Underneath the ludic exterior lurks a serious refutation of Laudianism as sensual, pompous, and illicit. The speaker comes to resemble that which he has defined himself staunchly against: "The oak leaves me embroider all … / And ivy, with familiar trails,/Me licks, and clasps, and curls, and hales./Under this antic cope I move/Like some great prelate of the grove" (74.587–592). Arrayed in all the accoutrements of his great prelacy, the speaker resembles that prelate (possibly Richard Neile) who inhabited "proud Cawood Castle" (46.363). Eroticism informs the ivy's sinuous envelopment of the speaker, as it licks and clasps onto him like an intertwining lover.[70] As Gary D. Hamilton has remarked, the sensuousness of the speaker's relation to the natural world invokes Laudianism.[71] Carnality was a charge often levied against the Laudian Church. Critics decried Laud as a "carnall man," and Laudian ceremonialism and support for the Book of Sports were thought to encourage carnal behaviour.[72]

A Laudian connotation can also be derived from the "antic cope" that the speaker furls about himself. The phrase alludes to John Milton's fifth anti-prelatical tract, *An Apology against a Pamphlet* (1642). At one point in the tract, Milton responds to his interlocutor's objection to a prayer not found in the "Service Book": "He dislikes it, and I therefore like it the better. It was theatricall, he sayes. And yet it consisted most of Scripture language: it had no Rubrick to be sung in an antick Coape upon the Stage of a High Altar. It was big-mouth'd he sayes; no marvell."[73] Milton sneers at the "beauty of holiness" and its theatricality and pomp; part of its ostentation includes the prominent placement of the altar and the cope. In "no marvell," it is clear why these particular sentences caught Marvell's attention. The "antick Coape" Milton derides, and to which Marvell alludes, is worn by a Laudian. The recurrence of complaints against the cope in anti-Laudian literature also suggests how the "antic cope" in *Upon Appleton House* has Laudian connotations.[74] For instance, in Peter Smart's 1640 petition to the Long Parliament, he offers this criticism of Richard Neile's governance of Durham Cathedral: "And they bought … another Cope which cost about ten groats, which had been a long time used by the Youth of Durham in their Sports and May games, a very fooles coat."[75] Smart portrays the prebends as particularly desperate for copes in their willingness to use discarded maypole streamers to assemble one. This desperation made it easy to regard the cope as a fixture of Laudianism. Summarizing Laudian "inventions" in part one of *The Rehearsall Transpros'd* (1672), Marvell lists "Candles, Crucifixes, Paintings, Images, Copes" among other innovations.[76] As these examples demonstrate, complaints about the cope and depictions of Laudians wearing it figure largely into anti-Laudian polemic. The place of the cope in that polemic, coupled with allusion to Milton's *An Apology*, support reading the "antic cope" in *Upon Appleton House* as having a Laudian identity.

The cope, an ornamental adornment signifying clericalism and separation between clergy and laity, represents the self-indulgent pomposity of this retreat. In his own mind, and bedecked in affirming garb, the speaker truly has become "great." Then, with the help of his technicolour dreamcope, he dissolves further into the monastic solitude of retreat before lapsing into the sexual impropriety the nuns practiced and of which Laud was accused: "Hide trifling youth thy pleasures slight./'Twere shame that such judicious eyes/Should with such toys a man surprise" (82.652–654).[77] Brilliantly expressing the result of his carnal ritualism and self-indulgent solipsism, the speaker's retreat into the wood becomes simply masturbatory. The parodying of Laudianism as carnal, pompous, and sexually illicit exposes its ascetic aspirations as mere affectation. The further degradation of Laudian asceticism, its exposure as failed and ultimately ineffective, anticipates the concluding presentation of Maria. Where Laudian asceticism fails, she will succeed terrifically – terrifyingly.

## V Maria: Vitrification and/as Asceticism

Scholars have often responded to Maria with a mixture of admiration, disbelief, and, at times, unease. She is, as Kitty Scoular notes, "superior" to all virgins "even to the Catholic Queen of Heaven."[78] She "is her father's fulfilment," Rosalie Colie discerns, "performing miracles as great as his and far more beautiful."[79] Perhaps most remarkably, in A.D. Cousins's description, "the logic of a Marian depiction of her points to her marriage as possibly bringing into post-revolutionary English society a child who will enact a religio-political messianic role."[80] The exalted terms in which Marvell praises Maria have left some critics incredulous. C.A. Patrides is "not certain I understand how a poem which advances from a cry of despair over the luckless apple tasted to a harrowing vision of fallen man's rampant destruction of nature, can abruptly introduce an idealized figure and expect us to assent without protest."[81] And protest some have. Most recently, Derek Hirst and Steven N. Zwicker have found that "every moment this celebration of virginal innocence spends in proximity to woman is marked by unease."[82] Even in critical accounts that view Maria positively, some sense of irregularity in her depiction emerges. Donald M. Friedman notes "the appearance of Mary Fairfax in stanza LXXXII draws [the speaker] back forcibly into the world of order and value that he left for the spiritual simplicity of the forest."[83] Nigel Smith remarks how Maria "utterly dominates our attention in the poem."[84] Maria's ability to dominate utterly, to draw back forcibly, and to represent uncontested superiority accomplishes her idealization. A sense of her as an overbearing, preponderant, and slightly oppressive figure structures even her positive reception. The following pages examine her fulfillment of asceticism with this preponderance in mind. While uncanny, her singular capacity to achieve the ends of asceticism criticizes the ascetic life and not Maria.

Maria utterly dominates from the moment of her appearance. Even the sun feels bashful in her presence and "loose Nature" must collect itself (83.657–664). The whole world seizes in a paroxysm of self-consciousness. "Loose" could mean, as Smith suggests, "unchaste."[85] It is not only nature's unchastity Maria corrects. Stanza eighty-seven invokes the sexual impropriety of the nuns and presents Maria as its antidote:

'Tis she that to these gardens gave
That wondrous beauty which they have;
She straightness on the woods bestows;
To her the meadow sweetness owes;
Nothing could make the river be
So crystal-pure but only she;
She yet more pure, sweet, straight, and fair,
Than gardens, woods, meads, rivers are. (87.689–696)

Maria's ability to make the River Wharfe "crystal-pure" glances backwards to the Prioress's temptation of Isabel Thwaites: "'Each night among us to your side/Appoint a fresh and virgin bride … / Where you may lie as chaste in bed,/As pearls together billeted./All night embracing arm in arm,/Like crystal pure with cotton warm'" (24.185–192). The crystal purity that Maria produces in the river reflects her own purity, the kind that causes "loose Nature" to become more chaste. It also contrasts sharply with the unchaste and putative crystal purity of the nuns. The "straightness" (i.e., rectitude) that Maria bestows, or perhaps imposes, on the natural world at Nun Appleton points backwards to the priory's homoeroticism.[86]

This stanza also recalls the monastery narrative and the nuns' lesbianism by alluding to John Donne's "Sappho to Philaenis."[87] Maria is "yet more pure, sweet, straight, and fair,/Than gardens, woods, meads, rivers are" (695–696). In Donne's poem, Sappho remarks about Philaenis "Thou art not soft and clear and straight and fair/As down, as stars, cedars and lilies are" (21–22).[88] Marvell takes Donne's negative comparison and confers on it a positive valence: "yet more" supplants "art not." Maria's capacity to be more exposes the lack and impoverishment of same-sex eroticism. Through their use of *versus rapportati*, lines 695–696 may also glance at the nuns' penchant for sewing and weaving. The interwovenness of the lines ("pure"/"rivers"; "sweet"/"meads"; "straight"/woods"; "fair"/"gardens") could recall the Prioress whose woven speech entices Isabel, and the nuns who "interweave" the holiness of saints into their lives (12.95, 16.126). In this way, Maria's purity cleanses the poem of the speaker's shameful eroticism, whatever looseness might exist in nature, and the same-sex erotics of the nuns.

Maria's effect on matter and the physical world explains her cleansing power. The poem compares nature's reaction to her with the effects of the halcyon: "The modest halcyon comes in sight,/Flying betwixt the day and night;/And such an horror calm and dumb,/Admiring Nature does benumb" (84.669–672). At Maria's arrival, like that of the halcyon, the world goes numb. The language associated with the halcyon in stanza eighty-five is that of density, adhesiveness, and rigidity: "viscous," "jellying," "compacts," "fix," "hang" (673–680). Far from fecund or generative – one way in which the Maria episode has been understood – these lines emphasize stagnation and inertia.[89] Maria renders matter inert. This anticipates the profound change materiality undergoes in the next stanza.

Stanza eighty-six describes a vitrification of the natural world, the kind that will occur after a final conflagration.[90]

> Maria such, and so doth hush
> The world, and through the ev'ning rush.
> No new-born comet such a train
> Draws through the sky, nor star new-slain.
> For straight those giddy rockets fail,
> Which from the putrid earth exhale,
> But by her flames, in heaven tried,
> Nature is wholly vitrified. (681–688)

The "hush" that Maria imposes on the world is familiar by now. Nature had been "wisht" (83.659) at her entrance; the halcyon, to which Maria is compared, produces a "horror calm and dumb" (84.671); and her attendants "with silent scene assist" (85.679). The silence Maria commands offers a marked contrast with the loquacity of Prioress Langton and perhaps even Lady Fairfax.[91] But while Lynn Staley describes the imposed silence as "the source of evening peace and stillness," it is the calm before the vitrification. It will, in fact, not bring peace but violent vitrifying.[92]

Vitrification represents the culmination of Maria's effect on the physical world and the stark power of her purity. It also possesses an ascetic connotation, for it contrasts with the candying that the Prioress identifies as a benefit of monastic life. By contrasting vitrification with candying, the poem elides the nature that Maria vitrifies with the human body the nuns' monastic asceticism acts upon.[93] In stanza twenty-two, the prioress offers this appraisal of the asceticism Isabel Thwaites will experience in the nunnery:

> 'Nor is our order yet so nice,
> Delight to banish as a vice.
> Here pleasure piety doth meet;
> One perfecting the other sweet.
> So through the mortal fruit we boil
> The sugar's uncorrupting oil:
> And that which perished while we pull,
> Is thus preservèd clear and full. (169–176)

In these lines, as Nigel Smith notes, "spiritual purification (and hence immortalization) is likened to the process of preserving fruit by boiling it in sugar."[94] To explain this idea, the notes refer the reader to Bunyan's *The Resurrection of the Dead* (1665). The comparison with Bunyan is apt, for it illustrates the inadequacy of the nun's version of purification. As Bunyan explains,

> you know, that things which are candied, by the Art of the Apothecary, they are so swallow'd up with the sweetness and vertue of that in which it is candied, that they are now as though they had no other Nature, than that in which they are boiled: When yet, in truth, the thing candied doth still retain its own proper Nature and Essence; though by vertue of its being candied, it loseth its former sourness, bitterness, stinking, smell, or the like.[95]

Bunyan outlines a process in which the substance does not change – though it might seem to – but only the accidents. Further illustrating candying's limitations, sweetness and virtue hardly engulf the spiritual life of the nun as she refuses to banish delight as a vice. Though the line does not strictly condemn delight as inherently flagitious, the types of activities (e.g., lesbian encounters) the nun finds delightful certainly do. The candying, then, is merely ornamental; the nuns' asceticism is but an excremental whiteness, one that reaches no farther than the cosmetic.[96]

In contrast to candying, the effects of Maria's spiritual purity are profoundly extensive. Whereas the nuns' ascetic lives produced a cloying external sweetness, Maria's purity results in fundamental transformation. The comparison with Bunyan is again illuminating. While candying preserves and purifies, "the thing candied doth still retain its own proper Nature and Essence."[97] That retention is not true of things vitrified: they, of course, become glass. The turning of matter to glass represents a culmination of the effects that Maria's entrance first began to produce in stanza eighty-two. Maria's indomitable presence stifles the eroticism of the speaker, nature, and the nuns. The conclusion of her redoubtable presence is vitrification, illustrating how the vitrifying has an ascetic (anti-erotic) charge. If asceticism represents one attitude towards materiality, one that is perennially suspicious of all types of matter (somatic and otherwise), then matter's vitrification signals an absolute triumph. Antagonism between the body and soul generates asceticism. Turning matter to brittle glass pacifies that antagonistic relationship by wholly redefining one of its elements. In effect, it completes asceticism.

Other early modern texts, on topics as diverse as cooking[98] and Revelation,[99] support the association of – and emphasize the stark contrast the poem draws between – vitrification and candying.[100] This contrast also derives from the capacity for vitrification to recall – in an ironic way – depictions of transubstantiation in the monastery narrative. Transubstantiation and vitrification constitute changes far more extensive than candying. James Kuzner has broadened the conception of what constitutes transubstantiality in *Upon Appleton House*: "[transubstantiation] could refer not simply to the transformation of bread into the body of Christ but to any utterance aimed at producing direct material effects on the bodies of the world."[101] *Pace* Kuzner, transubstantiation need not be limited to utterances producing those material effects. For example, Marvell expressly connects the nuns' use of transubstantial language and its capacity to "suck" Isabel Thwaites into the nunnery (25.200) with how the "viscous air" "sucks" Maria in stanza 85 (674). Partly as a result of that sucking, the "jellying stream compacts" and flies are "in crystal overta'en" (675–678). This process of compaction and crystallization finishes in stanza 86's description of vitrification. In this way, the nuns' transubstantial language corresponds to Maria's vitrification. As Kuzner observes, "Isabel is sucked in; Maria, as I have mentioned, is sucked from."[102] But as the variance indicates, vitrification does not simply repeat transubstantiation, either in the particular workings of the verb "suck" or in a more broadly conceptual way. Instead of turning bread into a body, Maria turns the world into glass. Vitrification ironically recasts transubstantiation, replacing its penchant for corporealization with Maria's glass-making. An element of parody and unseriousness informs this recasting.[103] That does not invalidate the poem's anti-Catholicism, but it does form a parallel – even if it is a negative one – with the practices of the nuns at the moment Maria supersedes them. Rather than a mere antagonism towards Roman Catholicism, Maria's anti-transubstantiation is more accurately described as an irreverence towards it. The irreverence accords with a poem whose greatest object of godly scorn is not, this chapter has argued, Roman Catholicism but its feeble resuscitation by Laudian asceticism. The association of Maria's vitrification with transubstantiation – along with the contrast the poem offers between the nuns' monastic candying and vitrifying – further emphasizes the profundity of the change Maria's version of asceticism denotes. In candying, as Bunyan explains, the accidents change but not the substance. In both vitrification and transubstantiation, the substance changes.

The most optimistic accounts of asceticism might imagine a transformation and spiritualization of bodily matter. For example, in *A prospect of eternity* (1654) John Wells writes, "did we seriously thinke of our future eternity ... Such thoughts would inflame the heart, raise the minde, fire the spirit, set on worke the affection, nay spiritualize and sublimate the body it self in holy services." Thoughts of eternity would cause believers to "nail their eyes to heaven in holy contemplation, chain their knees to the earth in prayer; and turn their flesh into iron in a constant adoration ... as one in the Primitive times." In addition to causing an imitation of patristic severity, those thoughts "would make us turne Anchorets in duty."[104] Incredulity frames the entirety of Wells's discussion of turning flesh into iron or the body into spirit. He bemoans the fact that no one ever seriously thinks about eternity in this way, or perhaps is capable of such painful introspection. Those capable of such thoughts belong to "Primitive times." The rarity and intensity of such austerity meet in Maria, and their meeting at once shows the impossibility of asceticism and her superlative virtue in making asceticism possible. Ascetic critique and Marian praise are inextricable.

Marvell's critique of asceticism derives from two sources: one, the exceptionalness of Maria; and two, the vitrifying form her asceticism takes. Maria's exceptional qualities are apparent in her being "the law/Of all her sex, her age's awe" (82.655–656). She also "precedes" all virgins (94.751), and she has been raised in a "domestic heaven ... where not one object can come nigh/But pure, and spotless as the eye" (91.722–726). As these lines acclaim, Maria attains to "perfection in temporal life."[105] The vaunted perfection of the nuns finds actual expression in her. Her awfulness and precedence complement a purity and spotlessness that seem positively anti-septic. What Rosalie Colie describes as "the objectification of the girl into a principle" renders her abstract, theoretical, and bloodless.[106] Maria's unapproachability as an imitative pattern supports what Ryan Netzley refers to as a "movement toward singularity and nonrelation" in Marvell's poetry.[107] Maria's status as an epitome makes her, by definition, inimitable. By her fulfillment of asceticism, she also obviates it. Marvell's critique of asceticism constitutes, in some ways, his most extravagant praise of Maria. While the poem emphasizes the impossibility of asceticism, it compliments Maria by showing her ability to fulfill it.

The brilliance of the poem's devastating critique also lies in its willingness to expose the dialectic that drives asceticism: namely, the antagonistic reciprocity between body and soul. The elevation of the soul comes through the deprivation of the body. But since the soul resides within the body, it must overcome the body *through* the body; this means of overcoming can perpetuate, rather than escape, the problem. An attempt to assert the independence of the soul results in recalling its dependency on the body. Asceticism ends up where it began. It seeks to escape the body, and the sexual urges burning within it, but only ends up affirming the soul's circumscription by the body. In addition to perpetuating this paradox of embodiment, asceticism may even exacerbate sexual desire. Coenobitic and hermitic monasticism provoke illicit desire in the monastery and during the speaker's retreat into the wood. To show that asceticism cannot hope to achieve what it claims, *Upon Appleton House* provides a mock-answer to the problem of overcoming the body through the body: it removes the materiality causing the problem. Glass is of course still matter, but it has been subject to such extreme modification that it no longer houses the eroticism pulsing through the somatic and natural world of the poem: it is inanimate; whatever was living in it – in a kind of burlesque of ascetic mortification – has been burned out. To liberate oneself from the recursive paradox of asceticism, the body must be scorched into glass.

This chapter began by considering scholarly accounts of Marvell's unease with sexuality and his possible ascetic proclivities. Some of those accounts emphasize the attraction asceticism held for Marvell. The preceding pages have sought to show how Marvell regards ascetic practices as largely unfeasible and impracticable. Only Maria – an inimitable extreme – can successfully adhere to those practices. She exhibits a perfect severity that both satisfies asceticism and, in the process, reveals the impossibility of ever really doing so. The poem dismantles asceticism from within: it takes seriously the conditions required to fulfill ascetic aims and meets them. But rather than only signaling an abandonment of asceticism, one possible conclusion drawn from this chapter's argument, *Upon Appleton House* may also demonstrate Marvell's commitment to imagining an existence beyond embodiment and sexuality. The conventional methods of escaping sexuality are simply not sufficient means of doing so. That Marvell exposes their insufficiency need not mean he disagrees with their basic project: namely, the extirpation of sexual desire, a release from the constraints (and demands) of the body. Marvell can occupy the seemingly irreconcilable positions of being at once fiercely anti-ascetic and determinedly asexual. In other words, Marvell's critique may be motivated by the fact that, for him, asceticism is not nearly ascetic enough.

# 5 Self-Denial, Monasticism, and *The Pilgrim's Progress*

*Upon Appleton House* reduces physical asceticism – monasticism and bodily purity – to an impossibility. This chapter examines how John Bunyan's *The Pilgrim's Progress* (1678) rethinks asceticism as a spiritual ideal. Bunyan is not, of course, responding to Marvell, but his allegory does respond to the kind of inadequacy *Upon Appleton House* locates in physical asceticism. So far, this book has focused on corporal austerity, bringing in spiritual asceticism as a hostile interlocutor to throw the physical version into greater relief. *The Pilgrim's Progress* represents one of the most sustained literary engagements with self-denial in the seventeenth century. That may come as something of a surprise. John Bunyan and his work have been read as illustrating the new importance interiority and the individual had in early modern England.[1] "*The Pilgrim's Progress*," Stuart Sim asserts, "is very much a celebration of individualism."[2] Roger Lundin also stresses the allegory's capacity to affirm individuality: "John Bunyan was one of those 'ordinary English men' who possessed an extraordinary gift for giving voice to what Charles Taylor has called that 'inexhaustible inner domain' of the self that was discovered in the sixteenth and seventeenth centuries."[3] Jason Crawford refers to this inner domain as an "autonomous subjectivity."[4] Bunyan's ability to articulate this autonomy has meant that his work focuses on "the experience of the individual, of the solitary self, to the exclusion almost of all other concerns."[5]

While some scholars might accept that Bunyan contributes to the emergence of subjectivity, they caution against locating an uncomplicated celebration of individuality in his work. Roger Pooley concludes that Bunyan "faces both ways in the late seventeenth century – back towards Puritanism and the folk tradition of storytelling, for example, and forward to the increasingly private inwardness of nonconformity, and to the emergent forms of autobiography and the novel."[6] Even cautious appraisals of Bunyan's relation to subjectivity often support the narrative of his individualism. For example, Margaret Breen writes, "in this case [i.e., *The Pilgrim's Progress*], the denial of the self entails the affirmation of the self as a reflection of the workings of divine grace upon the individual."[7] Constituting the self through a process of negation, or the importance of the self deriving from a desire to obliterate it, certainly contrast with the relation between the individual and *The Pilgrim's Progress* that some propose. Ultimately, though, whether the importance of subjectivity in Bunyan derives from a paradoxical rejection of the self that reconstitutes the self, or if it derives from an unabashed celebration of individualism, the result can be largely the same: Bunyan's allegory anticipates modern subjectivity. Linda Tredennick, who acknowledges the vexed position of interiority in Bunyan, nevertheless perceives its momentum as progressive: "For Puritans such as Milton, Bunyan, and White, the interior mind was neither safe nor essential, but rather a place as full of anxiety, instability, and danger as the public world. Given the prominence of psychoanalysis in the story of the modern individual, perhaps this is not such a surprise."[8] Chaotic interiority points to the incoherence of the early modern self and its coherence with the modern one. Even when not avowedly championing the self, Bunyan champions it nonetheless.

This chapter contests the claim that self-denial in *The Pilgrim's Progress* presages modern subjectivity. It shifts the critical discussion away from the mere fact of subjectivity remaining to what kind remains after the process of self-denial concludes. The following pages elaborate the monastic connotations of self-denial in *The Pilgrim's Progress*. Bunyan's allegory privileges self-denial, a primarily spiritual version of asceticism; but it often illustrates how this spiritual mode intersects with, and becomes largely identical to, physical asceticism.[9] If chapters 2 and 3 witnessed Milton's physical asceticism at times drifting towards spiritual expression, here the movement is reversed: spiritual asceticism leans towards corporal austerity. Rather than deposing corporal austerity, *The Pilgrim's Progress* reveals how self-denial and humiliation – primarily spiritual forms of asceticism – both retain and reinvent monasticism. If the newly discovered early modern self – chastened and affirmed through self-denial – strides into the marketplace of life and looks achingly towards modernity, then it does so with monasticism in tow.[10] This complicates the ease with which the modern and early modern selves can be elided or continuity established between them, seeing as how traditional asceticism helps actuate selfhood in the latter. As we have heard before, asceticism and modernity are incompatible, and that makes the task of establishing a recognizable continuity between the modern self and an ascetically inflected early modern one increasingly difficult.[11]

By illustrating that difficulty, this chapter contributes to the fraught status of subjectivity that histories of selfhood document in early modernity. For example, James Kuzner's *Open Subjects* emphasizes the vulnerability and fragility of the early modern self. He rejects the "deepening interior recesses and increasing autonomy" that other scholars have found to characterize subjectivity during the period.[12] Kuzner's articulation of an unprotected and unbounded self accords with the basic premise of self-denial: it assumes a self that is not so well-established and entrenched that it cannot be extirpated. As the compatibility of self-denial with Kuzner's vulnerable self illustrates, this chapter offers a provisional and highly fragile form of subjectivity, one perhaps scarcely recognizable to modern sensibilities. Another theorist of early modern selfhood clarifies why ascetic self-denial yields fragile subjectivity. In *Mirages of the Selfe: Patterns of Personhood in Ancient and Early Modern Europe*, Timothy J. Reiss enumerates many examples of strife between body and soul. In particular, throughout the work of Petrarch, Reiss locates frequent instances of the "soul's incessant struggle with the flesh" and the "corporeal incarceration" of the soul.[13] For Reiss, this incessant strife between body and soul vastly curtails the ability of the self to consolidate and to become autonomous: "At the same time, as the glass container denoted a prison for the soul, the fragility it betokened forbad belief in a separable *self*. Something had broken; with as yet no means of repair" (original emphasis).[14] If conflict between body and soul prohibits the self from separation, individuation, and internal unity, then early modern asceticism contributes to the provisional nature of selfhood during the period. It is only by removing asceticism from early modernity that the self attains the separability and invulnerability familiar to modern conceptions of selfhood. For example, as the introduction discussed, Charles Taylor's *Sources of the Self* relies on Weber's theory of a highly diminished asceticism to posit the increasing coherence of early modern subjectivity.

The existence of early modern asceticism also complicates Jerrold Seigel's investigation of subjectivity in *The Idea of the Self: Thought and Experience in Western Europe since the Seventeenth Century*. Seigel identifies Aristotle as "the ancient writer who exercised the strongest influence on European thinkers in medieval and early modern times." To describe that influence, Seigel points to the questions about subjectivity that did *not* occur to Aristotle:

> The questions that so troubled Descartes and many who followed him, how it was possible for an immaterial soul to be joined to a material body, or for one to have an effect on the other, never arose. The same can be

> said more generally of such issues – momentous for modern thinkers – as whether mind or body was more powerful in determining what a human being is, or which one holds the deeper truth about human nature.[15]

Seigel importantly brings to the fore the issue of whether an awareness of a radical divisibility between matter and spirit, body and soul, causes an introspection in whose inwardness modern selfhood might find a provenance. For Reiss, the troubled relation between body and soul signaled the tenuous nature of early modern subjectivity as opposed to presaging modern problems. If Seigel is right – that a modern disposition towards subjectivity can be found in contemplation of soul joined to body and the problems attendant thereupon – then the self has been modern long before modernity. And so Seigel must not be right, for ascetics have *always* deliberated and agonized over the questions that he regards as first raised by Descartes. Earlier still, those questions have been relevant at least since Paul first felt a law in his members rebelling against that of his mind (Romans 7:23).[16] This means that the strife between body and soul that Seigel associates with Descartes and concepts of selfhood so "momentous for modern thinkers" are, in fact, much older. It is only by ignoring the presence of asceticism in (and before) early modernity – and the thorny, dualistic questions it raises – that Seigel's idea of the self remains tenable and largely Cartesian. As this chapter argues, ascetic self-denial in *The Pilgrim's Progress* affirms the tenuous nature of subjectivity Kuzner and Reiss locate in early modernity and seriously limits the ability to discern modern subjectivity in early modern selves.

The primary reason for that difficulty results from the monastic connotations of the spiritual asceticism Bunyan articulates. The unrestrained eroticism of the prefatory poem to *The Pilgrim's Progress* supplies an explanatory context to understand this ascetic hybrid. With its frenetic references to sex and procreation and Pauline conception of sin's pervasiveness, the poem clarifies why Bunyan must draw on both spiritual and physical types of asceticism in the allegory.[17]

## I Tickling Trout

"The Author's Apology For His Book" (hereafter, the *Apology*) describes how Bunyan had initially set out to write about the "Way / And Race of Saints in this our Gospel-Day."[18] Whenever he wrote about that topic, however, another clamored for attention: an allegory about the saints' "Journey, and the way to Glory" (what would eventually become *The Pilgrim's Progress*). As soon as he wrote twenty things down about that journey,

This done, I twenty more had in my Crown,
And they again began to multiply,
Like sparks that from the coals of Fire do flie.
Nay then, thought I, if that you breed so fast,
I'll put you by your selves, lest you at last
Should prove *ad infinitum*, and eat out
The Book that I already am about. (1)

This is not just birth, but uncontrolled reproduction. When we think of Bunyan's putative topic, the "race of saints," some godly irony may be at work: regeneration is everywhere. But it is also more than a little unsettling in its capacity to "eat out" the book about the "Way/And Race of Saints." The rhyme of "out"/"about" has a certain eviscerating potential, as the former partially devours the latter. This is almost like Sin's description of her offspring in *Paradise Lost*: "for when they list into the womb/That bred them they return, and howl and gnaw/ My bowels, their repast" (2.798–800).[19] Instead of gnawing the womb that gave them birth (i.e., "Crown"), Bunyan's rival topics are poised to consume another offspring of that womb. To some extent, then, the matricide Milton recounts finds a similarly disturbing cannibalism in Bunyan's fratricidal births.

This unchecked procreation must be contained. Little, though, can prepare us for how the *Apology* goes about containing it:

Thus I set Pen to Paper with delight,
And quickly had my thoughts in black and white.
For having now my Method by the end;
Still as I pull'd, it came; and so I penn'd
It down, until it came at last to be
For length and breadth the bigness which you see. (1–2)

It does not take a lurid imagination to read these lines as positively teeming with obstetric and masturbatory implications. All of this pulling and coming seems inescapably sexual. The *Oxford English Dictionary* first records "come" as meaning "to experience sexual orgasm" in 1604, though Eric Partridge dates the usage to the 1590s.[20] In other words, finding a sexual meaning in "it came … it came" is not anachronistic. The coming that results from the arduous activity of pulling suggests a kind of ejaculation, the "bigness" a potential erection. As length and breadth become enlarged, swelling ruptures into orgasm. The framing of this whole episode with "delight" implies the kind of self-gratification that could license an autoerotic interpretation. The lines are at once masturbatory – conceiving of writing as orgasm and self-pleasuring – but also figure composition as a kind of midwifery. "Big" can refer to pregnancy. In this scenario, the pulling might describe helping a child from its mother's womb during the moment of birth.

These erotic themes intensify, as masturbatory pulling soon graduates into references to sex. When considering the advice he has received from others regarding publishing *The Pilgrim's Progress*, Bunyan argues that even those dissuading him from writing could benefit from his work. To prove this point, he offers the example of how the rain from both dark and bright clouds produces the same fruit.

> Yea, dark, or bright, if they their silver drops
> Cause to descend, the Earth, by yielding Crops,
> Gives praise to both, and carpeth not at either,
> But treasures up the Fruit they yield together:
> Yea, so commixes both, that in her Fruit
> None can distinguish this from that … (2–3)

Fruit is produced through a process of commixture that entails the silver drops from both the dark and bright clouds intermingling. Each contributes to the generation of "offspring." To gauge the genetic implications of these lines, consider how early modern science viewed the process of insemination. While discussing the hereditary transmission of diseases, *The method of chemical philosophie and physic* (1664) offers this account of fertilization: "for the seed of the Male and Female commix and become one seed."[21] A tragic theory of early modern female sexuality held that rape could not be proved if a child were begotten, for that indicated a willingness on the mother's part to accept the rapist's seed. In refutation of this point, *Aristoteles Master-piece* (1684) holds the following:

> But my opinion is, that poor silly Girls, strugling to defend themselves in case of such violence, and not in such fear and perplexity regarding the nicety of containing their Humour, the Seminary Vessels by an natural proneness will open, and the Seed in such cases, whether they desire it or not, will flow, to commix with the Mans in the Matrix, and by coagulating with the Blood that descends to nourish, it will form the Child.[22]

In light of these two examples, the *Apology*'s description of a fruit created by a commixture of two "seeds" (rain from two different clouds) aligns with how early modern science theorized the process of fertilization. The earth is a womb in which the seed of both parents mix, producing fruit. The process and the vocabulary have a genetic, seminary connotation. Even seemingly innocuous images of weather are pervaded with sexual stimulation in this *Apology*. It is, quite simply, obsessed with sex.

As Bunyan compares enticing readers to luring an elusive fish, the analogy also reflects that obsession:

> You see the ways the Fisher-man doth take
> To catch the Fish; what Engins doth he make?
> Behold! how he ingageth all his Wits;
> Also his Snares, Lines, Angles, Hooks and Nets:
> Yet Fish there be, that neither Hook, nor Line,
> Nor Snare, nor Net, nor Engin can make thine;
> They must be grop'd for, and be tickled too,
> Or they will not be catcht, what e're you do. (3)

On the one hand, these lines have a perfectly conventional meaning; they are about fish and the best method to catch them. As Randle Holme describes in *The academy of armory* (1688), "Grope, or Tickle; is a kind of Fishing by Diving under Water, or in shallow Waters where Fish is seen, by putting ones hand into the water holes, where Fish lieth: and when felt tickle them about the Gills, they will lie so quiet, that you may take them in your hands and cast them a Land."[23] But on the other, there is something erotic about stroking the fish and eccentric about the prolixity Bunyan uses when recounting it: engines, snares, lines, angles, hooks and nets not to mention, of course, the negation of all these ("Nor Snare, nor Net … "). The process, by virtue of its incessant labour and constant resourcefulness, seems seductive.

The sexual connotations of fish in the early modern period support this interpretation: "fish was often associated with sex, specifically female flesh and genitalia."[24] Fish can also refer, by an objectifying synecdoche, to prostitutes (hence Hamlet's reference to Polonius as a "fishmonger" [2.2.172]).[25] Reading the groping and tickling of fish as having sexual applications was not uncommon. In "The Bait," Donne compliments his beloved by writing, "Let coarse, bold hands from slimy nest/ The bedded fish in banks out-wrest … / For thee, thou need'st no such deceit,/For thou thyself art thine own bait;/That fish that is not caught thereby,/Alas, is wiser far than I" (21–28).[26] In *Speculum mundi* (1635), John Swan elaborates on why, of all fish, the trout is particularly susceptible to seductive flattery: "This is in some kinde a foolish fish, and an embleme of one who loves to be flattered: for when he is once in his hold, you may take him with your hands by tickling, rubbing, or clawing him under the bellie. I will not say who else is like this fish, for fear I should offend some squeamish dame: but let not her anger shew her wantonnesse."[27] What increases the potential for tickling fish having a sexual meaning is the frequency of those meanings in the *Apology*. Were it not for the commixing and swelling bigness, perhaps it would be possible *not* to take this seemingly banal reference to fishing as laden with innuendo. Contextually, that seems a very tall order indeed. The *Apology*'s treatment of sex runs the gamut from obstetric horror to hypersexuality. That evidences just how erratic the treatment is. How can we account for this?

The explosive carnality of the *Apology* corresponds to Bunyan's Pauline conception of the ubiquity of sin. Early in the *Apology*, Bunyan writes, "Neither did I but vacant seasons spend/In this my Scribble; Nor did I intend/But to divert my self in doing this,/From worser thoughts, which make me do amiss" (1). There is a sense here of the Pauline depravity in, and helplessness in the face of, sin. Writing about saints is the diversion; worse thoughts and doing amiss comprise the norm. This recalls Romans 7, a passage to which Bunyan makes frequent allusion. In *The Acceptable Sacrifice* (1689), Bunyan observes "the Broken-hearted is a sorrowful Man, for that he finds his Depravity of Nature strong in him, to the putting forth it self to oppose, and overthrow what his changed Mind doth prompt him to. When I would do Good, said Paul, Evil is present withe me, Rom. 7. 21."[28] Romans 7 does not define this struggle only in terms of good and evil, but also conceives of the conflict as between flesh and spirit: "But I see another law in my members, warring against the law of my mind, and bringing me into captivity to the law of sin which is in my members. O wretched man that I am! who shall deliver me from the body of this death?" (7:23–24). The "worser thoughts," the doing amiss to which Bunyan finds himself constantly subject, have a bodily connotation. "Those that are most sanctified," *The Advocateship of Jesus Christ* (1688) argues, "have yet, a Body of Sin and Death in them, Rom. 7. 24. and so also it will be while they continue in this World … This Body of Sin, strives to break out, and will break out, to the polluting of the Conversation."[29] The *Apology* suffers this pollution as it experiences bodily breakings forth.

Whether the breakouts are intentional is difficult to discern. Did Bunyan include them to illustrate the prevalence of sin? But as Romans 7 makes clear, intentionality is a moot point: "For that which I do I allow not: for what I would, that do I not; but what I hate, that do I" (7:15). When action cannot be traced back to motivation, there is little purpose in trying to determine intentionality. The only reality is the inescapable prevalence of sin: "there is in the Worlds best things, Righteousness and all, Nothing but Death and Damnation … Rom. 7."[30] Romans 7 provides one context in which to make sense of the inexplicable outburst of sinful carnality in the *Apology*. The carnal outbursts anticipate how Bunyan will fortify spiritual asceticism with physical throughout the allegory, marshalling all the ascetic resources at his disposal.[31] To appreciate that resourcefulness, though, it is first necessary to consider the paradigmatic moment of self-denial in the allegory.

## II Denying Self, Defying Logic

Christian's desertion of his family represents that paradigmatic moment. The analysis that follows is particularly attentive to the paradoxes that define Christian's self-denial. Those paradoxes – and the illogic they enclose – are informed by a central tenet of the doctrine: namely, that it requires a denial of reason. As Christopher Wilson writes in *Self Deniall* (1625), "this shewes us the difficulty of true Religion; for what can bee harder to man then to overcome himselfe, to deny his owne reason and choice, and wholly to subiect himselfe to Gods; to renounce his owne will, and to chuse and doe the will of God."[32] The paradoxes that characterize Christian's renunciation of self also deny reason: the abandonment of his family is actually a selfless act; his cries of "Life, Life Eternal Life" signal a death to the world; and the plugging of Christian's ears indicates a new capacity for hearing. In a brilliant way, Bunyan employs these logical reversals to challenge both Christian and the reader into confronting the antipathy between self-denial and reason.

At the beginning of the allegory, Christian is exposed to scripture and the advice of Evangelist. As a result of that exposure, he decides to abandon home and family for the Wicket-Gate and the promise of spiritual renewal:

> So I saw in my Dream, that the Man began to run; Now he had not run far from his own door, but his Wife and Children perceiving it, began to cry after him to return: but the Man put his fingers in his Ears, and ran on crying, Life, Life, Eternal Life: so he looked not behind him, but fled towards the middle of the Plain. (10)

These sentences effortlessly hold violently contrasting meanings in suspension, animating the scene with a palpable dramatic tension. For instance, Christian seems like a deadbeat dad, deserting his wife and children in a spectacular display of selfishness.[33] But contrasting with Christian's putative self-absorption is the denial of self that pervades his flight. Christian perfectly illustrates Bunyan's description of self-denial in *The resurrection of the dead and eternall judgement* (1665). To gauge whether one's name is written in the Book of Life, Bunyan asks, "what acts of self-denyal, hast thou done for the name of the Lord Jesus, among the Sons of men? I say, what house, what friend, what Wife, what Children, and the like, hast thou lost, or left, for the Word of God, and the Testimony of his truth in the World."[34] In "lost, or left," Bunyan's deferral of the second term probably reflects its greater degree of difficulty. There is a considerable difference between losing one's family for "the name of the Lord Jesus" and leaving it. Losing implies that family has been taken, perhaps in a time of persecution; leaving does not carry the same connotation of external compulsion. Christian's adoption of the latter reflects the severity of his self-denial.

Indeed, he seems especially severe by not looking behind him. In that detail, Bunyan alludes to Lot's wife (Genesis 19:17) being turned to a pillar of salt for looking back at the destruction of Sodom. Bunyan's catechetical *Instruction for the ignorant* (1675) discusses Lot's wife in the section on self-denial. When asked to provide examples of individuals who "have not denied themselves when called thereto," the interlocutor cites "Lot's wife for but looking behind her towards Sodom when God called her from it … therefore remember Lots Wife, Gen. 19. 17, 26."[35] Though it does not seem like a selfish action, Christian looking behind him at the miserable family he is deserting would signify an indulgence of self consonant with the disobedience of Lot's wife. It is precisely when Christian seems monstrously selfish that he denies himself.

The great interpretive challenge of this moment in *The Pilgrim's Progress* is that it requires a total transvaluation of what we would normally call selflessness. Christian's indifference, his blatant disregard for the ones he loves, witnesses self-denial. As Christian explains to Obstinate, who is shocked at the prospect of leaving "our Friends, and our Comforts" behind, "that all, which you shall forsake, is not worthy to be compared with a little of that that I am seeking to enjoy" (11). Indicating the faultiness of Obstinate's thinking, Christian remarks that "for there where I go, is enough, and to spare" (11). What Obstinate regards as "all" is not at all comprehensive; *its* supposed extensiveness cannot touch – cannot even begin to grasp – the enormity of what Christian seeks. The totality that Obstinate so highly values cannot enclose where Christian is going. If it were truly "all," then there would not be "enough, and to spare" remaining. Moreover, the repetition of "that" may also point to the puny misguidedness of Obstinate's reasoning. "*That* all" does not compare to "that that I am seeking." Christian's "that" proliferates; it is 100 per cent larger than that which Obstinate finds to be encompassing. Whereas the "that" of "that all" is terse and compact, the subordinate clause of "that I am seeking to enjoy" extenuates Christian's "that," extending its reach, prolonging its expression, and making it more capacious as a result. A demonstrative adjective, Obstinate's "that" merely modifies, while Christian's pronominal "that" *signifies*.

The various ways in which Christian derogates Obstinate's "all" suggest a certain disdain for the friends and comforts Obstinate is so solicitous about. Self-denial can manifest in shocking derogations of familial relationships. In *Vindiciae redemptionis* (1647), John Stalham describes the impetus for this disdain while discussing self-denial: "as for relative engagements to friends, parents, children, wives, husbands, kinred, house and family; these are set by, and not known in Christs cause; yea, there is a kinde of comparative hatred of them, in respect of the Pearl and Treasure."[36] The "comparative hatred" that Stalham urges to self-deniers also informs Christian's observation that friends and comforts – what Obstinate finds to be all – are "not worthy to be compared" with the kingdom of heaven (i.e., "Pearl and Treasure"). Bunyan is certainly subtler about advocating the difficult doctrine of this hatred than Stalham. It is nonetheless evident in Christian's use of the comparative construction, his denigration of Obstinate's all, and in deserting his family.

The paradoxes of self-denial are also evident in Christian's cries of "Life, Life, Eternal Life." In *Grace Abounding to the Chief of Sinners* (1666), Bunyan's spiritual autobiography, he writes about his endurance of affliction during imprisonment,

> that Saying 2 Cor. 1. 9, was of great use to me, But we had the sentence of death in our selves, that we might not trust in our selves, but in God that raiseth the dead: by this Scripture I was made to see, that if ever I would suffer rightly, I must first pass a sentence of death upon every thing that can properly be called a thing of this life, even to reckon my Self, my Wife, my Children, my health, my enjoyments, and all, as dead to me, and my self as dead to them.[37]

An acknowledgment of a sentence of death in oneself allows for faith in resurrection, in a life beyond death and in "God that raiseth the dead." Becoming dead to self, wife, and children witnesses this life, and may very well motivate Christian's "Life, Life, Eternal Life." *Instruction for the Ignorant* clarifies the role that self-denial plays in this vivification. While explaining self-denial, Bunyan counsels, "he that will save his life shall lose it, but he that will lose his life for my sake, saith Christ, shall save it unto life Eternal."[38] By losing one's life, eternal life is gained. Thomas Manton also expresses this paradox in *One hundred and ninety sermons on the hundred and nineteenth Psalm* (1681): "Self-denial, when upon Hopes of the World to come, they grow dead to present Interests, and can hazard them for God, and can forsake all for a naked Christ, the World thinketh this humorous Folly."[39] Christian's actions are certainly labeled as "humorous Folly" (and worse) by Obstinate, who compares the pilgrim to "Craz'd-headed Coxcombs" (11). As Manton flatly declares, hope of life in the world to come causes deadness in this one. One must evince a kind of zombie-like indifference towards the things of this world to care truly about those of the next; Christian must disdainfully dismiss Obstinate's "all" and, what's more, even hate it. His desertion, therefore, and his cries of "Life, Life, Eternal Life" are indicative of becoming dead to present interests. Paradoxically, death signifies life. This thoroughly unsettling moment challenges the reader in its brilliant capacity to hold contradictory meanings in paradoxical suspension. This is also evident in Christian's very gestures.

Christian putting his fingers in his ears, refusing to hear his family's pleas, constitutes one of the most memorable details of his flight. Like his refusal to turn around, the gesture indicates Christian's obstinate determination to remain implacably unmoved by his family's cries. Though I have not found evidence that it has been interpreted in this way, Christian's gesture alludes to Mark 7:32–34. In this passage, Jesus cures a blind and deaf man by placing his fingers into his ears and spitting on his tongue: "And they bring unto him one that was deaf, and had an impediment in his speech; and they beseech him to put his hand upon him. And he took him aside from the multitude, and put his fingers into his ears, and he spit, and touched his tongue; And looking up to heaven, he sighed, and saith unto him, EPHPHATHA, that is, Be opened."

Erasmus's discussion of Mark 7:33 in the *Paraphrases* (1548) is particularly applicable to Christian's experience:

> As Christe did, so in manour doe the teachers of the gospel. They take men and leade them away from the multitude, when they call them backe from the brode way (by the which very many walke unto damnacion) to the felowship of the litle flocke of true Christians. They put their fingers, into theyr eares, when perswadinge them to put no trust in thinges transitorie, they styrre and exhorte them to embrace the heavenly doctrine.[40]

By leaving the world behind, Christian accomplishes one of the primary meanings Erasmus attributes to this passage; namely, drawing believers away from the multitude.[41] Erasmus's warnings about the "brode way" are also repeated to Christian: "Then said Evangelist, pointing with his finger over a very wide Field, Do you see yonder Wicket-gate?" (10). The wicket-gate that lies across the wide field, and the "litle flocke" that congregate away from the "brode way," both allude to Matthew 7:13–14 and its depiction of the narrow way. Moreover, Erasmus interprets the gospel teacher (i.e., Evangelist) as simulating Christ's insertion of his fingers into the deaf man's ears. Exposure to the gospel

(8–10) enabling this ear-clearing is a chronology that also obtains in *The Pilgrim's Progress*. Christian's gesture signifies the effect the gospel has had on him: it has broken through a previous deafness to enliven his ears and heart with hearing. Erasmus also claims that those with open ears often exhibit the self-denying behaviour Christian adopts. Those who "forsoke all that ever they had and folowed him" had their ears open.[42] Christian's flight may be symptomatic of the effects Erasmus considers Mark 7:33 to have on believers.

Paradoxically, Christian putting his fingers into his ears, while it does have the effect of drowning out the cries of his family, ultimately indicates the aural (really, spiritual) sensitivity of his newfound hearing to gospel truth. Thomas Watson, the Marian Bishop of Lincoln, expresses the paradox in a sermon on baptism. Watson discusses how the ritual of the priest placing his fingers into the child's ears imitates "Christe when he healed the deafe and dombe manne." Only now "the Priest in the persone of Christe doth open the eares and touche the nose of the childe that is borne spiritually deafe and dombe, that he shoulde nowe begynne to heare the voyce and woorde of GOD."[43] The action that impairs hearing actually represents its increased sensitivity.

It is no coincidence that Watson's comments during a baptismal sermon are applicable to Christian. The fingering of ears during baptismal ceremony and the widespread use of Mark 7:33 to validate the ritual suggest how Christian's gesture might also be interpreted as a kind of baptism. Bunyan was, as Richard L. Greaves observes, an "open-membership, open communion Baptist with Reformed predestinarian views" (*ODNB*). As Bunyan argues (based on Mark 1:8) in *A Confession of my Faith* (1672) and *Differences in Judgment about Water-Baptism, No Bar to Communion* (1673), true baptism is performed by the Spirit and the ritual is only a perfunctory, exterior sign.[44] Bunyan elaborates on this view in *A Confession of my Faith*: "Now I say, he that believeth in Jesus Christ; that richer and better then that, viz. is dead to sin, and that lives to God by him, he hath the heart, power and doctrine of Baptism."[45] The heart and power of it mainly consist in the baptized knowing "that they have professed themselves, dead, and buryed, and risen with him to newness of life."[46] Since Bunyan believed that the newness of life conferred in baptism is accomplished by the Spirit, Mark 7:33 provides an effective means for articulating the belief. Christ's finger in Mark 7:33 is often interpreted as representing the Holy Spirit. The Danish Lutheran Niels Hemmingsen equates the two, noting, God's word "can neither be heard nor understood, unlesse our eares be opened by Chrystes finger, that is too say, unlesse the holy Ghoste doo open the eares of our hart."[47] Christian performing a common baptismal gesture, the ability of the allusion behind that gesture to express Bunyan's own baptismal views about the Spirit, and Christian's profession of baptismal regeneration ("Life, Life, Life Eternal") demonstrate his undergoing baptism.

The baptism also reinforces Christian's austere self-denial. R.J., in *Compunction or pricking of heart* (1648), observes a fundamental connection between baptism and self-denial: "Now Baptisme is a note of Christian profession, whereby we give our names, yea our selves to Christ, which I dare say it, none can ever truly do unless he deny himself; I speak of a powerfull profession, and such as in life answers that verbal profession made in our baptisme."[48] Giving oneself over to Christ in self-denial is answerable to baptismal re-birth. The presence of baptism empowers this moment with even more self-denying potential. As R.J. notes, it is a "powerfull profession." Christian does not simply deny himself. Rather, he dies to that self after being reborn in the newness of life. Dying to oneself resulting in a new birth articulates but another of the paradoxes that accompany Christian's self-denial. Bunyan employs paradox – in death signifying life, abandonment of family selflessness, and deafness a new ability to hear – as the means for expressing the renunciation of reason and logic that self-denial demands.

## III The Persistence of the Self?

A renunciation of logic exemplifies self-denial's difficulty and intensity. Does this indicate, therefore, the complete extirpation of subjectivity? In addition to the scene at the wicket-gate, the self-denial that characterizes Christian's baptism and flight are found throughout part I. These later references to self-denial, though, often contain qualifications to the doctrine, either pointing to its strenuous nature or Christian's inability to adhere completely to its rigours.

Referencing the indifference (even hatred) one must manifest towards his relations, at one point Christian responds to Mr. Worldly-Wiseman's question of "Hast thou a Wife and Children" by flatly declaring "I am as if I had none" (17). However, when Christian relates his conversation with Worldly-Wiseman to Evangelist, he says, "He asked me if I had a Family, and I told him: but, said I, I am so loaden with the burden that is on my back, that I cannot take pleasure in them as formerly" (21). This answer is quite different than Christian's response to Worldly-Wiseman. Not taking pleasure in family members ameliorates the intensity of declaring oneself without them. Evangelist notices the lessening severity of Christian's self-denial, of completely extricating himself from worldly entanglements, reminding him, "Thou must abhor his laboring to render the Cross odious unto thee." To impress this upon Christian, Evangelist quotes Luke 14:26: "he that comes after him, and hates not his father and mother, and wife, and children, and brethren, and sisters; yea, and his own life also, he cannot be my Disciple" (23). Evangelist's counsel expresses the comparative disdain/hatred evident in Christian's earlier explanation to Obstinate that his "all" cannot be compared to the "enough" of heaven.

Despite part I's constant affirmation of self-denial, Christian still acknowledges the arduous difficulty of the doctrine. In a moment reminiscent of the exchange with Worldly-Wiseman and Evangelist, Christian offers this response to Ignorance's assertion that he has left all: "That I doubt, for leaving of all, is an hard matter, yea a harder matter then many are aware of" (145). In *A holy life* (1684), Bunyan draws a similar conclusion about the practices associated with self-denial, arguing about 1 Corinthians 6:12, "But this is a hard lesson, and impossible to be done except thou art addicted to self-denial."[49] Ultimately, acknowledgments like these clearly evince Bunyan's genius for presenting the hardest of Christian truths in accessible forms. In *The Pilgrim's Progress*, the rigours of self-denial are enjoined with a degree of empathy; they are not just dictated with the unfeeling coldness of one who has never experienced – and perhaps even failed at – the challenge they pose. Maintaining self-denial at the extreme level of the allegory's opening is indeed a hard matter. Acknowledging the difficulty, perhaps even the impossibility of total self-denial, means that Christian does not expunge subjectivity entirely. As we have also seen, his confession to Evangelist of a waning commitment to renouncing family exemplified a similar impulse of the willful self. This is distinct from some spiritual ascetics who, drawing especially on Galatians 2:20, try to nullify and/or annihilate the self. A comparison of Christian with these staunch self-deniers reveals the complex persistence of the self in *The Pilgrim's Progress*.

Edward Polhill offers this rapturous exclamation about the self-debasement called for in scripture: "Oh! what manner of self-denial doth it call for? how doth it labour to un-selve, and as it were un-man us, that God may be all in all?"[50] Like Polhill, John Stalham posits an inverse relationship between the absence of the self and the omnipresence of God: "He that shall more annihilate himself, shall finde more the creatures all in Christ; Christs all in him, for him, to him."[51] Self-emptying often accompanies the process of annihilation that Polhill and Stalham depict as enabling God's fullness. In Thomas Watson's *The duty of self-denial* (1675), Watson asserts, "but a Man must deny himself; this self-emptying, or self-annihilation is the Strait Gate through which a Christian must enter into the Kingdom of God."[52] Here, Watson articulates the ascetic ideal of *kenosis* (κένωσις), or self-emptying. Based on Christ's emptying of himself in Philippians 2:7 – "But made himself of no reputation, and took upon him the form of a servant, and was made in the likeness of men" – many ascetics regarded this emptiness as the goal of their austerities. For instance, Timothy Manlove urges, "let this Mind be in us that was in Christ, who made himself of no Reputation … Let us exercise our selves frequently and solemnly in Self-Annihilation."[53] Watson's version of *kenosis* is particularly severe. He flatly asserts, "self is an Idol, and it is hard to sacrifice this Idol; but this must be done."[54] Iconoclasm energizes the intensity of Watson's annihilation of self.

John Howe supplies one of the fullest descriptions of the process of self-annihilation, particularly what comes after it and, more importantly, what does not. In *The blessednesse of the righteous* (1668), Howe describes self-annihilation as "a pure nullifying of self."[55] When the soul has been "trained up in acts of mortification … through a continued course, and series of self-denyall," then "nothing now appears more becoming, than such a self-annihilation." What eventuates from this contraction of the self to nothing is, paradoxically, *everything*: "Self gives place that God may take it, becomes nothing, that he may be all. It vanishes, that his glory may shine the brighter." In Howe's account, God's ubiquity simply supersedes, it nullifies, the self by an "overcoming sense of his boundless, alsufficient, every where flowing fullness." By emptying the self, one can be filled with the fullness of God. In a remarkable culmination of this fullness, Howe, a Calvinist, describes the experience in the following way: "'Tis to live at the rate of a God; a God-like life. A living upon immense fulnes, as he lives."[56] The apotheosis that Howe records does not correspond to the Calvinist belief in the depravity of man. In order to retain some notion of man's depraved condition in light of this deification, we must assume that self-annihilation is complete: the self has been totally eclipsed in order to facilitate this God-like state. It does not remain. Howe provides a corrective to the assumption that a process of self-denial ultimately entails affirming subjectivity.

In contrast with Howe and Polhill et al., Christian's experience of a self that remains even after denying it is closest to Richard Baxter's discussion of the self in *A Treatise of Self-Denial* (1659). For Baxter, self-denial initiates a paradoxical process of sanctification through which man actually finds himself:[57]

> The illuminated Soul is so much taken with the Glory and Goodness of the Lord, that it carrieth him out of himself to God, and as it were estrangeth him from himself, that he may have communion with God; and this makes him vile in his own eyes, and abhor himself in dust and ashes; He is lost in himself; and seeking God, he finds himself again in God.[58]

Estranged from himself, there he finds himself more truly and more strange. As Richard Valantasis remarks, "becoming a stranger … stands at the heart of ascetic activity."[59] In an interesting way, depravity does not preempt the estranged soul's communion with God; it facilitates it. As he is carried towards God (n.b., he is not "in God" at this point), the soul contemplates this potential communion and is overcome with abhorrence for itself. In this lost and desperately seeking state, God (and the self) is found.[60] Baxter's account of self-denial, though rigorous and alienating for one's subjectivity, does not work towards the self's complete nullification.

Something about the self also remains indomitable in *The Pilgrim's Progress*. Its resilience may testify to the increasing importance subjectivity came to have in early modernity. The self was becoming unavoidable. That a process of self-demolition, relentlessly pursued throughout *The Pilgrim's Progress*, could produce such self-awareness demonstrates a degree of ineluctable subjectivity. Before concluding that this ineluctability gestures towards the modern self, it is important to consider how monasticism and physical austerity inform self-denial.

## IV Self-Denial, Humiliation, and Monasticism

In the allegory, the process of self-demolition has strong connotations of monasticism, mixing spiritual and physical forms of asceticism. This hybrid asceticism has a source in the carnality of the *Apology*, but also in two tendencies within spiritual asceticism: one, the visceral metaphors spiritual ascetics often resort to when describing the virtual processes of self-denial and annihilation; and two, self-denial's monastic promotion of disregarding familial ties. Illustrating the first of these tendencies, in *A Lesson of Self-Deniall* (1650), John Collinges presents an especially harsh attitude towards the self, asking "were your soules ever in such a true bitternesse for sinne, that it wrought in thee an indignation against your selves; that you could even eat your owne flesh, to think you should ever have been such a vaine, wanton, wretch, such a proud sinner as you have been?"[61] Also employing the imagery of self-consumption, John Stalham attests, "joy in self, and joy in Christ, are heterogeneall, and of a contrary root and principle; And the later [sic] will and must (if the heart be upright) eat out, and consume the former."[62] In this grim communion, the self must be removed root and branch.

The self-destructive cannibalism that Collinges and Stalham implicate in self-denial also finds articulation in the violence that Christopher Wilson urges in *Self Deniall*. Wilson recounts the function of grace during this task: "Grace teaches us to take the Anotomizing knife of Gods word, and ripp up our owne hearts, and makes us willing and ready to acknowledge and confesse our sinnes unto the Lord."[63] Thomas Reeve adopts similar language of anatomization while discussing denying oneself: "And thus ye see, how repentance doth not onely anatomize, but atomize you, naught you, nusquam you, null you."[64] Self-denial vaporizes the individual. The intensity of the violence ("eat your owne flesh"; eat joy in self; "ripp up our owne hearts"; "atomize you") indicates a more extreme conception of self-denial as annihilation. These graphic metaphors illustrate two important points. They demonstrate the severity with which spiritual asceticism treats the self and that, even in the midst of a spiritual emphasis, physical austerity remains relevant. It also remains relevant in that zealous forms of self-denial could result in a monastic disregard for familial and matrimonial ties.[65]

Self-denial quite literally leads to the monastic life in Jeremiah Burrough's *Moses his self-denyall* (1641). The work relates a story of physical displacement that has several parallels with Christian. Burroughs details how, after hearing a sermon by the Italian reformer Peter Martyr, the Marquess of Vico, Marcus Galeacius, reads scripture obsessively and decides to "change his former company, and to make choise of better." Galeacius resolves to "leave court, and father, and honours, and inheritance, to joyne himself to a true Church of God; and according to this his resolution he went away." Burroughs then depicts a poignant scene where "much meanes were used to call him backe": "His children hung about him with dolefull cryes, his friends standing by with watery eyes, which so wrought upon his tender heart (hee being of a most loving and sweet disposition) that, as he hath often said, he thought that all his bowells rouled about within him ... but he denyed himself in all."[66] The rhyme of "cryes" and "eyes" heightens the scene's affective poignancy. In a cleverly synaesthetic way, it connects an aural phenomenon ("dolefull cryes") with an optical one ("watery eyes"), tangling the reader's emotional response in a complex and compelling web of sentiment and sensory crossings. The rhyme also reinforces the pathos evoked. "Eyes" and "cryes" are brought into close proximity through rhyme, and this results in a new compound that supplies the lines with another iteration of tearful grief: eyes *do* cry.

In its emotional intensity, the scene is reminiscent of Christian leaving his family. In fact, there exists an interesting correspondence between the two texts. Before Christian leaves, he confesses to his family, "O my dear Wife, said he, and you the Children of my bowels, I your dear friend am in my self undone" (8). Upon leaving, Galeacius's "bowells rouled about within him," and Christian addresses his children as being "of my bowels" before departing. Both texts emphasize the physical connection between father and children, making the forced disconnection seem unnatural and even more difficult. Henry Burton concludes in a sermon from 1641, "deny our selves in those things, which otherwise we are bound to love by the Law of Nature. Trample upon thy Father, cast off thy wife and children, saith a Father, if they seeke to draw thee from Christ."[67] The rolling of Galeacius's bowels, Christian referring to his children as "of my bowels" before leaving them, indicate how their actions require ignoring – if not outrightly rejecting – the law of nature. What that nature represents – children, wife, family – indicates how its denial corresponds to monastic asceticism. Monasticism, too, embraces that which is contrary to nature. As we saw Thomas Beard state in chapter 2, "for, whence ariseth this necessary conclusion, that the vow of single life is repugnant to nature."[68] Writing about how religious embrace "Austeritie of life," Girolamo Piatti observes how this austerity is repugnant to nature: "this severitie brings much profit with it; and first, by use of hard and paineful things, our nature is mortifyed and kept from flying out."[69] In its disassociation from the world and family, in its rejection of the law of nature, godly self-denial reproduces the eremitic life of monasticism.

John Everard also embraces the monastic life in *The Gospel treasury opened* (1657) while advocating self-denial. As distinct from Burroughs, though, Everard envisions a wholly internal state of monastic withdrawal. In one sermon in the work, he advocates self-annihilation as a way "to be emptie in our selves, to be Nothing."[70] To accomplish this emptying, what Everard refers to as "Iness or Selfness" must be removed: "but these things, Iness and Selfness, being let in, These, these things make us deformed; this is that makes us like the Devil himself."[71] The removal of "Iness" is achieved by a studied detachment from, and a disciplined indifference towards, the things of this world. The detached man "if he have Wife, Children, Honours, Riches, &c. he sets not his heart on them."[72] As Everard explains, "if ye love Father, Mother, Wife, Children, Goods, Honour, Credit, what great acts have ye done? what have you done more then Heathens do? But as ye are Christians, I injoyn you A Love above all these: You are to love, That Noble, that Divine, that Internal part that is in them." Not loving them, but loving God in them achieves the "abdication I speak of."[73] When one can manifest this disinterested detachment towards his relations and the world, one can reach the ultimate goal of self-annihilation, namely, to become "a sequestered man which hath lost all that ever he hath in this world."[74] Importantly, the use of "sequester" attributes a monastic connotation to the self-denial Everard describes. It is a word often applied to isolation (i.e., sequestration) in a monastery. In Robert Crofts's *The terrestriall paradise* (1639), he criticizes those who would "sequester our selves for fear / Into a Monastery."[75] By using "sequester," Everard attributes a monastic sensibility to self-denial.

As a result, self-annihilation in *The Gospel treasury opened* recreates coenobitic indifference towards the world in one's emotional disposition towards, not physical dislocation from, it. One does not leave his family, but loves them indifferently. This is the emotional and spiritual equivalent of monastic sequestration. While Max Weber argued that Protestant asceticism "no longer lived outside the world in monastic communities, but within the world and its institutions," that only partially accounts for Everard's experience. For Everard, self-denial is still very much otherworldly. The otherworldliness derives not from isolation in a monastery, but from the location of a monastic disregard for the world in the soul. Otherworldliness is resituated in the world. The door is not, finally, slammed on the monastery, for its passageway still stands open in the spiritual life of each sequestered man.[76] In the words of Richard Baxter, "every true Member of Christ is dead to the world, and not only Monks, or Votaries, or such like."[77] Everard's self-denial, much like the version found in Burroughs, retains a thoroughly monastic approach to the world. Spiritual asceticism draws on its physical counterpart, as we saw anticipated in the *Apology* and reflected in cannibalistic metaphors of self-denial.

In part II of the allegory, as the pilgrims journey to the Valley of Humiliation, a hybrid of spiritual and physical asceticism also applies. Humiliation and self-denial are often discussed as working in conjunction. "The most self-denying humiliation," Baxter concludes, "is the neerest way to heaven, and the most self-exalting Pride is the surest and neerest way to hell."[78] Humiliation is a godly sorrow and contrition for one's sins that precipitates the sinner's search for God. As Jeremiah Burroughs asks, did God "first prepare thy heart, by a work of humiliation to seek him, and make up thy peace with him?"[79] Mercie's account of what one may experience in the valley stresses the benefit of humiliation: "Here one may think, and break at Heart, and melt in ones Spirit, until ones Eyes become like the Fish Pools of Heshbon" (239).[80]

Mercie's allusion to the Song of Solomon in "Eyes become like the Fish Pools of Heshbon" (7:4) illustrates humiliation's capacity to effect beautifying transformation. In that respect, the allusion connects humiliation to other ascetic processes that also beautify. By understanding the Song of Solomon allegorically as a dialogue between the individual believer and Christ, analogy with the fish pools denotes the sinner's increasing pulchritude to the Bridegroom.[81] In his commentary on The Song of Solomon, John Robotham paraphrases verses 7:4–6 as "In summe, her beauty is wonderfull in all parts, she is comely throughout … she is beautifull in every part, she is wholly delectable and full of glory."[82]

In the poetry of Joseph Beaumont, asceticism makes Simeon Stylites more "delicious" to Christ. Though Simeon suffers from a gangrenous, worm-infested wound, he does not abate his ascetic exertions. Simeon's eventual triumph over the malady evidences his "Angelik Fervencie,/ Whose Mystik Power hath made Him now / All Soule: Sure Simeon feels no blow/Nor wound, but those, w^ch LOVE'S sweet Darts/Bestow on Saints Delicious Hearts."[83] A similar delectability results in Robotham's exegesis of The Song of Solomon and establishes a connection between Beaumont's Simeon and Bunyan's humiliated. In *The Pilgrim's Progress*, as eyes become like fish pools as a result of humiliation, an ascetic process beautifies the sinner in a way similar to Simeon's corporal mortification. It is no coincidence, then, that humiliation also invokes another form of physical asceticism, namely monastic retirement.

The delights that the Valley of Humiliation affords are similar to those offered by monastic life. About them, Mr. Great-heart says, "here a man shall be free from the Noise, and from the hurryings of this Life; all States are full of Noise and Confusion, only the Valley of Humiliation is that empty and Solitary Place. Here a man shall not be so let and hindred in his Contemplation, as in other places he is apt to be" (238). In the words of the Laudian Peter Hausted, contemplatives are happiest because they "hath no imployment, but onely to pray."[84] The contemplative life is, of course, shorthand for monasticism. Great-heart's conclusion about how the world interferes with contemplation resonates with the Jesuit Girolamo Piatti's observation about that interference in *The happines of a religious state* (1632). Piatti claims "the quiet of a Religious life" allows for "the studie of heavenlie knowledge," "For as no man can attentively think of anie thing in the midst of a great hurrie and noise, but in the dead of the night, or in a solitarie place, that verie silence and solitude doth invite a man to contemplation."[85] For Piatti, the great hurry and noise dissipate in the silence, solitude, and contemplation of the religious life. In the Valley of Humiliation, the same dissipation occurs. Piatti also claims the unique capacity of a religious life for "the voluntarie humiliation of ourselves."[86] Descriptions of monastic life that depict it in terms similar to the Valley of Humiliation – that is, as solitary, affording time for contemplation, and escaping the noise of the world – are commonplace.[87]

Based on these similarities, Bunyan employs monastic terminology when describing the Valley of Humiliation, and the impetus behind retirement to the Valley is consonant with monasticism. Part II locates the monastic ideal within the godly practice of humiliation; part I found it within self-denial. The withdrawal central to monastic practice has been appropriated and transformed; it does not entail physical dislocation, but relocating the solitary life within the soul. The otherworldliness of monasticism is retained, only resituated within the world.

In the introduction, I noted that Weber's thesis resulted in asceticism's spiritualization and diminishment, and that the idea of ascetic disappearance is an important narrative for (early) modernity. Those ideas deserve consideration again here. Does this secularization (otherworldly worldliness) constitute a diminution of the monastic life?[88] Is it a lessening of and, therefore, ultimately a movement away from asceticism: a journey out from underneath the cowl of a medieval and monastic past into modernity? Possibly. But it was also regarded at the time as a reformation, reclamation, and *intensification* of that past. Richard Baxter writes, "its one thing to creep into a Monks Cell, or an Anchorets Cave, or an Hermits Wilderness, or Diogenes Tub; and another thing truly to be Crucified to the world; and in the midst of the creatures to live above them unto God."[89] This is a reformation that also recommits. The crucifixion to the world that monks, anchorites, hermits, and even cynics claim to achieve through removal from it is still possible within it. What's more, *that* is the more rigorous ascetic task – to be *in* the world but not *of* it. As self-denial and humiliation throughout *The Pilgrim's Progress* illustrate, the secularization of monasticism is, paradoxically, a strengthening of it. The scrutiny of the self throughout the allegory, one that reflects and participates in the slow crawl towards a modern subjectivity, looks backwards as much as forwards. The monastic resources upon which self-denial draws make Bunyan's subject the object of reinvented modes of traditional asceticism.

*The Pilgrim's Progress* ultimately urges caution when deciding the modernity of the early modern self. Bunyan would find, as the previous analysis shows, the individualism for which his allegory has been celebrated repugnant. Whether that repugnance signals an intense engagement with subjectivity, with (à la Reiss) "who-ness," consonant with the emergence of selfhood is a thornier question with a less obvious answer.[90] But whatever form this early modern "self" takes, the preceding pages have sought to prove that asceticism contributes to its formation. Traditional modes of asceticism (i.e., monasticism) – the representative vestiges of the medieval past the self is thought to shed – are instrumental in the formation of early modern subjectivity.

In addition to its significance for histories of selfhood, self-denial in *The Pilgrim's Progress* affirms this book's argument about the nature of early modern asceticism. Bunyan's allegory offers the most thoroughly spiritualized version of asceticism this study documents. And yet, the allegory's spiritual asceticism incurs heavy debts to monasticism and physical austerity. As a result, Bunyan demonstrates the porous boundary separating spiritual and physical modes of the ascetic life.

The collapse of spiritual asceticism into physical austerity is symptomatic of a problem Marvell astutely observes. As asceticism seeks to escape the body, it must rely on the body for its mean of exit. The body circumscribes the soul; that is an ineluctable and inconvenient reality for both spiritual and physical ascetics alike. For physical ascetics, beating down the body intensifies – rather than liberates one from – relation to it. Milton's asceticism may lean in a spiritual direction for this reason. For spiritual ascetics, the circumscription means even the most avowedly spiritual versions of self-denial, such as that found in *The Pilgrim's Progress*, eventually drift towards conventional forms of severity. Circumscription yields an interdependence between body and soul that is at once begrudging and resentful. Whether the object of punitive ascetic force consists of the self or the body, the outcome is the same. Bunyan announces his preference for spiritual asceticism and then the nature of embodiment successively undermines that preference. No matter how much early modern Protestants wish to abandon severe forms of corporal austerity, they are incapable of relinquishing them.

# Conclusion

To explain how this book ends, I wish to summarize the argument so far by returning to an important historical moment from this study's beginning. At the Woodstock meeting in 1631, the Laudian movement raised questions about the nature of asceticism that, for some, already had clear answers. Preferment going to the unmarried suggested a preference for physical asceticism. Considering that the persons involved were priests, it also indicated that celibacy was more suited to such a holy profession than marriage. That struck a nerve with those Protestants who considered asceticism to be an internal, spiritual process that occasionally manifested in mild forms of physical expression such as fasts. Rigorous forms of corporal austerity – monasticism, bodily mortification, physical virginity – belonged to a pre-Reformation and benighted past. Internal asceticism not only redirected punitive energies that were wasted on the body, but it in fact represented a more difficult and challenging version of austerity.

These debates about early modern asceticism were not confined to theological controversy but, as the previous chapters have argued, became of significant cultural and literary moment. John Milton, in *A Mask* and *Lycidas*, deliberates the value of physical and spiritual asceticism. As chapters 2 and 3 argue, the frequent outcome of that deliberation – a sympathy with corporal austerity – revises Milton's religious affiliation as a staunch radical; it reveals him drifting – complicatedly and often equivocally – towards the Laudian Church. While Donne and Bunyan do not engage directly with Laudianism, the conflicted asceticism they depict, poised between physical and spiritual expression, surely does. Differences between the depiction of virginity in the stanza on "The Virgins" in "A Litany" and in "Since She Whom I Loved" encapsulate much of Protestantism's difficult relation to the single life. One wonders how Donne's celebration of Tilman as a "bless'd hermaphrodite" in 1618 might have struck Laud at Woodstock in 1631.

To conclude this study, the following pages consider what happens to early modern asceticism as the seventeenth century moves farther away from the fateful events at Woodstock and the Laudian moment that have been this book's focus. Do the tensions between spiritual and physical types of asceticism work themselves out, or become less relevant, the farther removed England becomes from the Reformation debates that surcharged those tensions with a renewed urgency? Ascetic types of living, of course, never go away. Asceticism's central question constantly renews its contemporaneity. As long as bodies and souls exist (or are thought to exist), the question of how they relate to each other, and beliefs about how they *should* relate to each other, make asceticism pertinent. Some of the inter- and intra-confessional pressures that inform ascetic practices do change, though, and it is the task of the following pages to describe those changes.

For example, if Laud painted puritans into an ascetic corner by advancing corporal austerities inimical to the spiritual asceticism they favoured, then the Restoration accomplished a similar portraiture. Charles II did not advance a rival version of asceticism, but rather unabashed libertinism. The "Bawdy House Riots" of 1668 were, to some extent, an ascetic reaction to that libertine lifestyle. The rioters, as Sarah Apetrei has written, "were overwhelmingly dissenters from the Church of England, appalled at the persecution of honest Protestants and their conventicles while fornication at court and prostitution on the streets of London were openly tolerated."[1] Much to his chagrin, Charles II probably did as much for the promotion of asceticism as his prudish father and the abstemious Laud.

It is in this environment that Anthony Horneck publishes *The happy ascetick* (1681), a work that exudes, but also seeks to overcome, many of the tensions – between spiritual and physical asceticism, and the inter- and intra-confessional affiliations they suppose – this study has traced. Horneck displays a unique circumspection and self-conscious awareness about asceticism's capacity to compromise seemingly hard and fast confessional distinctions. As a result, he evinces a palpable impatience for how advocating physical or spiritual asceticism could automatically trigger assumptions about intra-confessional allegiance. Apart from Marvell, no other writer in the pages of this book approaches such subtle commentary on austerity. Whereas Marvell probed the paradoxes of embodiment and asceticism, Horneck scrutinizes the confessional positions attached to each ascetic type. In so doing, *The happy ascetick* offers a glimpse of what an ascetic future might look like in the Restoration and beyond.

## I "Our Bodies Naturally Are Enemies to Our Souls"

Anthony Horneck (1641–1697) was born in the Lower Palatinate and educated at the University of Heidelberg, where he studied under the Calvinist theologian Friedrich Spanheim the Younger. He arrived in England in 1660 to study at Oxford "where," as W.R. Ward notes, "he caught the eye of the provost [of Queen's College], Thomas Barlow, who had the reputation of being a stiff Calvinist and also a patron of needy scholars" (*ODNB*). Eventually, Horneck became a chaplain to William III, but spent much of his career at various indigent livings. Ward identifies the driving impulse behind Horneck's theology as "working out rules of life for ordinary Christians" (*ODNB*). To that end, he promoted the formation of religious societies for young men and also supported the reformation of manners. *The happy ascetick* represents Horneck's commitment to working out those rules of life and manners in practical divinity.

*The happy ascetick* contains fifteen chapters on what it calls the "ordinary Exercises of Godliness" and four chapters on "extraordinary" ascetic exercises.[2] Each of the four chapters outlines a different practice, including vowing, fasting, watching, and self-revenge (the latter is a catch-all term for miscellaneous practices of mortification). It is significant that Horneck even includes these chapters. Based upon his godly pedigree, we might not expect him to engage so openly with physical asceticism. More significant still is the evident favour in which the chapters hold corporal austerity. Horneck regards extraordinary exercises as essential because of the nature of embodiment and how he defines the relationship between body and soul: "That using severities upon our selves is sometimes necessary, is evident from hence, because our Bodies naturally are enemies to our Souls, and nothing is so great a clog to our Spirits, as our sensual Appetite." As a result, Horneck considers bodily satisfaction inimical to soulful piety: "The more the Body is denied, the freer is the Soul in her Motions."[3] Antipathy between body and soul helps explain why severe ascetic practices are met with general approbation in *The happy ascetick*.

They include, for instance, the story of "a holy Man in Egypt, who being tempted by a Harlot to acts of uncleanness, and feeling the temptation work, lighted a Candle, and burnt his Fingers one by one, till by the smart and pain of his Flesh, he forgot all thoughts of impurity."[4] Horneck's respect for patristic asceticism extends to Jerome "beating" his body into submission and Chrysostom, who "absconded himself in a desert place" to master the "Lusts of the Flesh."[5] *The happy ascetick* clearly admires this austerity, and at times its admiration even borders on amazement and disbelief: "In Egypt especially men used such severities upon themselves, that we that never tryed them, would scarce believe, that ever there were such men, or that they did those mighty things which are recorded in History."[6] Despite his regard for such heroic and "mighty things," Horneck does not definitively endorse these practices. He is very solicitous about their misuse, noting especially that they should not be regarded as meritorious or as expiating sin. He does, though, offer this statement about them: "I cannot and dare not press these severities as absolutely necessary, yet thus much I will be bold to tell you, that the Saints of old thought Heaven could not be had without them."[7] They are not "*absolutely* necessary": only heaven hangs in the balance. He makes this remark after spending the preceding twenty pages explaining how these severities should be handled "with very great cautiousness and circumspection."[8] Some dissonance exists, no doubt, between these two positions: the cautiousness on one hand, heaven dependent on the other. That dissonance – embracing physical asceticism while still keeping it at arm's length – reflects the tension between physical and spiritual asceticism that this study has examined. But Horneck also desires to move beyond it.

He complains that "the age we live in is so very apt to call all things Superstition, and Rags of the Whore of Babylon, that looks like Self-denial."[9] That is usually a complaint levied against Laudians by godly critics of physical asceticism, not one used by the godly to exonerate their own preference for corporal austerity. Horneck labeling the ascetic practices "self-denial," the godly term for spiritual asceticism, is symptomatic of the misalignment, or rather the *re*-alignment he attempts.

Throughout Horneck's writing, there is a sense that rash determinations about ascetic superstition have become nothing more than an excuse:

> The Age we live in will not bear these severities, Mens Lusts have made that necessary, which heretofore would scarce have been thought convenient, so strangely is Religion alter'd from what it was, and let no Man tell me here; that to Preach up severities, is to teach People to turn Heathens again; for the Priests of Baal cut themselves with Knives and Laucers, till the Blood gush'd out upon them, 1 Reg. 18. 28. we urge no such severities, as shall disable the Body from doing the Work, that's proper for it, nor do we look upon God as a Tyrant, or a Deity, that delights in Blood, as those Heathens did, much less do we think that any such severities merit God's favour, or his Audience, as they did; no, the severities which we recommend to Christians are such as the Primitive Fathers used, severities, which nothing but love to God produces, and a

> hatred of Sin, and a willingness to be rid of those Lusts, and Temptations, which do so easily beset us.[10]

Horneck's fatigue and frustration with conventional ascetic discourse are evident: "and let no Man tell me here; that to Preach up severities, is to teach People to turn Heathens again." One gets the sense that the paganism card has been played frequently against his ascetic arguments. Instead of just rejecting that argument (which he does), Horneck signals its tiredness. In other words, he envisions a possibility beyond this ascetic polemic that has now become clichéd. He also outlines how to move beyond the polemic while still retaining a godly sense of vocation ("as shall disable the Body from doing the Work"), soteriology ("any such severities merit God's favour"), and depravity ("hatred of Sin") alongside an acknowledgment of ascetic severity. Throughout this study, those things have often been held in conflict *not* compatibility. While one element might have been harmonized with physical asceticism, I do not recall an instance of all three reconciled to its rigours. For example, as we saw in Donne's Bridgewater sermon, he recommends "Disciplines, and Mortifications" for those attempting to remain continent, but with this caveat: "(which Disciplines and Mortifications, every state and condition of life is not bound to exercise, because such Mortifications as would overcome their Concupiscences, would also overcome all their naturall strength, and make them unable to doe the works of their callings)."[11] In the Washington and Nethersole sermons, Donne does not limit the mortifications and disciplines with a consideration of calling. Horneck claims "we urge no such severities, as shall disable the Body." But the "severities" he recommends are those "such as the Primitive Fathers used," raising serious questions about the feasibility of avoiding disablement. For Horneck, in contrast with Donne, the relationship between the rigour of the proposed severities and the ability to perform one's calling is not inversely proportional. That may be baldly contradictory, but it is also evidence of Horneck's desire to recalibrate ascetic discourse, throwing over some of its truisms.

Within the model Horneck proposes, spiritual and physical modes of the ascetic life can exist together. Physically demanding actions have an overarching spiritual impulse to inform and guide them: love of God. Horneck achieves a degree of stasis between two previously warring ascetic factions not through some dizzying flight of intellectual insight, but through a recognition of the self-evident fact that these superstitiously popish or High Church Protestant severities can easily serve Godly – not just godly – ends (and vice versa). The dark glasses of polemic and politics obscured that fact.

Even while expressing exhaustion with the polemical positions that imperil ascetic discourse, Horneck's writing cannot fully escape them. The formulation "necessary … convenient" engages the exegetical tradition surrounding 1 Corinthians 7:35. In that verse, and about his advice regarding the married and single life, Paul concludes, "and this I speak for your own profit; not that I may cast a snare upon you, but for that which is comely, and that you may attend upon the Lord without distraction." Paul says this after arguing "he that is unmarried careth for the things that belong to the Lord," and the married for those of "the world" (7:32–33). There is perhaps a bit of ground to be made up for proponents of marriage. *Annotations upon the Holy Bible* (1685), based upon the Presbyterian Matthew Poole's *Synopsis criticorum aliorumque sacrae scripturae interpretum* (1669), offers this commentary on the passage's use of the word "comely": "but in this place the word signifies most largely the same with profitable and convenient. For marriage is a state which neither is in it self indecent, nor ever was so reputed in the World by any Nation, and the Scripture tells us, that Marriage is honourable amongst all."[12] Stressing marriage's profitability and convenience, *Annotations* is eager to make up that ground. Also in response to 1 Corinthians, the anonymous *An Account of marriage* (1672) contends, "if upon all these considerations, Sir marriage appears so convenient and necessary for the World, they must have slender pleas who admire unsociable and solitatary [sic] tempers."[13] *An Account of marriage* argues for both marriage's convenience and necessity, while *Annotations* asserts its convenience in the face of Paul's seeming denigration.

Horneck, in what is largely a reversal of *An Account of marriage*'s rhetoric, uses the "necessary" and "convenient" formula to claim asceticism's exigence. He is not anxious about protecting matrimony from slipping into potential Pauline disrepute. In light of how the terms are used in *Annotations* and *An Account of marriage,* it is more than a little ironic that strenuous assertions of marriage's *convenience* are now replaced by declarations of asceticism's *necessity*; not only does asceticism replace marriage, but it commands where matrimony was only commended. That represents a rather dim view of marriage, but one consistent with a work that praises primitive Christianity for holding remarriage in the following esteem: "There was hardly a Widow among them, that complained of Solitariness, or sought Comfort in a second Husband, and second Marriage was counted little better than Adultery."[14] It does not take a third widowhood for these women to embrace retiredness. How asceticism usurps marriage's place in the "necessary … convenient" formulation, coupled with Horneck's attitude towards remarriage, reveals an antipathy between the ascetic life and matrimony. The privileging of asceticism results in the devaluing of marriage.

That privileging endangers any attempt to supersede previous ascetic tensions. In fact, it triggers those tensions. One of the chief objections Protestants had to Roman Catholic asceticism was its elevation of virginity by means of disparaging marriage.[15] The sanctity of virginity need not detract from the holiness of matrimony. In the irony of "necessary … convenient," *The happy ascetick* walks right into this polemical morass. The conventions of traditional ascetic discourse still circumscribe Horneck's criticism of it. The commitment to ascetic severity that causes such circumscription has a source in Horneck's biography.

## II The Happy Ascetic

The demanding austerity outlined throughout *The happy ascetick* reflects the equally demanding personal piety of its author. While *The happy ascetick* might not be wholly effective in its attempt to synthesize corporal austerity with godly principles, Horneck did achieve that synthesis – rather spectacularly and movingly – in his own person. Bishop Kidder's biography attests to Horneck's personal adoption of the strict rules of life he enjoined on others. Kidder describes Horneck as a "Conqueror" of the world and its fleshly blandishments, who spent much time "in watchings and great austerities." According to Kidder, he "led an Ascetick Life, kept under his Body, and with great industry advanced in Holiness, and a Life that was spiritual and heavenly."[16]

The most remarkable instance of Horneck keeping under his body comes when Kidder recounts Horneck's endurance of kidney stones, especially in the time preceding his death. The stones were so painful that Horneck "walked with difficulty," "could hardly bear a Coach," and "made very little, and that a bloody Water."[17] Despite the agony he must have been in, Horneck did not remit from his labours. During the Christmas preceding his death on 31 January, "his work increased upon him, and whereas other men's labours are then intermitted, his were augmented." Instead of retiring from these exertions, or performing them with grudging reluctance, Horneck "nevertheless went through all this labour and trouble, with as great chearfulness as was possible."[18] He was particularly concerned about the well-being of the poor in his parish during the Christmas season.

After preaching on 23 January 1697, and after the exertions he had undergone, Horneck took a turn for the worse. As Kidder records, at this point his urine had "totally stopped." But when Horneck was asked if he was experiencing the agony that he most assuredly was, he replied, "the pain he felt was tolerable."[19] In Horneck's measured reply, there is something of Simeon's indifference to gangrenous worms. Horneck's labeling of the pain as "tolerable" partly reflects what Christopher Wilson identifies as self-denial's most difficult task: "as on the contrary, when our affections carry us to the mislike off [sic], and flying from a thing as grievous, yet to imbrace that with joy and delight: o how happie a thing it is? this is a worke farre passing the severest Popish Discipline, which in their blinde devotions men inflict on themselves."[20] Wilson's comments help make sense of Horneck titling his work *The happy ascetick.* The seemingly oxymoronic combination of "happy" and "ascetick" expresses the ascetic transvaluation of deleterious and painful things as welcome and joyful ones. A response such as "the pain he felt was tolerable" attempts to accomplish that welcoming.

What Horneck endured must have been excruciating. A post-mortem examination of his body found the following:

> Both his Ureters were stopped: One of them was stopped as a Bottle with a Cork, with a Stone that entered the top of the Ureter with a sharp end, the upper part of which was thick and much too big to enter any farther: The other was stopped also with Stones, of much less firmness and consistence than the other.[21]

In light of this discovery, Horneck's ability to function cheerfully and work tirelessly is remarkable. It does raise the question, though, of whether Horneck is guilty of the extreme asceticism he cautions against in *The happy ascetick.* One of the caveats Horneck offers while discussing corporal austerity is that "weak or sickly persons" should only use them with "moderation." The body should not be "disabled."[22] In fact, Kidder mentions how, before the extraordinary exertions of Christmas 1696, he persuades Horneck that "he could not long continue under the labour which he underwent." Horneck proves "sensible" of this fact, but nonetheless "went on in his accustomed labours to Christmas, 1696."[23] Had he taken his own advice, instead of continuing (and in some ways redoubling) his efforts, Horneck's life might have been prolonged. There is, no doubt, a note of the hagiographic throughout Kidder's account. But whether this constitutes the construction of an ideal or reality, the biography documents an ascetic life as physically and spiritually demanding as any found in *The happy ascetick.*

Of the texts considered in the preceding pages, the work closest to *The happy ascetick* is William Watts's *Mortification apostolicall* (1637), examined at length in the introduction. William Prynne's *Canterburies doome* (1646) describes Watts as one of a number of "Clergy men infected with Arminianisme, Popery, and devoted to Popish Ceremonies."[24] What is significant about the comparison of Horneck with Watts is that in the former we find godly advocacy of the ascetic practices that the godly had previously decried in the latter. Horneck's work does not primarily redefine asceticism, appropriating it to, and altering it within, a godly framework. It reclaims it *en masse*, situating it within that godly framework. For that to be possible, for Watts and Horneck to switch places, the cultural tensions this study has described must no longer be – or must be differently – applicable. Horneck's work holds out the possibility of an asceticism in which Calvinist spirituality stands alongside the corporal austerity often branded as Laudian or Roman Catholic. He imagines a fully integrated ascetic future, of body and soul, physical and spiritual. With his desire for a godly asceticism that embraces corporal austerity, and his impatience with the objections to such a syncretic formulation, Horneck stands at the end of the cultural moment of asceticism this book has examined.

To some extent, Horneck stretches asceticism past its logical breaking point: primitive austerity that does not disable one in his or her calling; Calvinist depravity coupled with severe ascetic exertion. In pushing asceticism so far, Horneck is anticipated by Andrew Marvell. *Upon Appleton House* asks profound questions about the nature of embodiment and the possibility of escaping the demands of the body. For Marvell, the ascetic life provides only a partial release from those demands; every ascetic act serves to highlight the dependency of the soul on the body. That dependence means asceticism cannot provide what it claims to. Both Horneck and Marvell probe the limits and the (im)possibilities of asceticism. Their difference lies in Marvell perceiving something inadequate in asceticism itself; namely, a body and soul dynamic that endlessly recurs. Horneck's asceticism discovers constraints in the confessional categories that would receive and taxonomize it. In ways that are similar to Laud's pan-asceticism from the introduction, in which Laud encompassed aspects of both physical austerity and self-denial, Horneck's is a voracious ascetic appetite that explodes confessional categories (the difference with Laud is that the cleric's mild concessions to self-denial are hardly explosive). For Marvell, then, asceticism is the problem; for Horneck, our reception of asceticism is what is deficient.

Despite these particular differences, Horneck and Marvell both raise serious, and potentially catastrophic, questions about the practicability of the ascetic life. In many ways, this is what is at stake in the cleavage of asceticism into its various physical and spiritual instantiations, and the inter- and intra-confessional strife that accompanies them: Is asceticism possible? At its broadest, that seems to me the problem with which this book – at nearly every moment – is preoccupied. Does asceticism constitute a futile revolt against the ineluctability of sexuality, or does it achieve a state beyond the turbidity of human desire? In their own way, each work examined in this book poses this challenging – and still relevant – question.

# Notes

## Notes to Introduction

1 At this point, Laud was essentially the *de facto* Archbishop of Canterbury. George Abbot, his predecessor, was archbishop in name only. Accidentally shooting a gamekeeper while hunting in 1621, Abbot had been deemed a "man of blood" by his fellow bishops and, since the accession of Charles I to the throne of England in 1625, had found himself in increasing disfavour with the new regime.

2 Peter Heylyn, *Cyprianus anglicus* (London, 1668), 224. See also Arthur Christopher Benson, *William Laud Sometime Archbishop of Canterbury, A Study* (London: Kegan Paul, Trench, Trübner & Co., 1897), 186. Quotations have been modernized with respect to f/s, u/v, and italicization.

3 Quotations of and references to the Bible are from *King James Study Bible*, ed. Kenneth Barker (Michigan: Zondervan, 2002).

4 See also Oxford, Queen's College Library, MS 390 fo. 58; Charles Edward Mallet, *The Sixteenth and Seventeenth Centuries*, in *A History of the University of Oxford* (London: Methuen, 1924), 2:305; William Laud, *Works*, 7 vols. (Oxford: John Henry Parker, 1847–1860; New York: AMS, 1975), 3:214. All quotations of Laud's works are from this edition.

5 Oxford, Bodleian Library, Jones MS 17 fo. 304[r]. See also Kenneth Fincham and Nicholas Tyacke, *Altars Restored: The Changing Face of English Religious Worship, 1547–c. 1700* (Oxford: Oxford University Press, 2007), 185.

6 Heylyn, *Cyprianus anglicus*, 224. If Heylyn is wrong about Laud's comments, is he also wrong about this wedding? The two did get married, and the level of elaboration seems inconsistent with misremembrance; the account reads as though Heylyn were in attendance. See the *ODNB* entry on Thomas Turner.

7 It is also possible that Heylyn was present at the Woodstock meeting; by this time, he was a chaplain-in-ordinary to Charles I. As Anthony

Milton notes, Heylyn was a master of using "the divisions of the 1630s to secure the humiliation of his opponents." The Rector of Exeter College John Prideaux, whom Milton describes as Heylyn's "bête noire of the 1620s," was on the chopping block at Woodstock for encouraging anti-ceremonialism. Anthony Milton, *Laudian and Royalist Polemic in Seventeenth-Century England: The Career and Writings of Peter Heylyn* (Manchester: Manchester University Press, 2007), 48.

8 Helen Parish, *Clerical Celibacy in the West: c. 1100–1700* (Surrey: Ashgate, 2010), 144. See also Helen Parish, *Clerical Marriage and the English Reformation: Precedent, Policy, and Practice* (Surrey: Ashgate, 2000), 167; Peter Marshall, *The Catholic Priesthood and the English Reformation* (Oxford: Clarendon Press, 1994), 142; John K. Yost, "The Reformation Defense of Clerical Marriage in the Reigns of Henry VIII and Edward VI," *Church History* 50 (1981): 152–165.

9 See also Heather Dubrow's observation that "the relative valuation of celibacy and marriage ... was far more complex in Protestant England than most scholars have acknowledged." *A Happier Eden: The Politics of Marriage in the Stuart Epithalamium* (Ithaca: Cornell University Press, 1990), 259.

10 Joseph Hall, *The honor of the married clergie* (London, 1620), sig. A2[v].

11 John Jewel, *A defence of the Apologie of the Churche of Englande* (London, 1567), 163, see 163–190.

12 John Foxe, *Actes and monuments* (London, 1583), 2:1165 (first half).

13 Heinrich Bullinger, *The golde[n] boke of christen matrimony* (London, 1542), sig. A4[v].

14 I am not intentionally drawing on Hegel's concept of *aufhebung* here. In asceticism, the body is not lifted up but beaten down. For an example of Hegelian *aufhebung*, see his *Phenomenology of Spirit*, transl. A.V. Miller (Oxford: Oxford University Press, 1977), "Consciousness," para. 107.

15 See Sarah Apetrei, "'The Life of Angels': Celibacy and Asceticism in Anglicanism, 1660-c. 1700," *Reformation & Renaissance Review* 13 (2011): 247–274, 270. Apetrei discerns a tension between pro- and anti-ascetic currents in Restoration culture.

16 See Basil's letter 2 to Gregory. *The Fathers of the Church*, ed. Roy Deferrari, vol. 13, *Letters*, transl. Sister Agnes Clare Way (Washington, D.C.: The Catholic University of America Press, 1951; Washington, D.C.: The Catholic University of America Press, 1965), 5–11. *Patrologiae Graeca*, ed. J.-P. Migne (Paris: Imprimerie Catholique, 1857), 32:cols. 223–234.

17 Some scholars still associate puritanism with conventional forms of corporal austerity. See Jennifer Waldron, *Reformations of the Body: Idolatry, Sacrifice, and Early Modern Theater* (New York: Palgrave Macmillan, 2013), 2.

18 Timothy J. Reiss, *Mirages of the Selfe: Patterns of Personhood in Ancient and Early Modern Europe* (Stanford: Stanford University Press, 2003), passim. See the discussion of self-denial and subjectivity in chapter 5.

For discussion of the Cartesian self, in which body and soul exist as "two independent substances," see Udo Thiel, *The Early Modern Subject: Self-Consciousness and Personal Identity from Descartes to Hume* (Oxford: Oxford University Press, 2011), 36–43. For ascetics, body and soul might be radically divisible, but they are not independent.

19 William Gouge, *A learned and very useful commentary on the whole epistle to the Hebrews* (London, 1655), 428 [commentary on chapter 10 of Hebrews].

20 John Tombes, *Fermentvm Pharisaeorvm* (London, 1643), 5.

21 Thomas James, *A manuduction, or introduction vnto diuinitie containing a confutation of papists by papists, throughout the important articles of our religion* (London, 1625), 84.

22 This is especially true of puritans, who celebrate married sexuality. See William Whately, *A Bride-Bush* (London, 1619), 14, 18; William Gouge, *Of domesticall duties* (London, 1622), 221. See also Daniel Doriani, "The Puritans, Sex, and Pleasure," in *Christian Perspectives on Sexuality and Gender*, ed. Adrian Thatcher and Elizabeth Stuart (Herefordshire: Fowler Wright Books, 1996), 33–52, esp. 38–39. For commentary on Protestantism's relationship to matrimony, see Levin L. Schücking, *The Puritan Family: A Social Study from the Literary Sources*, transl. Brian Battershaw (London: Routledge & Kegan Paul, 1969); William Haller and Malleville Haller, "The Puritan Art of Love," *Huntington Library Quarterly* 5 (1942): 235–272; Roland Mushat Frye, "The Teachings of Classical Puritanism on Conjugal Love," *Studies in the Renaissance* 2 (1955): 148–159; Marshall, *The Catholic Priesthood and the English Reformation*, 164.

23 Earlier Reformers vigorously protested the idea that virginity was universally applicable. William Tyndale shrinks the applicability of chastity by remarking in "The dutie of Kynges, and of the Iudges and Officers" that "… chastity is an exceeding seldom gift." *The vvhole workes of W. Tyndall, Iohn Frith, and Doct. Barnes* (London, 1573), 133.

24 For calling and vocation, see William Charke and William Fulke, *A treatise against the Defense of the censure* (Cambridge, 1586), 174; Andrew Willet, *Synopsis papismi* (London, 1592), 250. For liberty, see Willet, *Synopsis papismi*, 249; William Perkins, *A golden chaine* (London, 1591), sig. G2[r]; John Donne, *The Sermons of John Donne*, 10 vols., ed. George R. Potter and Evelyn M. Simpson (Berkeley: University of California Press, 1953–1962), 4:153. And for denial, see Thomas Lupton, *The Christian against the Iesuite* (London, 1582), 48; William Prynne, *Canterburies doome* (London, 1646), 335.

25 I will expand on this in chapter 5 below where I examine spiritual ascetics' visceral metaphors of self-cannibalization. Max Weber, *The Protestant Ethic and the Spirit of Capitalism*, ed. Richard Swedberg, transl. Talcott Parsons (New York: W.W. Norton & Company, 2009), 60.

26 Wilson's text is largely a paraphrase of Thomas Brightman's *The Art of Self-Deniall: or, A Christian's First Lesson* (London, 1646). There is no *ODNB*

entry for Wilson, and this is his only publication. Brightman, a prolific author and major millennial thinker, died in 1607, so I would assume (but am not certain) that authorship belongs to him.

For self-denial as a response to corporal austerity, see William Negus, *Mans actiue obedience* (London, 1619), 262.

27 Christopher Wilson, *Self Deniall: or, A Christians Hardest Taske* (London, 1625), sig. E2ʳ.
28 Wilson, *Self Deniall*, sig. E2ᵛ.
29 Wilson, *Self Deniall*, sig. E4ʳ.
30 Wilson, *Self Deniall*, sigs. L2ʳ⁻ᵛ. Cf. Brightman, *The Art of Self-Deniall*, 53–55.
31 Tom Webster observes an "experiential radicalisation" in "the voluntary devotions of Puritans in England" during the 1630s. Tom Webster, "Early Stuart Puritanism," in *The Cambridge Companion to Puritanism*, ed. John Coffey and Paul C.H. Lim (Cambridge: Cambridge University Press, 2008), 48–66, 60–61. See also Christopher Durston, "'For the Better Humiliation of the People': Public Days of Fasting and Thanksgiving during the English Revolution," *The Seventeenth Century* 7 (1992): 129–149.
32 Thomas Cartwright, *The holy exercise of a true fast* (Scotland?, 1582), 15–17.
33 Arthur Hildersam, *The doctrine of fasting and praier* (London, 1633), 58.
34 Humphrey Chambers, *A divine balance to weigh religiovs fasts in applyed to present vse in a sermon preached before the honourable House of Commons in S. Margarets Westminster at their publique fast Sept 27, 1643* (London, 1643), 16.
35 William Attersoll, *Three treatises* (London, 1633), 37.
36 R.J., *Compunction or pricking of heart* (London, 1648), 318.
37 Samuel Smith, *The Character of a weaned Christian. Or The Evangelical Art of promoting Self-denial* (London, 1675), 56–57.
38 George Downame, *The Christians sanctuarie* (London, 1604), 55.
39 Downame, *The Christians sanctuarie*, 44.
40 Downame, *The Christians sanctuarie*, 55.
41 For previous discussions of Laudianism's ascetic predilections, see Austin Warren, *Richard Crashaw: A Study in Baroque Sensibility* (Ann Arbor: University of Michigan Press, 1939; Ann Arbor: University of Michigan Press, 1957), 8–10; Anthony Milton, *Catholic and Reformed: The Roman and Protestant Churches in English Protestant Thought, 1600–1640* (Cambridge: Cambridge University Press, 1995), 317–318. Deborah Shuger finds an affinity between the avant garde and ecumenical nature of Laudianism and the monastic life practiced at Little Gidding. My claim differs in that I find something ascetic in Laudianism itself. See Deborah Shuger, "Laudian Feminism and the Household Republic of Little Gidding," *Journal of Medieval and Early Modern Studies* 44 (2014): 69–94.
42 See Henry Mason, *Christian Humiliation* (London, 1625), 27–28; Peter Hausted, *Ten Sermons* (London, 1636), 176–177.

43 For criticism of Jerome's view of virginity, see William Fulke, *A defense of the sincere and true translations of the holie Scriptures into the English tong* (London, 1583), 412; George Abbot, *The reasons vvhich Doctour Hill hath brought, for the vpholding of papistry* (Oxford, 1604), 408; Thomas Wilson, *A commentarie vpon the most diuine Epistle of S. Paul to the Romanes* (London, 1614), 1120–1121; Edward Leigh, *A systeme or body of divinity consisting of ten books* (London, 1654), 743n; Edward Bulkley, *An answere to ten friuolous and foolish reason* (London, 1588), 47.

44 For a discussion of Laudian anti-Calvinism, see Nicholas Tyacke, *Anti-Calvinists: The Rise of English Arminianism c. 1590–1640* (Oxford: Oxford University Press, 1987).

45 It is for this reason that I do not think humoralism and, more broadly, Galenic physiology provide an adequate framework through which to understand the ascetic body. Ascetics frequently sacrifice their own health to austere endeavour; this rejects what Michael Schoenfeldt identifies as the guiding principle behind Galenic humoralism: "good health could emerge from good living." Asceticism achieves the health of the soul to the detriment of the body. Michael C. Schoenfeldt, *Bodies and Selves in Early Modern England: Physiology and Inwardness in Spenser, Shakespeare, Herbert, and Milton* (Cambridge: Cambridge University Press, 1999), 7.

46 There is patristic precedent for finding the aesthetic in abstinence. See Peter Brown, *The Body and Society: Men, Women and Sexual Renunciation in Early Christianity* (New York: Columbia University Press, 1988), 173. See also Jacob of Serug's (c. 449–521 C.E.) sermon on Simeon Stylites: Susan Ashbrook Harvey (transl.), "Jacob of Serug, *Homily on Simeon the Stylite,*" in *Ascetic Behavior in Greco-Roman Antiquity: A Sourcebook*, ed. Vincent L. Wimbush (Minneapolis: The Fortress Press, 1990), 15–28, esp. 20–22. See also Joseph P. Amar (transl.), "On Hermits and Desert Dwellers," in *Ascetic Behavior in Greco-Roman Antiquity: A Sourcebook*, ed. Vincent L. Wimbush (Minneapolis: The Fortress Press, 1990), 66–80, 72. For a more general discussion of asceticism and aesthetics, see Geoffrey Galt Harpham, *The Ascetic Imperative in Culture and Criticism* (Chicago: University of Chicago Press, 1987), 24; Patricia Cox Miller, "Dreaming the Body: An Aesthetics of Asceticism," in *Asceticism*, ed. Vincent L. Wimbush and Richard Valantasis (Oxford: Oxford University Press, 1998), 281–300, 290.

47 See Robert Skinner, *A Sermon Preached Before the King at White-Hall* (London, 1634), 6; Samuel Hoard, *The Churches Authority Asserted* (London, 1637), 55–56.

48 Watts (c. 1590–1649) is perhaps most well-known for having been Prince Rupert's chaplain and writing an account of the prince's adventures in the 1640s. Watts was also a committed Laudian. He wrote a tract defending the surplice, and the end of *Mortification apostolicall* criticizes those who

too highly value sermons. See Kenneth Fincham, "William Laud and the Exercise of Caroline Ecclesiastical Patronage," *Journal of Ecclesiastical History* 51 (2000): 69–93, 81 on Watts's preferment.

49 For similar commentary on physical mortification, see also John Pocklington, *Altare Christianum* (London, 1637), 38, 04 [sic, i.e., 40]; see Richard Montagu, *Immediate addresse vnto God alone* (London, 1624), 182 for his approval of *scleragogie.*

50 William Watts, *Mortification apostolicall* (London, 1637), 6. Subsequent references to page numbers will appear in-text.

51 Thomas Mason, *Christs victorie ouer Sathans tyrannie* (London, 1615), 387. In the dedication to Abbot and Coke, Mason states, "I have herein abridged many bookes, but especially the Booke of Martyrs" (sig. A3[v]).

52 For other adverse reactions to Origen's self-castration, see Joseph Hall, *Christian moderation* (London, 1640), 30; Meredith Hanmer (transl.), *The auncient ecclesiasticall histories of the first six hundred yeares after Christ, wrytten in the Greeke tongue by three learned historiographers* (London, 1577), 124n.

53 See also Joseph Beaumont's poem on Gregory Nazianzen, "S. Gregorie Nazianzen," in *The Minor Poems of Joseph Beaumont, D.D., 1616–1699*, ed. Eloise Robinson (Boston: Constable & Company, 1914). For discussion of the comparison of virgins and angels, see Richard Robinson, *The vineyarde of vertue* (London, 1579), 42; *The holie Bible*, transl. Gregory Martin (Douai, 1609–1610), 531 [annotations on Isaiah 56:3]; Richard Broughton, *The iudgement of the Apostles and of those of the first age* (Douai, 1632), 331; William Austin, *Devotionis Augustinianae flamma* (London, 1635), 9.

54 The quotation is from Gregory's funeral oration for Basil of Caesarea (c. 329–379 C.E.).

55 Girolamo Piatti, *The happines of a religious state* (Rouen, 1632), 1–2.

56 Gervase Babington, *A very fruitfull exposition of the Commaundements* (London, 1583), 335.

57 Jean-Louis Quantin, *The Church of England and Christian Antiquity: The Construction of a Confessional Identity in the 17th Century* (Oxford: Oxford University Press, 2009), 170. See also Julian Davies, *The Caroline Captivity of the Church: Charles I and the Remoulding of Anglicanism* 1625–1641 (Oxford: Oxford University Press, 1992), 51.

58 Watts's work can be found in Oxford, Bodleian Library, MS Tanner 262 fo. 43[r]. See also Foulke Robartes, *Gods Holy House and Service, According to the primitive and most Christian forme thereof* (London, 1639), 68.

59 Of many examples, see for instance Laud's *Articles to be inquired of in the metropoliticall visitation of the most reverend father, VVilliam, by Gods providence, Lord Arch-bishop of Canterbury* (London, 1635), sig. A3[r].

60. Richard Culmer, *Cathedrall newes from Canterbury* (London, 1644), 19.

61 William Laud (spurious), *The recantation of the prelate of Canterbury* (London, 1641), 3.
62 Dwalphintramis [Richard Bernard], *The anatomie of the service book* (s.l., 1641), 67.
63 Oxford, Bodleian Library, MS Tanner 262 fo. 43[r].
64 Henry Burton, *A replie to a relation, of the conference between William Laude and Mr. Fisher the Jesuite* (Amsterdam, 1640), 105–106.
65 Gouge, *A learned and very useful commentary on the whole epistle to the Hebrews*, 428.
66 Jeremy Taylor, *The great exemplar of sanctity and holy life according to the Christian institution* (London, 1649), 125.
67 Kevin Sharpe, "Archbishop Laud," in *Reformation to Revolution: Politics and Religion in Early Modern England*, ed. Margo Todd (London: Routledge, 1995), 71–77, 76.
68 Thomas Fuller, *The Church History of Britain* (London: Thomas Tegg and Son, 1837), 3:475. Nineteenth and early 20th-century biographies of Laud (many of them hagiographies) also comment on Laud's personal severity. See Benson, *William Laud*, 159; W.L. Mackintosh, *Life of William Laud* (London: Masters & Co. Ltd., 1907), 132; John Baines, *The Life of William Laud, Archbishop of Canterbury, and Martyr* (London: Joseph Masters, 1855), 208.
69 Fuller, *The Church History of Britain*, 3:477.
70 See L.E. Semler, "Who is the Mother of 'Eliza's Babes' (1652)? 'Eliza,' George Wither, and Elizabeth Emerson," *JEGP* 99 (2000): 513–536, 516; L.E. Semler, "The Creed of Eliza's Babes (1652): Nakedness, Adam, and Divinity," *Albion* 33 (2001): 185–217.
71 All quotations of Eliza's poetry are from L.E. Semler (ed.), *Eliza's Babes: or The Virgin's Offering* (Madison: Fairleigh Dickinson University Press, 2001). In-text references are to line numbers.
72 Also repeated at Mark 12:25 and Matthew 22:30.
73 Henry Burton, *Truth's triumph ouer Trent* (London, 1629), 105–114. See also George Sikes, *The life and death of Sir Henry Vane* (London, 1662), 58.
74 Joseph Alleine, *The way to true happiness* (London, 1675), 195–197.
75 Peter Heylyn, *Theologia veterum* (London, 1654), 479–480. Austin, *Devotionis Augustinianae flamma*, 194, 198. William Austin, *Haec Homo* (London, 1637), 181. For Roman Catholic interpretation of this passage, see Leonardus Lessius, *The treasure of vowed chastity in secular persons* (Saint-Omer, 1621), 54. Cf. Piatti, *The happines of a religious state*, 466.
76 Beaumont, *The Minor Poems of Joseph Beaumont, D.D., 1616–1699*, 40. For other poems praising virginity, see "S. Gregorie Nazianzen," "S. Joseph," and "Annunciatio B.V."
77 For evidence of her Calvinism, see Eliza's prose meditations. In the meditations, she emphasizes her own depravity (107 [n.b. references are to

page numbers]) and God's omnipotence (117), and she inveighs against an Arminian view of the relationship between salvation and works (123).

78 Sophie Read, *Eucharist and the Poetic Imagination in Early Modern England* (Cambridge: Cambridge University Press, 2013), 4. Scholars such as Ethan Shagan, Timothy Rosendale, Regina Schwartz, Molly Murray, Ryan Netzley, and Brooke Conti (among others) have offered important qualifications to a Protestant versus Roman Catholic binary in early modern religion and literature. Ethan H. Shagan, *Popular Politics and the English Reformation* (Cambridge: Cambridge University Press, 2003); Regina Schwartz, *Sacramental Poetics at the Dawn of Secularism: When God Left the World* (Stanford: Stanford University Press, 2008); Timothy Rosendale, *Liturgy and Literature in the Making of Protestant England* (Cambridge: Cambridge University Press, 2007); Molly Murray, *The Poetics of Conversion in Early Modern English Literature* (Cambridge: Cambridge University Press, 2009); Ryan Netzley, *Reading, Desire, and the Eucharist in Early Modern Religious Poetry* (Toronto: University of Toronto Press, 2011); Brooke Conti, *Confessions of Faith in Early Modern England* (Philadelphia: University of Pennsylvania Press, 2014).

79 Milton, *Catholic and Reformed*, 346.

80 For the claim that asceticism disappears, see Charles H. George and Katherine George, *The Protestant Mind of the English Reformation* 1570–1640 (Princeton: Princeton University Press, 1961), 111–112; Patrik Hagman, "The End of Asceticism: Luther, Modernity and How Asceticism Stopped Making Sense," *Political Theology* 14 (2013): 174–187, 175. For the idea of increased bodily liberation, see Richard Strier, "The Refusal to be Judged in Petrarch and Shakespeare," in *A Companion to Shakespeare's Sonnets*, ed. Michael Schoenfeldt (Oxford: Blackwell Publishing Ltd., 2007), 73–89; Stephen Greenblatt, *The Swerve: How the World Became Modern* (New York: W.W. Norton & Company, 2011). This is not, of course, to deny that attitudes towards the body did change; that change, however, need not obviate asceticism. See Charles H. Parker, "Diseased Bodies, Defiled Souls: Corporality and Religious Difference in the Reformation," *Renaissance Quarterly* 67 (2014): 1265–1297.

81 In addition to the examples that follow, see also Hughes Oliphant Old, *The Reading and Preaching of the Scriptures in the Worship of the Christian Church* (Grand Rapids, MI: William B. Eerdmans, 2002), 4:216.

82 Richard Strier, *The Unrepentant Renaissance: From Petrarch to Shakespeare to Milton* (Chicago: University of Chicago Press, 2011), 36–38. It is undeniable that anti-ascetic strains exist within the Reformation, and that Renaissance humanism sits uncomfortably alongside ascetic deprivation. See John Hindle's discussion of this idea in the thought of Jacob Burckhardt. *Jacob Burckhardt and the Crisis of Modernity* (Montreal: McGill-Queen's University Press, 2000), 23.

83 See Achsah Guibbory's discussion and conflation of Pauline flesh and spirit in *Ceremony and Community from Herbert to Milton: Literature, Religion, and Cultural Conflict in Seventeenth-Century England* (Cambridge: Cambridge University Press, 1998), 23–24. Some early modern authors insist on distinguishing the Pauline flesh and spirit from body and soul; see Anthony Burgess, *A treatise of original sin* (London, 1658), 475. But others do not; see Joseph Hall, *Three tractates* (London, 1646), 250–251; Nicholas Mosley, *Psychosophia* (London, 1653), 216. For splitting the difference between the two positions, where soul could become allied with either flesh or spirit, see Thomas Hooker, *Heautonaparnumenos* (London, 1646), 33.

84 Strier, *The Unrepentant Renaissance*, 37–38.

85 Michel Foucault, *The Hermeneutics of the Subject: Lectures at the Collège de France*, 1981–82, ed. Frédéric Gros, transl. Graham Burchell (New York: Palgrave, 2005), 333.

86 Richard Baxter, *A Treatise of Self-Denial* (London, 1659), 67.

87 Weber, *The Protestant Ethic and the Spirit of Capitalism*, 80. For discussion about the applicability of Weber's theories to the medieval and early modern periods, see Caroline Walker Bynum, *Fragmentation and Redemption: Essays on Gender and the Human Body in Medieval Religion* (New York: Zone Books, 1992), 71–74; Janel Mueller, "The Saints," in *Cultural Reformations: Medieval and Renaissance in Literary History*, ed. Brian Cummings and James Simpson (Oxford: Oxford University Press, 2010), 166–187, 186.

88 Thomas Rist, "Topical Comedy: On the Unity of *Love's Labour's Lost*," *Ben Jonson Journal* 7 (2000): 65–87, 74–75.

89 Thomas Nipperdey, "The Reformation and the Modern World," in *Politics and Society in Reformation Europe: Essays for Sir Geoffrey Elton on his Sixty-Fifth Birthday*, ed. E.I. Kouri and Tom Scott (London: Macmillan, 1987), 535–552, 546.

90 Charles Taylor, *Sources of the Self: The Making of the Modern Identity* (Cambridge, MA: Harvard University Press, 1989), 218.

91 Taylor, *Sources of the Self*, 290.

92 Taylor, *Sources of the Self*, 222.

93 See John Rogers, "The Enclosure of Virginity: The Poetics of Sexual Abstinence in the English Revolution," in *Enclosure Acts: Sexuality, Property, and Culture in Early Modern England*, ed. Richard Burt and John Michael Archer (Ithaca: Cornell University Press, 1994), 229–250; Kathleen Coyne Kelly and Marina Leslie (eds.), *Menacing Virgins: Representing Virginity in the Middle Ages and Renaissance* (Newark: University of Delaware Press, 1999); Bonnie Lander Johnson, *Chastity in Early Stuart Literature and Culture* (Cambridge: Cambridge University Press, 2015); Jenna Lay, *Beyond the Cloister: Catholic Englishwomen and Early Modern*

*Literary Culture* (Philadelphia: University of Pennsylvania Press, 2016). These works focus largely on virginity and not on other acts of corporal mortification. Exceptions to this narrow focus, both in terms of ascetic practices considered and the larger relevance of asceticism in the period, include Apetrei, "'The Life of Angels'"; Joshua Phillips, "Monasticism and Idleness in Spenser's Late Poetry," *SEL* 54 (2014): 59–79; Amy Appleford, "Asceticism, Dissent, and the Tudor State: Richard Whitford's Rule for Lay Householders," *Journal of Medieval and Early Modern Studies* 46 (2016): 381–404.

94 Theodora A. Jankowski, *Pure Resistance: Queer Virginity in Early Modern English Drama* (Philadelphia: University of Pennsylvania Press, 2000), 11.

95 John Calvin, *The institution of Christian religion*, transl. Thomas Norton (London, 1561), fo. 59[v].

96 John Rogers, *The Matter of Revolution: Science, Poetry, and Politics in the Age of Milton* (Ithaca: Cornell University Press, 1996), 80. See Peter Lake, "Lancelot Andrewes, John Buckeridge, and Avant-garde Conformity at the Court of James I," in *The Mental World of the Jacobean Court*, ed. Linda Levy Peck (Cambridge: Cambridge University Press, 1991), 113–133.

97 "CŒLEBS HINC MIGRAVIT AD AUREOLAM CŒLESTEM." For the full inscription, written by Matthew Wren, see Lancelot Andrewes, *Two Answers to Cardinal Perron, and Other Miscellaneous Works of Lancelot Andrewes*, ed. Henry Isaacson (Oxford: John Henry Parker, 1854), xxxii–xxxiii.

98 Lay, *Beyond the Cloister*, 16.

99 David Hillman, "Staging Early Modern Embodiment," in *The Cambridge Companion to the Body in Literature*, ed. David Hillman and Ulrika Maude (Cambridge: Cambridge University Press, 2015), 41–57, 44. I disagree with attempts to normalize body-soul relations. See Sarah E. Johnson, *Staging Women and the Soul-Body Dynamic in Early Modern England* (Surrey: Ashgate, 2014), 19.

100 See Jankowski, *Pure Resistance*; Melissa E. Sanchez, *Erotic Subjects: The Sexuality of Politics in Early Modern English Literature* (Oxford: Oxford University Press, 2011); Mario DiGangi, *Sexual Types: Embodiment, Agency, and Dramatic Character from Shakespeare to Shirley* (Philadelphia: University of Pennsylvania Press, 2011).

101 Will Stockton and James M. Bromley, "Introduction: Figuring Early Modern Sex," in *Sex before Sex: Figuring the Act in Early Modern England*, ed. James M. Bromley and Will Stockton (Minneapolis: University of Minnesota Press, 2013), 1–24, 8–9.

102 Bill Burgwinkle, "Medieval Somatics," in *The Cambridge Companion to the Body in Literature*, ed. David Hillman and Ulrika Maude (Cambridge: Cambridge University Press, 2015), 10–23, 19.

103 See Judith H. Anderson, *Words That Matter: Linguistic Perception in Renaissance English* (Stanford: Stanford University Press, 1996); Theresa M. DiPasquale, *Literature and Sacrament: The Sacred and the Secular in John Donne* (Pittsburgh: Duquesne University Press, 1999); Robert Whalen, *The Poetry of Immanence: Sacrament in Donne and Herbert* (Toronto: University of Toronto Press, 2002); Judith H. Anderson, *Translating Investments: Metaphor and the Dynamic of Cultural Change in Tudor-Stuart England* (New York: Fordham University Press, 2005); Gary Kuchar, *Divine Subjection: The Rhetoric of Sacramental Devotion in Early Modern England* (Pittsburgh: Duquesne University Press, 2005); Schwartz, *Sacramental Poetics at the Dawn of Secularism*; Netzley, *Reading, Desire, and the Eucharist in Early Modern Poetry*; Read, *Eucharist and the Poetic Imagination in Early Modern England*; and Kimberly Johnson, *Made Flesh: Sacrament and Poetics in Post-Reformation England* (Philadelphia: University of Pennsylvania Press, 2014).

104 Read, *Eucharist and the Poetic Imagination in Early Modern England*, 181.

105 *John Milton: Complete Shorter Poems*, ed. Stella Revard (Oxford: Wiley-Blackwell, 2009).

106 See Schwartz, *Sacramental Poetics*, 87–116; Read, *Eucharist and the Poetic Imagination in Early Modern England*, 81.

107 Caroline Walker Bynum, "The Female Body and Religious Practice in the Later Middle Ages," in *Fragments for a History of the Human Body*, ed. Jonathan Crary, Michel Feher, Hal Foster, and Sanford Kwinter, vol. 1, *Part One*, ed. Michel Feher (New York: Zone, 1989), 1:160–219, 1:189.

108 See Willet, *Synopsis papismi*, 539; Anthony Wotton, *A defence of M. Perkins booke, called A reformed Catholike* (London, 1606), 500. For later examples of this argument, see George Tully, *An answer to a discourse concerning the celibacy of the clergy* (Oxford, 1688), 15; Henry Wharton, *A treatise of the celibacy of the clergy* (London, 1688), 18.

109 Ben Saunders, *Desiring Donne: Poetry, Sexuality, Interpretation* (Cambridge: Harvard University Press, 2006), 60.

## 1. John Donne and Asceticism

1 Rebecca Ann Bach, "(Re)placing John Donne in the History of Sexuality," *ELH* 72 (2005): 259–289. Ben Saunders, *Desiring Donne: Poetry, Sexuality, Interpretation* (Cambridge: Harvard University Press, 2006), 60. William Kerrigan, "What Was Donne Doing?" *South Central Review* 4 (1987): 2–15, 8.

2 Achsah Guibbory, "Erotic Poetry," in *The Cambridge Companion to John Donne*, ed. Achsah Guibbory (Cambridge: Cambridge University Press, 2006), 133–148, 143. See also her essay "Donne, Milton, and Holy Sex," in *Returning to John Donne* (Surrey: Ashgate, 2015), 107–124. See also Regina

Schwartz, *Sacramental Poetics at the Dawn of Secularism: When God Left the World* (Stanford: Stanford University Press, 2008), 89.

3 Ilona Bell, "Gender Matters: The Woman in Donne's Poems," in *The Cambridge Companion to John Donne*, ed. Achsah Guibbory (Cambridge: Cambridge University Press, 2006), 201–216, 212.

4 Ramie Targoff, "Facing Death," in *The Cambridge Companion to John Donne*, ed. Achsah Guibbory (Cambridge: Cambridge University Press, 2006), 217–232, 224.

5 John Donne, *The Sermons of John Donne*, 10 vols., ed. George R. Potter and Evelyn M. Simpson (Berkeley and Los Angeles: University of California Press, 1953–1962), 7:106. Donne associates this flesh with the body. As he soon makes clear, treating all flesh as sinful does not lead him to endorse "inordinate abstinencies."

6 Donne, *Sermons*, 3:68. See also Donne, *Sermons*, 3:131.

7 Gervase Babington, *A very fruitfull exposition of the Commaundements* (London, 1583), 343–344.

8 Donne, *Sermons*, 2:63.

9 See "La Corona," "Elegy upon the Death of Mistress Bulstrode," and "A Funeral Elegy" for Elizabeth Drury. All quotations of Donne's poetry are from *The Complete Poems of John Donne*, ed. Robin Robbins (Harlow: Longman, 2010). In-text parenthetical references are to line numbers.

10 Virginity intensifies – it is complicit in the changes of – Lady Markham's alchemical purification.

11 For other considerations of Donne and asceticism, see Kitty Datta, "Love and Asceticism in Donne's Poetry: The Divine Analogy," *Critical Quarterly* 19 (1977): 5–25; and Felecia Wright McDuffie, *"To Our Bodies Turn We Then": Body as Word and Sacrament in the Works of John Donne* (New York: Continuum, 2005), 64–69.

12 See Richard Halpern, "The Lyric in the Field of Information: Autopoiesis and History in Donne's *Songs and Sonnets*," in *Critical Essays on John Donne*, ed. Arthur F. Marotti (New York: G.K. Hall & Co., 1994), 49–76, 66; Saunders, *Desiring Donne*, 57. See also Janel Mueller, "Women among the Metaphysics: A Case, Mostly, of Being Donne For," *Modern Philology* 87 (1989): 142–158.

13 For the holistic claim, see Richard Strier, "Radical Donne: 'Satire III,'" *ELH* 60 (1993): 283–332, 292.

14 Charis Charalampous, "Thinking (of) Feelings in Donne's Poetry: The Signifying Rift and 'The Evidence of Things Not Seen,'" *Religion & Literature* 47 (2015): 61–98, 87. See Brian Cummings's discussion of, and skepticism about, "the turn of the body" in Donne studies, "Donne's Passions: Emotion, Agency and Language," in *Passions and Subjectivity in Early Modern Culture*, ed. Brian Cummings and Freya Sierhuis (Surrey: Ashgate, 2013), 51–74, 62.

15 Siobhán Collins, *Bodies, Politics and Transformations: John Donne's Metempsychosis* (Surrey: Ashgate, 2013), 5.
16 Ramie Targoff, *John Donne, Body and Soul* (Chicago: University of Chicago Press, 2008), 5. See also John Carey, *John Donne: Life, Mind and Art* (New York: Oxford University Press, 1981), 162; *The Poems of John Donne*, ed. Herbert J.C. Grierson (Oxford: Clarendon Press, 1912), 2:xlvi; Blaine Greteman, "'All this seed pearl': John Donne and Bodily Presence," *College Literature* 37 (2010): 26–42, 27.
17 For arguments that Donne's work is anti-ascetic, see John Klause, "Hope's Gambit: The Jesuitical, Protestant, Skeptical Origins of Donne's Heroic Ideal," *Studies in Philology* 91 (1994): 181–215, 201; Catherine Gimelli Martin, "The Erotology of Donne's 'Extasie' and the Secret History of Voluptuous Rationalism," *SEL* 44 (2004): 121–147, 128. For resistance to Donne's sexual modernity, see Diane Treviño Benet, "Sexual Transgression in Donne's Elegies," *Modern Philology* 92 (1994): 14–35; Bach, "(Re)placing John Donne in the History of Sexuality."
18 Donne, *Sermons*, 4:226.
19 Quotations of and references to the Bible are from *King James Study Bible*, ed. Kenneth Barker (Michigan: Zondervan, 2002).
20 Donne, *Sermons*, 4:228. For other comments critiquing the retired life, see 1:209, 1:247, 7:104, 9:337.
21 Without the soul, the body is a mere carcass ("A Nocturnal upon Saint Lucy's Day being the Shortest Day," 27); the body is external apparel for the soul ("Satyre I," 43).
22 Donne is not wholly consistent on this point. See *Sermons*, 7:106, where he rejects treating the body as a prison for the soul.
23 James Grantham Turner, *One Flesh: Paradisal Marriage and Sexual Relations in the Age of Milton* (Oxford: Clarendon Press, 1987), 115.
24 Elizabeth M.A. Hodgson, *Gender and the Sacred Self in John Donne* (Newark: University of Delaware Press, 1999), 102.
25 Guibbory, *Returning to John Donne*, 114.
26 Ralph Houlbrooke, "The Family and Pastoral Care," in *A History of Pastoral Care*, ed. G.R. Evans (London: Cassell, 2000), 262–293, 286.
27 Donne, *Sermons*, 2:339.
28 Anthony Wotton, *A defence of M. Perkins booke, called A reformed Catholike* (London, 1606), 500.
29 For other arguments about the obtainability of chastity, see Arthur Golding, *The vvarfare of Christians* (London, 1576), 9–10; Thomas Bentley, *The fift lampe of virginitie* (London, 1582), 6–7.
30 Pierre Du Moulin, *The accomplishment of the prophecies* (Oxford, 1613), 18.
31 See John Calvin, *The sermons of M. Iohn Caluin vpon the fifth booke of Moses called Deuteronomie* (London, 1583), 829; John Foxe, *Actes and monuments* (London, 1583), 2:1159 (first half); Andrew Willet, *Synopsis papismi*

(London, 1592), 249; Wotton, *A defence of M. Perkins booke, called A reformed Catholike*, 494; Thomas Beard, *A retractiue from the Romish religion* (London, 1616), 22–23.

32 Peter Marshall, *The Catholic Priesthood and the English Reformation* (Oxford: Clarendon Press, 1994), 164.

33 William Perkins, *Christian oeconomie* (London, 1609), 17.

34 Donne, *Sermons*, 3:243.

35 John Calvin, *The institution of Christian religion*, transl. Thomas Norton (London, 1561), fo. 89[r]. See also Willet, *Synopsis papismi*, 247. Abraham Woodhead rejects this logic. See R.H. [Abraham Woodhead], *Two discourses* (Oxford, 1687), 7 [second discourse]; Thomas Bell, *The suruey of popery* (London, 1596), 261, 263.

36 Calvin, *The sermons of M. Iohn Caluin vpon the fifth booke of Moses called Deuteronomie*, 829.

37 Donne, *Sermons*, 8:100–101.

38 Cf. Donne, *Sermons*, 2:301.

39 George Downame, *The Christians sanctuarie* (London, 1604), 3, 7.

40 Willet, *Synopsis papismi*, 250.

41 Donne, *Sermons*, 3:244.

42 Donne also gives these disciplines and mortifications a wide berth at *Sermons*, 4:153, 9:166.

43 Theodore Beza, *A briefe and piththie summe of the Christian faith* (London, 1565), 118[v]. The work is translated by the Marian exile to Geneva Robert Fills.

44 John Merbecke, *A booke of notes and common places* (London, 1581), 682.

45 Andrew Willet, *Tetrastylon papisticum* (London, 1593), 14.

46 Merbecke, *A booke of notes and common places*, 674.

47 See Bald's discussion of Ann Donne's death. R.C. Bald, *John Donne: A Life* (Oxford: Oxford University Press, 1970), 324–328.

48 Izaak Walton, *The lives of Dr. John Donne, Sir Henry Wotton, Mr. Richard Hooker, Mr. George Herbert* (London, 1675), 41–42. I am quoting from the revised and expanded reprinting.

49 Donne, *Sermons*, 2:244.

50 William Perkins, *A commentarie or exposition, vpon the fiue first chapters of the Epistle to the Galatians* (Cambridge, 1604), 632–633. For connecting Galatians 6:14 to a rejection of Roman Catholic asceticism, see Andrew Willet, *A catholicon* (Cambridge, 1602), 102–104.

51 Perkins, *A commentarie or exposition, vpon the fiue first chapters of the Epistle to the Galatians*, 632–633.

52 Willet, *Synopsis papismi*, 247.

53 Robbins, *The Complete Poems of John Donne*, 573n.

54 See also Paul R. Sellin, "The Mimetic Poetry of Jack and John Donne: A Field Theory for the Amorous and the Divine," in *Sacred and Profane:*

*Secular and Devotional Interplay in Early Modern British Literature*, ed. Helen Wilcox, Richard Todd, and Alasdair MacDonald (Amsterdam: VU University Press, 1996), 163–172, 170.

55 See Theresa M. DiPasquale's discussion of the "twisted" emotional logic of these lines. "Ambivalent Mourning in 'Since she whome I lovd,'" in *John Donne's "desire of more,"* ed. M. Thomas Hester (Newark: University of Delaware Press, 1996), 183–195, 191.

56 Perkins, *Christian oeconomie*, 16.

57 For marriage not being inimical to heavenly cares, see Bell, *The suruey of popery*, 248.

58 Anthony Stafford, *The femall glory* (London, 1635), 148–149.

59 Jennifer Radden (ed.), *The Nature of Melancholy from Aristotle to Kristeva* (Oxford: Oxford University Press, 2000), 56, 62.

60 Robbins, *The Complete Poems of John Donne*, 715n.

61 *Oxford English Dictionary*, s.v. "obtain, v.," accessed November 10, 2018, http://www.oed.com.proxy.lib.siu.edu/view/Entry/130002?redirectedFrom=obtain.

62 *John Donne: The Complete English Poems*, ed. A.J. Smith (London: Penguin Books, 1971; London: Penguin Classics, 1986), 641n.

63 For discussion of this, see Arthur L. Clements, *Poetry of Contemplation: John Donne, George Herbert, Henry Vaughan, and the Modern Period* (New York: State University of New York Press, 1990), 79. See also Donne, *Sermons*, 7:109. For a version of chastity that is almost entirely spiritual, see Daniel Featley, *The Honour of Chastity* (London, 1632).

64 Sellin, "The Mimetic Poetry of Jack and John Donne: A Field Theory for the Amorous and the Divine," 163.

65 Achsah Guibbory, "Reconsidering Donne: From Libertine Poetry to Arminian Sermons," *Studies in Philology* 114 (2017): 561–590, 590. See also Mary Arshagouni Papazian, "The Augustinian Donne: How a 'Second S. Augustine?,'" in *John Donne and the Protestant Reformation: New Perspectives*, ed. Mary Arshagouni Papazian (Detroit: Wayne State University Press, 2003), 66–89, 84n.

66 Thomas Becon, *A new postil* (London, 1566), fo. 45[v].

67 Girolamo Piatti, *The happines of a religious state* (Rouen, 1632), 4. See also Robert Baillie, *Ladensium Autokatakrisis* (Amsterdam, 1640), 69. See page 71 of the first London printing (1641).

68 John Donne, *The Divine Poems*, ed. Helen Gardner, 2nd ed. (Oxford: Clarendon Press, 1952; Oxford: Clarendon Press, 1978), 101n.

69 Henry Hammond, *A practicall catechisme* (Oxford, 1645), 260.

70 Richard Younge, *A counterpoyson* (London, 1641), 318.

71 Marshall, *The Catholic Priesthood and the English Reformation*, 142.

72 For Renaissance love poetry, see A.R. Cirillo, "The Fair Hermaphrodite: Love-Union in the Poetry of Donne and Spenser," *SEL* 9 (1969): 81–95; for

the Trinity, see Jillian Kearney, "Donne's *Devotions* in the Context of His Early Sermons: A Revelation of St John the Divine" (D. Phil. Thesis, Oxford University, 1995), 179; for Geoffrey of Vinsauf, see R.P. McGerr, "Donne's 'Blest Hermaphrodite' and the *Poetria Nova*," *Notes and Queries* 33 (1986): 349.

73 *Pseudodoxia Epidemica*, in *The Works of Sir Thomas Browne*, new ed., ed. Geoffrey Keynes (London: Faber and Faber, 1928; Chicago: University of Chicago Press, 1964), 2:215. See also Andrew Breeze, "Donne's 'Blest Hermaphrodite' and Psalms 'More Harsh,'" *John Donne Journal* 22 (2003): 249–254, 250.

74 Gregory of Nyssa, *A Select Library of Nicene and Post-Nicene Fathers of the Christian Church*, 2nd ser., ed. Philip Schaff and Henry Wace, vol. 5, *On the Making of Man*, transl. William Moore and Henry Austin Wilson (New York: Christian Literature Company, 1893; Grand Rapids, MI: Wm. B. Eerdmans Publishing Company, 1961) 22.4, 5:412; Gregory of Nyssa, *De hominis opificio* 22, in *Patrologiae Graeca*, ed. J.-P. Migne (Paris: Imprimerie Catholique, 1863), 44:col. 205b. Οὐ γὰρ ὅτε τὸ κατ' εἰχόνα ἐποίησε, τότε τὴν τοῦ αὐξάνεσθαι καὶ πληθύνεσθαι δύναμιν τῷ ἀνθρώπῳ προσέθηχεν, ἀλλ' ὅτε διέκρινε τῇ κατὰ τὸ ἄρρεν καὶ θῆλυ διαφορᾷ, τότε φησίν· 'Αὐξάνεσθε καὶ πληθύνεσθε, καὶ πληρώσατε τὴν γῆν.'

75 Peter Brown, *The Body and Society: Men, Women and Sexual Renunciation in Early Christianity* (New York: Columbia University Press, 1988), 294.

76 Gregory of Nyssa, *On the Making of Man* 22.4, 5:412. *Patrologiae Graeca*, 44:col. 205b. οὐκ ἂν τοῦ τοιούτου τῆς γεννήσεως εἴδους προσεδεήθημεν, δι' οὗ γεννᾶται τὰ ἄλογα.

77 Gregory of Nyssa, *On the Making of Man* 17.2, 5:407; *Patrologiae Graeca*, 44:col. 189a. Οὐκοῦν κατὰ τὸν αὐτὸν τρόπον, εἴπερ μηδεμία παρατροπή τε καὶ ἔκστασις ἀπὸ τῆς ἀγγελιχῆς ὁμοτιμίας ἐξ ἁμαρτίας ἡμῖν ἐγένετο, οὐκ ἂν οὐδὲ ἡμεῖς τοῦ γάμου πρὸς τὸν πληθυσμὸν ἐδεήθημεν. 'Αλλ' ὅστις ἐστὶν ἐν τῇ φύσει τῶν ἀγγέλων τοῦ πλεονασμοῦ τρόπος, ἄρρητος μὲν καὶ ἀνεπινόητος στοχασμοῖς ἀνθρωπίνοις, πλὴν ἀλλὰ πάντως ἐστίν· οὗτος ἂν καὶ ἐπὶ τῶν βραχύ τι παρ' ἀγγέλους ἠλαττωμένων ἀνθρώπων ἐνήργησεν, εἰς τὸ ὡρισμένον ὑπὸ τῆς βουλῆς τοῦ πεποιηκότος μέτρον τὸ ἀνθρώπινον αὔξων.

78 See John Scottus Eriugena, *De divisione Naturae* 4.12, in *Patrologia Latina*, 2nd ser., ed. J-.P. Migne (Paris: Garnieri Fratres, 1853), 122:col. 799b. See also Alexandre Leupin, *Barbarolexis: Medieval Writing and Sexuality*, transl. Kate M. Cooper (Cambridge, MA: Harvard University Press, 1989), 11. For the influence of Gregory of Nyssa on Eriugena, see Frances M. Malpezzi, "Adam, Christ, and Mr. Tilman: God's Blest Hermaphrodites," *The American Benedictine Review* 40 (1989): 250–260, 252.

79 See Roberta Albrecht, "Alchemical Augmentation and Primordial Fire in Donne's 'The Dissolution,'" *SEL* 45 (2005): 95–115.

80 Cynthea Masson, "Text as Stone: Desire, Sex, and the Figurative Hermaphrodite in the *Ordinal* and *Compound of Alchemy*," in *Sexual Culture in*

the *Literature of Medieval Britain*, ed. Amanda Hopkins, Robert Allen Rouse, and Cory James Rushton (Cambridge: D.S. Brewer, 2014), 111–126, 117.

81 I am inspired by Deirdre Carabine's use of "wholeness" in a similar context. See *John Scottus Eriugena* (Oxford: Oxford University Press, 2000), 83.

82 See lines 5–8 of "The Canonization" and 13–16 of "To Mr Tilman after he had Taken Orders."

83 *Threnoikos* (London, 1640), 404.

84 John Florio, *A vvorlde of wordes* (London, 1598), 22.

85 *Oxford English Dictionary*, s.v. "convey, v.1," accessed July 16, 2018, http://www.oed.com.proxy.lib.siu.edu/view/Entry/40805?rskey=4x68E5&result=2&isAdvanced=false.

## 2. A Mask, Asceticism, and Caroline Culture

1 See John Leonard, "Milton's Vow of Celibacy: A Reconsideration of the Evidence," in *Of Poetry and Politics: New Essays on Milton and His World*, ed. P.G. Stanwood (New York: Medieval & Renaissance Texts & Studies, 1995), 187–202, 187n.

2 Milton publishes *An apology against a pamphlet* in April 1642; his fateful trip to Forest Hill, Oxfordshire takes place in June 1642. *The Complete Prose Works of John Milton*, ed. Don M. Wolfe (New Haven: Yale University Press, 1953), 1:892–893 (hereafter, *CPW*).

3 Brooke Conti, "Milton, Jerome, and Apocalyptic Virginity," *Renaissance Quarterly* 72:1 (2019), 194–230, 195. My thanks to Brooke Conti for allowing me to read the article in advance of its publication.

4 William Kerrigan, *The Sacred Complex: On the Psychogenesis of Paradise Lost* (Cambridge, MA: Harvard University Press, 1983), 34. For another example of a psychoanalytic perspective on Milton's asceticism, see John Rumrich, *Milton Unbound: Controversy and Reinterpretation* (Cambridge: Cambridge University Press, 1996), 88.

5 David Quint, "Expectation and Prematurity in Milton's 'Nativity Ode,'" *Modern Philology* 97 (1999): 195–219, 211.

6 For the influence of Revelation 14:4, see J. Martin Evans, *The Road from Horton: Looking Backwards in "Lycidas"* (Victoria, B.C.: University of Victoria Press, 1983), 59. See also Edward Le Comte, *Milton and Sex* (New York: Columbia University Press, 1978), 22.

7 James Holly Hanford, "The Youth of Milton: An Interpretation of His Early Literary Development," in *Studies in Shakespeare, Milton and Donne* (New York: Macmillan, 1925; New York: Haskell House, 1964), 87–164, 154.

8 Hanford, "The Youth of Milton," 143. See E.M.W. Tillyard, *Milton* (London: Chatto & Windus, 1930; London: Chatto & Windus, 1946), 380–381, 383.

9 John Milton, *Paradise Lost*, rev. 2nd ed., ed. Alastair Fowler (Harlow: Longman, 1971; New York: Routledge, 2007).

10 Hanford, "The Youth of Milton," 160.
11 Hanford, "The Youth of Milton," 155.
12 Denis Saurat goes back even farther to locate the source of Miltonic asceticism: namely, the world of primitive myth. *Milton: Man and Thinker* (London: J. Cape, 1924; New York: Haskell House, 1970), 9.
13 Ernest Sirluck, "Milton's Idle Right Hand," *Journal of English and Germanic Philology* 60 (1961): 749–785, 767.
14 Barbara Lewalski, *The Life of John Milton: A Critical Biography* (Oxford: Blackwell, 2000; Oxford: Blackwell, 2003), 74.
15 *John Milton: Complete Shorter Poems*, ed. Stella Revard (Oxford: Wiley-Blackwell, 2009), 112n. Quotations of Milton's poetry are from this edition. For discussion of this tendency, see J. Martin Evans, *The Miltonic Moment* (Lexington: The University Press of Kentucky, 1998), 48–49.
16 See Maryann Cale McGuire, *Milton's Puritan Masque* (Athens: University of Georgia Press, 1983); Cedric C. Brown, *John Milton's Aristocratic Entertainments* (Cambridge: Cambridge University Press, 1985); Leah S. Marcus, "Milton's Anti-Laudian Masque," in *The Politics of Mirth: Jonson, Herrick, Milton, Marvell, and the Defense of Old Holiday Pastimes* (Chicago: University of Chicago Press, 1986), 169–212; Stella Revard, *Milton and the Tangles of Neaera's Hair: The Making of the* 1645 *Poems* (Columbia: University of Missouri Press, 1997), 155; Achsah Guibbory, *Ceremony and Community from Herbert to Milton: Literature, Religion, and Cultural Conflict in Seventeenth-Century England* (Cambridge: Cambridge University Press, 1998), 161; Barbara Lewalski, "Milton's *Comus* and the Politics of Masquing," in *The Politics of the Stuart Court Masque*, ed. David Bevington and Peter Holbrook (Cambridge: Cambridge University Press, 1998), 296–320; Martin Butler, *The Stuart Court Masque and Political Culture* (Cambridge: Cambridge University Press, 2008), 357. Anne Baynes Coiro, however, argues that Milton finds the "centrality of women in Caroline theatrical culture" a source of "powerful creative intensity" in his masque. Ann Baynes Coiro, "'A thousand fantasies': The Lady and the *Mask*," in *The Oxford Handbook of Milton*, ed. Nicholas McDowell and Nigel Smith (Oxford: Oxford University Press, 2009), 89–111, 111.
17 Marina Leslie, "Evading Rape and Embracing Empire in Margaret Cavendish's *Assaulted and Pursued Chastity*," in *Menacing Virgins: Representing Virginity in the Middle Ages and Renaissance*, ed. Kathleen Coyne Kelly and Marina Leslie (London: Associated University Presses, 1999), 179–197, 180.
18 Lewalski, "Milton's *Comus* and the Politics of Masquing," 310.
19 On the ascetic investments of the court, see Steven N. Zwicker, "The Day that George Thomason Collected His Copy of the *Poems of Mr. John Milton, Both English and Latin, Compos'd at Several Times*," *RES*, n.s., 64 (2012): 231–245, 240. For a failure to perceive the connection among Laudianism,

asceticism, and *A Mask*, see Elizabeth Hodgson, "Milton Takes the Veil," in *Milton and Questions of History: Essays by Canadians Past and Present*, ed. Feisal G. Mohamed and Mary Nyquist (Toronto: University of Toronto Press, 2012), 311–326, 318.

20 For more general discussion of *A Mask* and its performative and/or theatrical context, see John G. Demaray, *Milton and the Masque Tradition: The Early Poems, Arcades, and Comus* (Cambridge, MA: Harvard University Press, 1968); M.S. Berkowitz, "An Earl's Michaelmas in Wales: Some Thoughts on the Original Presentation of *Comus*," *Milton Quarterly* 13 (1979): 122–125; Brown, *John Milton's Aristocratic Entertainments*; Ann Baynes Coiro, "Anonymous Milton, or, A 'Mask' Maskd," *ELH* 71 (2004): 609–629; Blair Hoxby, "The Wisdom of Their Feet: Meaningful Dance in Milton and the Stuart Masque," *English Literary Renaissance* 37 (2007): 74–99; Joseph M. Ortiz, *Broken Harmony: Shakespeare and the Politics of Music* (Ithaca: Cornell University Press, 2011), 216–220; John Creaser, "The Original Sabrina?" *Milton Quarterly* 46 (2012): 15–20.

21 Quotations of and references to the Bible are from *King James Study Bible*, ed. Kenneth Barker (Michigan: Zondervan, 2002).

22 Louis Richeome, *The pilgrime of Loreto* (Saint-Omer, 1629), 204.

23 Anthony Stafford, *The femall glory* (London, 1635), 28.

24 Jeremy Taylor, *The rule and exercises of holy living* (London, 1650), 89–90. For connecting charity to spiritual virginity, see Donald Lupton, *The glory of their times* (London, 1640), 335.

25 For discussion of *A Mask* and chastity/virginity, see Kerrigan, *The Sacred Complex*, 22–72; Marcus, *The Politics of Mirth*, 203; Christopher Kendrick, "Milton and Sexuality: A Symptomatic Reading of *Comus*," in *Re-membering Milton: Essays on the Texts and Traditions*, ed. Mary Nyquist and Margaret W. Ferguson (New York: Methuen, 1987), 43–73; Kathleen Wall, "*A Mask Presented at Ludlow Castle*: The Armor of Logos," in *Milton and the Idea of Woman*, ed. Julia M. Walker (Urbana: University of Illinois Press, 1988): 52–65; John Leonard, "Saying 'No' to Freud: Milton's *A Mask* and Sexual Assault," *Milton Quarterly* 25 (1991): 129–140; John Rogers, "The Enclosure of Virginity: The Poetics of Sexual Abstinence in the English Revolution," in *Enclosure Acts: Sexuality, Property, and Culture in Early Modern England*, ed. Richard Burt and John Michael Archer (Ithaca: Cornell University Press, 1994), 229–250; Lewalski, "Milton's *Comus* and the politics of masquing"; Lauren Shohet, "Figuring Chastity: Milton's Ludlow Masque," in *Menacing Virgins: Representing Virginity in the Middle Ages and Renaissance*, ed. Kathleen Coyne Kelly and Marina Leslie (Newark: University of Delaware Press, 1999), 146–164; Ross Leasure, "Milton's Queer Choice: *Comus* at Castlehaven," *Milton Quarterly* 36 (2002): 63–86; Andrew Escobedo and Beth Quitslund (eds.), "*The Faerie Queene* at Ludlow," special issue *Milton Quarterly* 37 (2003): 179–244; Kathryn

Schwarz, "Chastity, Militant and Married: Cavendish's Romance, Milton's Masque," *PMLA* 118 (2003): 270–285; Catherine Thomas, "Chaste Bodies and Poisonous Desires in Milton's *Mask*," *SEL* 46 (2006): 435–459; N.K. Sugimura, *"Matter of Glorious Trial": Spiritual and Material Substance in Paradise Lost* (New Haven: Yale University Press, 2009), 90–102; Astrid Giugni, "The 'Holy Dictate of Spare Temperance': Virtue and Politics in Milton's *A Masque Presented at Ludlow Castle*," *Journal of Medieval and Early Modern Studies* 45 (2015): 395–418; Catherine Gimelli Martin, *Milton's Italy: Anglo-Italian Literature, Travel, and Religion in Seventeenth-Century England* (New York: Routledge, 2017), 192–198.

26 Revard, *John Milton: Complete Shorter Poems*, 54n.

27 Girolamo Piatti, *The happines of a religious state* (Rouen, 1632), "Preface" sig. [illegible letter]1$^{v}$.

28 Richard Baxter, *The crucifying of the world by the cross of Christ* (London, 1658), 9.

29 Heinrich Bullinger, *Fiftie godlie and learned sermons* (London, 1577), 225–226.

30 Richard Ward, *Theologicall questions, dogmaticall observations, and evangelicall essays, vpon the Gospel of Jesus Christ, according to St. Matthew* (London, 1640), 234.

31 Thomas Beard, *A retractiue from the Romish religion* (London, 1616), 24–25. See also Joseph Hall, *The honor of the married clergie* (London, 1620), 63.

32 Hall, *Christian moderation*, 33.

33 Hall, *Christian moderation*, 37–38.

34 Hall, *Christian moderation*, 34.

35 Hall, *Christian moderation*, 48.

36 Hall, *Christian moderation*, 21–33.

37 John Leonard sees a possible reference to marriage in the Lady mentioning Juno at line 701. In addition to being the goddess of marriage, Juno is also the protector of women. Moreover, the Lady might be ironically referencing Comus's ventriloquism of Protestant defenses of matrimony were Juno meant to invoke marriage. *The Value of Milton* (Cambridge: Cambridge University Press, 2016), 36.

38 Ambrose of Milan, *A Select Library of Nicene and Post-Nicene Fathers*, 2nd ser., ed. Philip Schaff and Henry Wace, vol. 10, *Concerning Virgins*, transl. Rev. H. De Romestin (New York: The Christian Literature Company, 1896; Grand Rapids, MI: Wm. B. Eerdmans Publishing Company, 1955), 2.3.19, 10:376. The Latin reads, "naturam etiam bestiarum virginitatis veneratione mutavit." *De Virginibus* 2.3.19, in *Patrologia Latina*, 1$^{st}$ ser., ed. J.-P. Migne (Paris: Garnieri Fratres, 1845), 16:col. 211c.

39 Juan Luis Vives, *A very frutefull and pleasant boke called the Instructio[n] of a Christen woma[n]* (London, 1529), sig. G1$^{v}$. See also Nicolas Caussin, *The holy court* (London, 1650), 106.

40 Thomas Heywood, *Londini artium & scientiarum scaturigo* (London, 1632), sig. B2$^{v}$.

41 Harriett Hawkins, "The Seductions of Comus," in *Style: Essays on Renaissance and Restoration Literature and Culture in Memory of Harriet Hawkins*, ed. Allen Michie, Eric Buckley, and Harriet Hawkins (Newark: University of Delaware Press, 2005), 60–68, 63.
42 Kerrigan, *The Sacred Complex*, 35. The phrase "sublimation of flesh" is also Kerrigan's. For an opposing view, see Sugimura, *"Matter of Glorious Trial,"* 107.
43 Alexandra Walsham, *The Reformation of the Landscape: Religion, Identity, and Memory in Early Modern Britain and Ireland* (Oxford: Oxford University Press, 2011), 263.
44 Henry Cogan (transl.), *The court of Rome* (London, 1654), 210.
45 Thomas Manton, *A fourth volume containing one hundred and fifty sermons on several texts of Scripture in two parts* (London, 1693), 252. See also 294.
46 Thomas Lupton, *The Christian against the Iesuite* (London, 1582), 48.
47 Kerrigan, *The Sacred Complex*, 57.
48 William Shullenberger, *Lady in the Labyrinth: Milton's Comus as Initiation* (Cranbury, NJ: Associated University Presses, 2008), 273. See also Revard, *Milton and the Tangles of Neaera's Hair*, 151; Sue P. Starke, *The Heroines of English Pastoral Romance* (Cambridge: D.S. Brewer, 2007), 168–169; Louis Schwartz, *Milton and Maternal Mortality* (Cambridge: Cambridge University Press, 2009), 150.
49 Bullinger, *Fiftie godlie and learned sermons*, 226.
50 Kerrigan, *The Sacred Complex*, 60.
51 For the Marian resonance of the "Sun-clad power of Chastity" (782), see Brown, *John Milton's Aristocratic Entertainments*, 138.
52 John Stoughton, *XI. choice sermons* (London, 1640), 47.
53 *Eniautos, or, A course of catechizing* (London, 1664), 72.
54 Robert Bellarmine (Saint), *An ample declaration of the Christian doctrine* (Roan, 1604), 26.
55 *Oxford English Dictionary*, s.v. "side, n.1.," accessed November 10, 2018, http://www.oed.com.proxy.lib.siu.edu/view/Entry/179258?rskey=yIs78A&result=1&isAdvanced=false.
56 David N. Dickey, *A Study in the Place of Women in the Poetry and Prose Works of John Milton* (Lewiston, NY: The Edwin Mellen Press, 2000), viii; see also 43–44.
57 Stafford, *The femall glory*, sig. C1$^{v}$.
58 John Donne, *The Sermons of John Donne*, 10 vols., ed. George R. Potter and Evelyn M. Simpson (Berkeley and Los Angeles: University of California Press, 1953–1962), 9:339.
59 Vives, *A very frutefull and pleasant boke called the Instructio[n] of a Christen woma[n]*, sig. F4$^{v}$.
60 Stewart A. Baker, "Eros and the Three Shepherds of *Comus*," *Rice University Studies* 61 (1975): 13–26, 23. See Nancy Lindheim, "Milton's Garden of Adonis: The Epilogue to the Ludlow Masque," *Milton Studies* 35 (1997): 21–41, for reading the conclusion as temporal allegory.

61 Coiro, "'A thousand fantasies,'" 105.
62 Gordon Teskey, *The Poetry of John Milton* (Cambridge, MA: Harvard University Press, 2015), 138.
63 Maggie Kilgour, *Milton and the Metamorphosis of Ovid* (Oxford: Oxford University Press, 2012), 92.
64 Maggie Kilgour, "Virgil and Ovid," in *The Oxford History of Classical Reception in English Literature*, ed. David Hopkins and Charles Martindale, vol. 2 (1558–1660), ed. Patrick Cheney and Philip Hardie (Oxford: Oxford University Press, 2015), 2:517–538, 2:534. See also Kilgour, *Milton and the Metamorphosis of Ovid*, 93; Kerrigan, *The Sacred Complex*, 58.
65 Quotations of Spenser are from *The Faerie Queene*, ed. A.C. Hamilton (New York: Longman, 1977).
66 See Kerrigan, *The Sacred Complex*, 56.
67 John Guillory, *Poetic Authority: Spenser, Milton, and Literary History* (New York: Columbia University Press, 1983), 91.
68 See also Karen Britland, "Recent Studies of the Life and Cultural Influence of Queen Henrietta Maria," *English Literary Renaissance* 45 (2015): 303–321. For discussions of Caroline court culture and sexuality, see R. Malcolm Smuts, *Court Culture and the Origins of a Royalist Tradition in Early Stuart England* (Philadelphia: University of Pennsylvania Press, 1987), 193, 196; Anne Coiro, "'A ball of strife': Caroline Poetry and Royal Marriage," in *The Royal Image: Representations of Charles I*, ed. Thomas N. Corns (Cambridge: Cambridge University Press, 1999), 26–46; Joshua Scodel, *Excess and the Mean in Early Modern English Literature* (Princeton: Princeton University Press, 2002), 164–169; Butler, *The Stuart Court Masque and Political Culture*, 152.
69 I do not mean to supplant one oversimplification with another. A great deal of court life was libertine. My interests are in establishing a connection between a particular court discourse and asceticism.
70 Hanford, "The Youth of Milton," 144. Greater attention to ascetic themes might help balance out a view of Caroline masques as purely wasteful and excessive. See Balachandra Rajan, "Ludlow Revisited: Milton and Eco-Justice," in *Milton and Questions of History: Essays by Canadians Past and Present*, ed. Feisal G. Mohamed and Mary Nyquist (Toronto: University of Toronto Press, 2012), 379–393, 380. For contemporary, negative reactions to Caroline Neoplatonism and culture, see Henry Burton, *A tryall of priuate deuotions* (London, 1628), sigs. B2$^{v}$–B3$^{r}$; John Rogers, *A Treatise of Love* (London, 1629), 96; William Prynne, *Histrio-mastix* (London, 1633), fo. 547$^{v}$; Richard Johnson, *The pilgrimage of man* (London, 1635), sig. C1$^{v}$; *A mis-led King, and a memorable Parliament* (London, 1643), sig. A1$^{r}$; William Prynne, *The fourth part of The soveraigne povver of parliaments and kingdoms* (London, 1643), 53. For a more comprehensive discussion of the puritan response to perceived Caroline libertinism, see G.F. Sensabaugh, *The Tragic Muse of John Ford* (Stanford: Stanford University Press, 1944), 140–151.

71 Bonnie Lander Johnson, *Chastity in Early Stuart Literature and Culture* (Cambridge: Cambridge University Press, 2015), 153. Johnson ultimately finds Milton critical of court culture.

72 For other discussions of how church and court are connected, see Erica Veevers, *Images of Love and Religion: Queen Henrietta Maria and Court Entertainments* (Cambridge: Cambridge University Press, 1989), 174; Benedict S. Robinson, "The 'Turks,' Caroline Politics, and Philip Massinger's *The Renegado*," in *Localizing Caroline Drama: Politics and Economics of the Early Modern English Stage*, 1625–1642, ed. Adam Zucker and Alan B. Farmer (New York: Palgrave Macmillan, 2006), 213–238, 229; Butler, *The Stuart Court Masque and Political Culture*, 286; Reid Barbour, *Literature and Religious Culture in Seventeenth-Century England* (Cambridge: Cambridge University Press, 2002), 111; R. Malcolm Smuts, "Force, Love and Authority in Caroline Political Culture," in *The 1630s: Interdisciplinary Essays on Culture and Politics in the Caroline Era*, ed. Ian Atherton and Julie Sanders (Manchester: Manchester University Press, 2006), 28–49, 35; Karen Britland, *Drama at the Courts of Queen Henrietta Maria* (Cambridge: Cambridge University Press, 2006), 148; Rebecca A. Bailey, *Staging the Old Faith: Queen Henrietta Maria and the Theatre of Caroline England*, 1625–1642 (Manchester: Manchester University Press, 2009), 91, 148. For further discussion of Laud's relation to Henrietta Maria, see Britland, "Recent Studies of the Life and Cultural Influence of Queen Henrietta Maria," 305–306.

73 Scholars have long recorded the connection between taming the lusts of the body in (neo)Platonic doctrines – particularly in Plato's *Phaedo* and the *Enneads* of Plotinus – and the earliest forms of Christian asceticism. On Plato, see John M. Dillon, "Rejecting the Body, Refining the Body: Some Remarks on the Development of Platonist Asceticism," in *Asceticism*, ed. Vincent L. Wimbush and Richard Valantasis (Oxford: Oxford University Press, 1998), 80–87. On Plotinus, see Joseph Ward Swain, *The Hellenic Origins of Christian Asceticism* (New York: The New Era Printing Company, 1916), 128–139. Several works – by court poets and clerics alike – illustrate church and court's shared ascetic interests. See Thomas Carew, *Coelum Britannicum* (London, 1634); William Davenant, *The temple of love* (London, 1634); Thomas Nabbes, *Microcosmus* (London, 1637); and William Strode, *The Floating Island* (London, 1655).

74 Sensabaugh, *The Tragic Muse of John Ford*, 144.

75 Reid Barbour, *English Epicures and Stoics: Ancient Legacies in Early Stuart Culture* (Amherst: The University of Massachusetts Press, 1998), 107.

76 Peter M. Daly and Mary V. Silcox, "William Marshall's *Emblems* (1650) Rediscovered," *English Literary Renaissance* 19 (1989): 346–374, 373.

77 Robert Crofts, *The Lover; or, Nuptiall love* (London, 1638), sig. A7[r].

78 Ben Jonson, *Loues triumph through Callipolis* (London, 1631), 1.

79 Aurelian Townshend, *Tempe restord* (London, 1632), 13.
80 Robert Crofts, *The way to happinesse on earth* (London, 1641), 257.
81 Crofts, *The Lover*, sig. C8$^{r}$.
82 Crofts, *The Lover*, sigs. D1$^{v}$-D2$^{r}$.
83 Peter Heylyn, *Cyprianus anglicus* (London, 1668), 224.
84 Crofts, *The Lover*, sig. D2$^{r}$.
85 Crofts, *The Lover*, sig. E7$^{v}$.
86 Crofts, *The Lover*, sig. F4$^{v}$.
87 Crofts, *The Lover*, sig. F3$^{r}$.
88 Crofts, *The Lover*, sigs. D2$^{v}$, E3$^{r}$.

## 3. The Virgin's Body and the Natural World in *Lycidas*

1 Christopher Hill, *Milton and the English Revolution* (New York: Faber & Faber, 1978), 50.
2 Anna Beer, *Milton: Poet, Pamphleteer, and Patriot* (London: Bloomsbury, 2008), 87; Nicholas McDowell, "How Laudian was the Young Milton?" *Milton Studies* 52 (2011): 3–33; John Leonard, *The Value of Milton* (Cambridge: Cambridge University Press, 2016), 42. For a select bibliography of arguments resisting the identification of the young Milton as a puritan radical, see John Spencer Hill, *John Milton: Poet, Priest and Prophet: A Study of Divine Vocation in Milton's Poetry and Prose* (New Jersey: Rowman and Littlefield, 1979); Annabel Patterson, "'Forc'd fingers': Milton's Early Poems and Ideological Constraint," in *"The Muses Common-Weale": Poetry and Politics in the Seventeenth Century*, ed. Claude J. Summers and Ted-Larry Pebworth (Columbia, MO: University of Missouri Press, 1988), 9–22; Jonathan Goldberg, "Dating Milton," in *Soliciting Interpretation: Literary Theory and Seventeenth-Century English Poetry*, ed. Elizabeth D. Harvey and Katherine Eisaman Maus (Chicago: University of Chicago Press, 1990), 199–220; Gordon Campbell and Thomas N. Corns, *John Milton: Life, Work, and Thought* (Oxford: Oxford University Press, 2008); Catherine Gimelli Martin, *Milton among the Puritans: The Case for Historical Revisionism* (Surrey: Ashgate, 2010).
3 Jeffrey Alan Miller, "Milton and the Conformable Puritanism of Richard Stock and Thomas Young," in *Young Milton: The Emerging Author, 1620–1642*, ed. Edward Jones (Oxford: Oxford University Press, 2013), 72–106, 90.
4 James Holly Hanford, "The Youth of Milton: An Interpretation of His Early Literary Development," *Studies in Shakespeare, Milton and Donne* (New York: Macmillan, 1925; New York: Haskell House, 1964), 87–164, 156.
5 Colin Burrow, "Poems 1645: The Future Poet," in *The Cambridge Companion to Milton*, ed. Dennis Danielson (Cambridge: Cambridge University Press, 1989; Cambridge: Cambridge University Press, 1999), 54–69, 60.

6 Sanctity inhering in the natural world in *Lycidas* contrasts strongly with Milton's later views. See *Paradise Lost* 11.829–39. *Paradise Lost*, ed. Alastair Fowler, rev. 2nd ed. (Harlow: Longman, 1971; New York: Routledge, 2007).

7 I am alluding to the title of Alexandra Walsham's *The Reformation of the Landscape: Religion, Identity, and Memory in Early Modern Britain and Ireland* (Oxford: Oxford University Press, 2011), a work that has influenced my own thinking on the topic.

8 Edward Elton, *An exposition of the Epistle of St Paule to the Colossians deliuered in sundry sermons* (London, 1615), 960–962. See also William Tyndale, *An answere vnto Sir Thomas Mores dialoge* (Antwerp, 1531), fos. xxxviii$^{v}$–xxxix$^{r}$.

9 Walsham, *The Reformation of the Landscape*, 82.

10 See also William Gearing, *The arraignment of pride* (London, 1660), 103–104; James Howell, *Thērologia* (London, 1660), 134.

11 Edward Muir, *Ritual in Early Modern Europe* (Cambridge: Cambridge University Press, 1997; Cambridge: Cambridge University Press, 2005), 73.

12 See Nathan J. Ristuccia, *Christianization and Commonwealth in Early Medieval Europe* (Oxford: Oxford University Press, 2018), 95–96. Ristuccia argues that the identification of rogation with Ambarvalia, while accepted by modern historians and medieval and early modern writers alike, is historically inaccurate.

13 For more on its Catholic connotations, see John Canne, *A necessitie of separation from the Church of England, prooved by the nonconformists principles* (Amsterdam, 1634), 111; William Perkins, *A treatise vnto a declaration whether a man be in the estate of damnation or in the estate of grace* (London, 1590), 314 [irregular pagination]. See Ronald Hutton, *The Rise and Fall of Merry England: The Ritual Year* 1400–1700 (Oxford: Oxford University Press, 1994), 85.

14 John Jewel, *Iniunctions giuen by the Reuerend Father in Christ John by Gods prouidence, Bishop of Sarisburie* (London, 1569), sig. B4$^{r}$. See also Church of England, *Articles ecclesiasticall* [Westfaling] (Oxford, 1592), sig. Aiii$^{v}$; John Parkhurst, *Iniunctions* (London, 1569), sig. Aii$^{v}$.

15 Richard Bancroft, *Articles, to be enquired of vvithin the dioces of London* (London, 1604), sig. A3$^{r}$.

16 Kenneth Fincham (ed.), *Visitation Articles and Injunctions of the Early Stuart Church*, 2 vols. (Suffolk: Boydell & Brewer, 1994–1998), 1:209.

17 See William Laud, *Articles to be enquired of vvithin the dioces of London* (London, 1631), sig. A3$^{v}$; William Laud, *Articles to be enquired of in the metropoliticall visitation of the most reverend father, VVilliam* (London, 1633), sig. A4$^{v}$; William Laud, *Articles to be inquired of in the metropoliticall visitation* (London, 1635), sig. A4$^{v}$; William Laud, *Articles to be inquired of in the first trienniall visitation of the most reverend father VVilliam* (London, 1637), sig. A5$^{v}$.

18 See Fincham, *Visitation Articles and Injunctions of the Early Stuart Church*, vol. 2.
19 See Walsham, *The Reformation of the Landscape*, 263.
20 Margaret Stieg, *Laud's Laboratory: The Diocese of Bath and Wells in the Early Seventeenth Century* (Lewisburg: Bucknell University Press, 1982), 195.
21 Henry Mason, *The epicures fast* (London, 1626), 48.
22 William Prynne, *A briefe suruay and censure of Mr Cozens his couzening deuotions* (London, 1628), 16.
23 Ristuccia, *Christianization and Commonwealth in Early Medieval Europe*, 72.
24 Quotations of and references to the Bible are from *King James Study Bible*, ed. Kenneth Barker (Michigan: Zondervan, 2002).
25 John Rawlinson, *The foure summons of the Shulamite* (Oxford, 1606), 8.
26 Anne Pratt, *The Flowering Plants of Great Britain* (London, 1855), 1:195.
27 Quotations of Milton's poetry are from *John Milton: Complete Shorter Poems*, ed. Stella Revard (Oxford: Wiley-Blackwell, 2009).
28 Joad Raymond, *Milton's Angels: The Early-Modern Imagination* (Oxford: Oxford University Press, 2010), 242.
29 George Wither, *The hymnes and songs of the Church* (London, 1623), 191–192.
30 Herodotus, *Histories I*, ed. J.H. Sleeman (Cambridge: Cambridge University Press, 1909; London: Bristol Classical Press, 2002), 1.23.
31 See Walter Burkert, *Homo Necans: The Anthropology of Ancient Greek Sacrificial Ritual and Myth*, transl. Peter Bing (Berkeley: University of California Press, 1983), 199–200.
32 See *Virgil: Georgics I and IV*, ed. H.H. Huxley (London: Methuen & Co. Ltd., 1963), 1.338–350, 110n; *The Elegies of Albius Tibullus*, ed. Kirby Flower Smith (New York: American Book Company, 1913), 2.1.
33 Lancelot Andrewes, *A learned discourse of ceremonies retained and used in Christian churches* (London, 1653), 59.
34 David Pareus, *A commentary upon the divine Revelation of the apostle and evangelist, Iohn* (Amsterdam, 1644), 215.
35 See M. Bradford Bedingfield, *The Dramatic Liturgy of Anglo-Saxon England* (Suffolk: The Boydell Press, 2002), 200.
36 For this date, see *The Annotated Book of Common Prayer*, ed. John Henry Blunt (London: Longmans, Green, 1895), 297. Rogation was instituted in England slightly later, at the Council of Cloveshoo in 747.
37 Alexander Ross, *Pansebeia* (London, 1655), 463. Compared with the 1653 first printing, the 1655 edition contains an expanded section 13 on the Church of Rome.
38 Arthur Hopton, *A concordancy of yeares* (London, 1612), 149.
39 Richard Taverner, *The Epistles and Gospelles with a brief postil vpon the same from after Easter tyll Aduent* (London, 1540), xxxiii[v].
40 Wither, *The hymnes and songs of the Church*, 191.
41 See Thomas North, *The Church Bells of Northamptonshire* (Leicester: Samuel Clarke, 1878), 139–140.

42 Church of England, *Articles ecclesiasticall* [Westfaling], sig. Aiii[v]. Church of England, *Articles ecclesiastical* (London, 1621), sig. B3[r].
43 Samuel Purchas, *Purchas his pilgrims* (London, 1625), 2:1274.
44 Steve Hindle, "Beating the Bounds of the Parish: Order, Memory, and Identity in the English Local Community, c. 1500–1700," in *Defining Community in Early Modern Europe*, ed. Michael J. Halvorson and Karen E. Spierling (Aldershot: Ashgate, 2008), 205–228, 219.
45 Felice Lifshitz, *The Norman Conquest of Pious Neustria* (Toronto: PIMS, 1995), 153.
46 Eamon Duffy, *The Stripping of the Altars: Traditional Religion in England c. 1400–c. 1580* (New Haven: Yale University Press, 1992), 279.
47 Hindle, "Beating the Bounds of the Parish," 222.
48 Hutton, *The Rise and Fall of Merry England*, 75.
49 Pilgrimage to the Mount during Rogationtide was a frequent pre-Reformation custom. See Nicholas Orme, *The Saints of Cornwall* (Oxford: Oxford University Press, 2000), 194. Milton would not have known the primary historical source for the ritual (Nicholas Roscarrock's *Lives of Saints*). But local studies of Cornwall did exist and, judging from how rarefied Milton's allusion to the "vision of the guarded Mount" is, he might well have had a strong interest in Cornwall lore. See Raymond, *Milton's Angels*, 231; Robert Whiting, *The Blind Devotion of the People: Popular Religion and the English Reformation* (Cambridge: Cambridge University Press, 1989; Cambridge: Cambridge University Press, 1991), 239; Richard Carew, *The survey of Cornvvall* (London, 1602).
50 *Oxford English Dictionary*, s.v. "rogation, n.," accessed October 21, 2018, http://www.oed.com.proxy.lib.siu.edu/view/Entry/166876?redirectedFrom=rogation.
51 Godfrey Goodman, *Bishop Goodman his proposition in discharge of his own dutie and conscience both to God and man* (London, 1650), sig. D1[r].
52 In the 1638 version, "whelming" is "humming," but the ponderousness is still supplied by visiting the bottom of the world. *Justa Edouardo King Naufrago* (Cambridge, 1638), 24.
53 Ronald Hutton, *The Stations of the Sun: A History of the Ritual Year in Britain* (Oxford: Oxford University Press, 2001), 286.
54 Muir, *Ritual in Early Modern Europe*, 73.
55 John Brand, *Observations on Popular Antiquities*, rev. Sir Henry Ellis (London: F.C. and J. Rivington, 1813), 1:175n.
56 Hindle, "Beating the Bounds of the Parish," 225–226.
57 For a description of those in Revelation 7 as saints, see Henry Ainsworth, *Annotations upon the five bookes of Moses, the booke of the Psalmes, and the Song of Songs, or, Canticles* (London, 1627), 103.
58 See William Troughton, *The mystery of the marriage song and mutuall spirituall embraces between Christ & his spouse opened* (London, 1656), 77.

59 Alison A. Chapman, *Patrons and Patron Saints in Early Modern English Literature* (New York: Routledge, 2013), 155.
60 John Sergeant, *Of devotion* (London, 1678), 131–132.
61 George Downame, *A godly and learned treatise of prayer* (London, 1640), 64.
62 Downame, *A godly and learned treatise of prayer*, 62.
63 William Prynne, *Canterburies doome* (London, 1646), 328–329. The passage is from Richard Clerke's *Sermons* (1637). For discussion of Laudians censoring Clerke, see his *ODNB* entry.
64 Walsham, *The Reformation of the Landscape*, 254.
65 Sarah Beckwith, *Signifying God: Social Relation and Symbolic Act in the York Corpus Christi Plays* (Chicago: University of Chicago Press, 2001), 36.
66 See John Fisher (Saint), *A sermon had at Paulis* (London, 1526), sig. G2[v]; Cyprian, *The discipline and habit of virgins* (London, 1697), 5.
67 See *The New Testament*, transl. Gregory Martin (Douai, 1582), sig. Eeeee1[v].
68 Hanford, "The Youth of Milton," 153; Ernest Sirluck, "Milton's Idle Right Hand," *Journal of English and Germanic Philology* 60 (1961): 749–785, 768; J. Martin Evans, *The Road from Horton: Looking Backwards in "Lycidas"* (Victoria, B.C.: University of Victoria Press, 1983), 60.
69 Brooke Conti, "Milton, Jerome, and Apocalyptic Virginity," *Renaissance Quarterly* 72:1 (2019): 194–230, 195.
70 Nicholas McDowell, "'Lycidas' and the Influence of Anxiety," in *The Oxford Handbook of Milton*, ed. Nicholas McDowell and Nigel Smith (Oxford: Oxford University Press, 2009), 112–135, 130n.
71 John Leonard, "Milton's Vow of Celibacy: A Reconsideration of the Evidence," in *Of Poetry and Politics: New Essays on Milton and His World*, ed. P.G. Stanwood (Binghamton: State University of New York Press, 1995), 187–202, 193.
72 E.M.W. Tillyard, *Milton* (London: Chatto & Windus, 1930; London: Chatto & Windus, 1946), 376. See also Brooke Conti, "Milton, Jerome, and Apocalyptic Virginity."
73 *Novum Testamentum Graece* (Stuttgart: Deutsche Bibelgesellschaft, 1993). "And they sung as it were a new song before the throne, and before the four beasts, and the elders: and no man could learn that song but the hundred and forty and four thousand, which were redeemed from the earth."
74 *A Greek-English Lexicon*, 9th ed. (Oxford: Oxford University Press, 1996), s.v. "μανθάνω."
75 Euripides, *Electra*, in *Fabulae*, ed. J. Diggle (Oxford: Clarendon Press, 1981), vol. 2.
76 Evert van Emde Boas, *Language and Character in Euripides'* Electra (Oxford: Oxford University Press, 2017), 109.

77 Gerhard Kittel (ed.), *Theological Dictionary of the New Testament*, transl. Geoffrey W. Bromiley (Grand Rapids, MI: Wm. B. Eerdmans Publishing Company, 1967; Grand Rapids, MI: Wm. B. Eerdmans Publishing Company, 1968), s.v. "μανθάνω in the New Testament," 4:407–408.
78 Anthony Stafford, *Staffords Niobe* (London, 1611), 75.
79 See the introduction, note 43.
80 Jerome, *A Select Library of Nicene and Post-Nicene Fathers*, 2nd ser., ed. Philip Schaff and Henry Wace, vol. 6, *Against Jovinianus*, transl. W.H. Fremantle (New York: The Christian Literature Company, 1892; Grand Rapids, MI: Wm. B. Eerdman's Publishing Company, 1954), 1.13, 6:358. Jerome, *Adversus Jovinianum* 1.13, in *Patrologia Latina*, 1st ser., ed. J.-P. Migne (Paris: Garnieri Fratres, 1845), 23:col. 232b.
81 Stafford, *Staffords Niobe*, 76–78.
82 Jeremy Taylor, *The rule and exercises of holy living* (London, 1650), 82–83.
83 John Bale, *The image of bothe churches after reulacion of saynt Iohan the euangelyst* (s.l., 1545), 78[v].
84 Arthur Dent, *The ruine of Rome: or An exposition vpon the whole Reuelation* (London, 1603), 201. See Thomas Wilson, *A Christian dictionarie* (London, 1612), 158; Richard Sibbes, *Bovvels opened* (London, 1639), 192; Lucas Osiander, *A manuell or briefe volume of controuersies of religion betweene the Protestants and the Papists* (London, 1606), 429–430; George Lawson, *Theo-politica* (London, 1659), 165.
85 William Fulke, *Praelections vpon the sacred and holy Reuelation of S. Iohn* (London, 1573), 92[r]. See also John Donne, *The Sermons of John Donne*, 10 vols., ed. George R. Potter and Evelyn M. Simpson (Berkeley and Los Angeles: University of California Press, 1953–1962), 2:214, 5:137, 5:169, 9:188, and 10:43.
86 Pareus, *A commentary upon the divine Revelation of the apostle and evangelist, Iohn*, 336.
87 Taylor, *The rule and exercises of holy living*, 82–83.
88 Pareus, *A commentary upon the divine Revelation of the apostle and evangelist, Iohn*, 334.
89 See Edward Le Comte, "Translations: Obsequies for Edward King," *Milton Quarterly* 35 (2001): 198–217, 211.
90 Le Comte, "Translations: Obsequies for Edward King," 200.
91 *Justa Edouardo King Naufrago*, sig. A4[v].
92 *A Greek-English Lexicon*, s.v. "παρθένος."
93 It is used at Matthew 1:23; Matthew 25:1, 25:7, 25:11; Luke 1:27; Acts 21:9; 1 Corinthians 7:25, 7:28, 7:34, 7:36–38; 2 Corinthians 11:2. David Pareus notes the oddity of this word. See *A commentary upon the divine Revelation of the apostle and evangelist, Iohn*, 334.
94 See Michael Lloyd, "Justa Edouardo King," *Notes and Queries* 5 (1958): 432–434.

95 Lycophron, *Lycophronis Alexandra*, ed. L. Mascialino (Leipzig: B.G. Teubneri, 1964).

96 See also Harris Francis Fletcher, "John Milton's Copy of Lycophron's *Alexandra* in the Library of the University of Illinois," *Milton Quarterly* 23 (1989): 129–158, 141.

97 See J. Martin Evans, *The Miltonic Moment* (Lexington: The University Press of Kentucky, 1998), 148n.

98 See John Reeve, *Hymnes and spiritual songs extracted from Scripture* (London, 1682), 72; Sir Henry Vane, *The retired mans meditations* (London, 1655), 121.

99 I have found only one commentator who interprets the "voice of a great multitude" in Revelation 19:6 as a "song." See I.F., *A sober inquiry* (London, 1660), 84.

100 Leonard, "Milton's Vow of Celibacy," 199.

101 Miles Coverdale, *The newe testamente both Latine and Englyshe ech correspondent to the other after the vulgare texte, communely called S. Ieroms* (Southwarke, 1538), fo. 301[r].

102 Newton observes that Milton follows the Vulgate with place names. John Milton, *Paradise Lost*, ed. Thomas Newton (London, 1750), 1:224–225n.

103 Methodius of Olympus, *The Symposium*, ed. and transl. H. Musurillo (New York: Paulist Press, 1958), 12.

104 Methodius of Olympus, *The Symposium*, 95.

105 Methodius of Olympus, *Le banquet*, ed. V.H. Debidour and H. Musurillo, *Sources chrétiennes* 95 (Paris: Cerf, 1963).

106 Methodius of Olympus, *The Symposium*, 95.

107 See Theodoret of Cyrrhus, *Théodoret de Cyr. L"histoire des moines de Syrie*, ed. P. Canivet and A. Leroy-Molinghen, 2 vols. (Paris: Cerf, 1977–1979), "vita xxix." For translation, see Theodoret of Cyrrhus, *A History of the Monks of Syria*, transl. R.M. Price (Michigan: Cistercian Publications, 1985), 185.

108 *A Greek-English Lexicon*, s.v. "βακχεύω."

109 *Oxford Latin Dictionary* (repr. with corrections, Oxford: Oxford University Press, 1996; Oxford: Oxford University Press, 2006), s.v. "bacchor."

110 See Julian Davies, *The Caroline Captivity of the Church: Charles I and the Remoulding of Anglicanism* 1625–1641 (Oxford: Oxford University Press, 1992), 52.

111 Augustine Lindsell, *Theophylaktou Archiepiskopou Boulgarias Exegesis ton Epistolon tou Hagiou Paulou* (London, 1636). Patrick Young, *Catena Graecorum patrum in beatum Iob collectore Niceta Heracleae* (London, 1637).

112 See H.R. Trevor-Roper, *Archbishop Laud*, 1573–1645 (London: Macmillan & Co. Ltd., 1963), 275.

113 Eleazar Duncon, *Of worshiping God towards the altar* (London, 1660), 31.

## 4. *Upon Appleton House* and the Impossibility of Asceticism

1 Derek Hirst and Steven N. Zwicker, *Andrew Marvell, Orphan of the Hurricane* (Oxford: Oxford University Press, 2011), 98.

2 Hirst and Zwicker, *Andrew Marvell, Orphan of the Hurricane*, 94.

3 John Michael Disanto, "Andrew Marvell's Ambivalence towards Adult Sexuality," *SEL* 48 (2008): 165–182, 167. See also Diane Purkiss, "Thinking of Gender," in *The Cambridge Companion to Andrew Marvell*, ed. Derek Hirst and Steven N. Zwicker (Cambridge: Cambridge University Press, 2011), 68–86, 81.

4 Nigel Smith, *Andrew Marvell: The Chameleon* (New Haven: Yale University Press, 2010), 342.

5 George Klawitter, *Andrew Marvell, Sexual Orientation, and Seventeenth-Century Poetry* (London: Rowman & Littlefield, 2017), 175.

6 Paul Hammond, "Marvell's Sexuality," *The Seventeenth Century* 16 (1996): 87–123, 117. For another discussion of Marvell moving outside the bounds of human sexuality, see Stephen Guy-Bray, "Animal, Vegetable, Sexual: Metaphor in John Donne's 'Sappho to Philaenis' and Andrew Marvell's 'The Garden,'" in *Sex before Sex: Figuring the Act in Early Modern England*, ed. James M. Bromley and Will Stockton (Minneapolis: University of Minnesota Press, 2013), 195–212.

7 Gary D. Hamilton, "Marvell, Sacrilege, and Protestant Historiography: Contextualizing 'Upon Appleton House,'" in *Religion, Literature, and Politics in Post-Reformation England, 1540–1688*, ed. Donna B. Hamilton and Richard Strier (Cambridge: Cambridge University Press, 1996), 161–186, 171. See also David Norbrook, *Writing the English Republic: Poetry, Rhetoric and Politics*, 1627–1660 (Cambridge: Cambridge University Press, 1999), 289.

8 Leah S. Marcus, *The Politics of Mirth: Jonson, Herrick, Milton, Marvell, and the Defense of Old Holiday Pastimes* (Chicago: University of Chicago Press, 1986), 246–247. See also James Turner, *The Politics of Landscape: Rural Scenery and Society in English Poetry* 1630–1660 (Cambridge, MA: Harvard University Press, 1979), 118.

9 Hugh Jenkins, "Two Letters to Lord Fairfax: Winstanley and Marvell," in *The English Civil Wars in the Literary Imagination*, ed. Claude J. Summers and Ted-Larry Pebworth (Columbia: University of Missouri Press, 1999), 144–158, 151.

10 Switching the object of greatest religious scorn from Roman Catholicism to Laudianism is consistent with the complicated anti-Catholicism James Kuzner finds in the poem. See James Kuzner, *Open Subjects: English Renaissance Republicans, Modern Selfhoods, and the Virtue of Vulnerability* (Edinburgh: Edinburgh University Press, 2011; Edinburgh: Edinburgh University Press, 2012), 138.

11 For millennial depictions of Fairfax triumphing over a Laudian anti-Christ, see Patrick J. McGrath, "A Religious House: 'Upon Appleton House,' Laudianism, and Exodus," *The Andrew Marvell Society Newsletter* 5 (2013): 4–16.

12 For a more general discussion of Marvell's religion, see William Lamont, "The Religion of Andrew Marvell: Locating the 'Bloody Horse,'" in *The Political Identity of Andrew Marvell*, ed. Conal Condren and A.D. Cousins (Aldershot: Scolar Press, 1990), 135–156.

13 Ronald A. Marchant, *The Puritans and the Church Courts in the Diocese of York*, 1560–1642 (London: Longmans, 1960), 262.

14 See William Prynne, *A short sober pacific examination of some exuberances in, and ceremonial appurtenances to the Common prayer* (London, 1661), 89–91.

15 Marchant, *The Puritans and the Church Courts*, 262. See also Nicholas von Maltzahn, *An Andrew Marvell Chronology* (New York: Palgrave Macmillan, 2005), 25–26; Andrew Marvell, *The Complete Works in Verse and Prose of Andrew Marvell*, ed. Rev. Alexander B. Grosart (London: Robson and Sons, Printers, 1872; New York: AMS Press, 1966), 1:xxv.

16 Pauline Burdon, "The Second Mrs Marvell," *Notes & Queries* 227 (1982): 33–44.

17 Andrew Marvell, *The Prose Works of Andrew Marvell*, ed. Annabel Patterson, Martin Dzelzainis, N.H. Keeble, and Nicholas von Maltzahn (New Haven: Yale University Press, 2003), 1:289. See also Smith, *Andrew Marvell*, 20; von Maltzahn, *An Andrew Marvell Chronology*, 92. All quotations of Marvell's prose are from the Yale edition.

18 Andrew Hopper, *'Black Tom': Sir Thomas Fairfax and the English Revolution* (Manchester: Manchester University Press, 2007), 154.

19 George W. Johnson (ed.), *The Fairfax Correspondence* (London: Richard Bentley, New Burlington Street, 1848), 1:335–336.

20 Hopper, *'Black Tom,'* 154.

21 See Hopper, *'Black Tom,'* 154.

22 Marchant, *The Puritans and the Church Courts*, 239.

23 Marchant, *The Puritans and the Church Courts*, 293.

24 Jonathan Crewe, "The Garden State: Marvell's Poetics of Enclosure," in *Enclosure Acts: Sexuality, Property, and Culture in Early Modern England*, ed. Richard Burt and John Michael Archer (Ithaca: Cornell University Press, 1994), 270–289, 284.

25 See Alison Shell, *Oral Culture and Catholicism in Early Modern England* (Cambridge: Cambridge University Press, 2007), 31–32; Brian Patton, "Preserving Property: History, Genealogy, and Inheritance in 'Upon Appleton House,'" *Renaissance Quarterly* 49 (1996): 824–839; Douglas D.C. Chambers, "'To the Abbyss': Gothic as a Metaphor for the Argument about Art and Nature in 'Upon Appleton House,'" in *On the Celebrated and Neglected Poems of Andrew Marvell*, ed. Claude J. Summers and Ted-Larry

Pebworth (Columbia: University of Missouri Press, 1992), 139–153, 146; Patsy Griffin, "'Twas No Religious House till Now': Marvell's 'Upon Appleton House,'" *SEL* 28 (1988): 61–76, 61.

26 Andrew Marvell, *The Poems of Andrew Marvell*, rev. ed., ed. Nigel Smith (London: Longman, 2003; London: Longman, 2007). All quotations of Marvell's poetry are from this edition.

27 See C.H. Simpkinson, *Life and Times of William Laud, Archbishop of Canterbury* (London: John Murray, Albemarle Street, 1894), 168.

28 Graham Parry, *Glory, Laud and Honor: The Arts of the Anglican Counter-Reformation* (Suffolk: The Boydell Press, 2006), 83.

29 See William Prynne, *Canterburies doome* (London, 1646), 65–66. For Laudian overreaching and vainglory, see John Browne, *A discovery of the notorious proceedings of William Lavd Archbishop of Canterbury* (London, 1641), sig. A3[r]; William Laud (spurious), *The recantation of the prelate of Canterbury* (London, 1641), 6.

30 See William Jones, *A commentary vpon the Epistles of Saint Paul to Philemon, and to the Hebrewes* (London, 1635), 438; William Prynne, *Lord bishops, none of the Lords Bishops* (Amsterdam, 1640), sigs. I/J4[v] –K1[r]; John Lilburne, *An Answer to nine arguments* (London, 1645), 43.

31 Henry Burton, *For God, and the King* (Amsterdam, 1636), 32.

32 *Mercuries message, or, The coppy of a letter sent to William Laud, late Archbishop of Canterbury, now prisoner in the Tower* (London, 1641), sig. A3[r].

33 *Oxford English Dictionary*, s.v. "lightly, adv.," accessed November 10, 2018, http://www.oed.com.proxy.lib.siu.edu/view/Entry/108225?rskey=fyvom2&result=4&isAdvanced=false.

34 H.R. Trevor-Roper, *Archbishop Laud*, 1573–1645 (London: Macmillan & Co. Ltd., 1963), 364. Charles Carlton differs on the reason of Archie's expulsion. *Archbishop William Laud* (London: Routledge & Kegan Paul, 1987), 154–155.

35 Archie Armstrong, *Archy's Dream* (London, 1641), sig. A2[r].

36 Prynne, *Canterburies doome*, 257.

37 Prynne, *Canterburies doome*, 335.

38 *Canterburie[s] pilgrimage* (London, 1641).

39 Richard Culmer, *Cathedrall newes from Canterbury* (London, 1644), 21.

40 Various classical writers (Dio, Vitruvius, Macrobius) make reference to the hut, so Marvell would have had access to these facts.

41 Catharine Edwards, *Writing Rome: Textual Approaches to the City* (Cambridge: Cambridge University Press, 1996), 34.

42 Jenna Lay, *Beyond the Cloister: Catholic Englishwomen and Early Modern Literary Culture* (Philadelphia: University of Pennsylvania Press, 2016), 146. See also David Wallace, "Nuns," in *Cultural Reformations: Medieval and Renaissance in Literary History*, ed. Brian Cummings and James Simpson (Oxford: Oxford University Press, 2010), 502–526, 502.

43 Lay, *Beyond the Cloister*, 148.

44 See Griffin, "'Twas No Religious House till Now'"; Anne Cotterill, "Marvell's Watery Maze: Digression and Discovery at Nun Appleton," *ELH* 69 (2002): 103–132.
45 Jeremy Taylor, *The rule and exercises of holy living* (London, 1650), 82–83.
46 Strode's Laudian inclinations are evidenced by his play *The Floating Island,* possibly commissioned by Laud to celebrate Charles I's visit to Oxford in 1636. See Strode's *ODNB* entry.
47 William Strode, *A sermon preached at a visitation held at Lin in Norfolk, June the 24th anno* 1633 (London, 1660), 7.
48 Anthony Stafford, *The femall glory* (London, 1635), 149.
49 Stafford, *The femall glory*, 148.
50 Robert Shelford, *Five Pious and Learned Discourses* (Cambridge, 1635), 124.
51 See Richard Braithwaite, *The English gentlevvoman* (London, 1631), 146–147; William Austin, *Devotionis Augustinianae flamma* (London, 1635), 194. For the pre-Reformation occurrence of the comparison, see Helen L. Parish, *Clerical Marriage and the English Reformation: Precedent, Policy, and Practice* (Surrey: Ashgate, 2000), 166.
52 Robert Baillie, *Ladensium Autokatakrisis* (Amsterdam, 1640), 69.
53 See Henry Burton, *A full and satisfactorie ansvvere to the Arch-bishop of Canterbvries speech* (London, 1645), 22; Prynne, *Canterburies doome*, 209–210; Zacharias Ursinus, *The summe of Christian religion* (London, 1645), 511 (this work was printed partly to contest Arminianism).
54 Charges of witchery also discredit monasticism at Nun Appleton (26.205–206). Edward Fairfax, Lord General Thomas's uncle, wrote a tract on witchcraft that circulated in manuscript, perhaps influencing the poem's depiction of witchcraft. Edward Fairfax, *Daemonologia: A Discourse on Witchcraft*, ed. William Grainge (Harrogate: R. Ackrill, Printer and Publisher, Herald Office, 1882).
55 See James Holstun, "'Will you Rent our Ancient Love Asunder': Lesbian Elegy in Donne, Marvell, and Milton," *ELH* 54 (1987): 835–867 for same-sex eroticism; for mention of the impropriety, see Smith, *The Poems of Andrew Marvell*, 222n.
56 Claire Cross and Noreen Vickers, *Monks, Friars and Nuns in Sixteenth Century Yorkshire* (Yorkshire: The Yorkshire Archaeological Society, 1995), 587.
57 A.G. Dickens, *Reformation Studies* (London: The Hambledon Press, 1982), 147.
58 See John Bale, *The apology of Iohan Bale agaynste a ranke papyst* (London, 1550), xliiii.
59 See Melissa E. Sanchez, "'She Straightness on the Woods Bestows': Protestant Sexuality and English Empire in Marvell's 'Upon Appleton House,'" in *Atlantic Worlds in the Long Eighteenth Century: Seduction and Sentiment*, ed. Toni Bowers and Tita Chico (New York: Palgrave Macmillan, 2012), 81–96, 87.

60 See also *The Arminian Nunnery* (London, 1641), 9.
61 William Prynne, *A breviate of the life, of VVilliam Laud Arch-Bishop of Canterbury* (London, 1644), 13.
62 William Prynne, *Histrio-mastix* (London, 1633), 213–214.
63 William Laud, *Works*, 7 vols. (Oxford: John Henry Parker, 1847–1860; New York: AMS, 1975), 3:134.
64 Prynne, *A breviate of the life, of VVilliam Laud*, 29.
65 Prynne, *A breviate of the life, of VVilliam Laud*, 30.
66 William Prynne, *Diotrephes catechized* (London, 1646), 4.
67 See Andrew Marvell, *Miscellaneous Poems* (London, 1681), 93.
68 Cf. Diane Kelsey McColley, *Poetry and Ecology in the Age of Milton and Marvell* (Hampshire: Ashgate, 2007), 32.
69 See Frank J. Warnke, "The Meadow-Sequence in 'Upon Appleton House': Questions of Tone and Meaning," in *Approaches to Marvell: The York Tercentenary Lectures*, ed. C.A. Patrides (London: Routledge & Kegan Paul, 1978), 234–250, 238 for a discussion of the disruption.
70 See M.C. Bradbrook, "Marvell and the Poetry of Rural Solitude," *RES* 17 (1941): 37–46, 39.
71 Hamilton, "Marvell, Sacrilege, and Protestant Historiography," 177.
72 See *A prophecie of the life, reigne, and death of VVilliam Laud, Archbishop of Canterbury* (London, 1644), 4; Burton, *For God, and the King*, 156; John Bastwick, *The answer of John Bastvvick, Doctor of Phisicke, to the information of Sir Iohn Bancks Knight* (Leiden, 1637), 14.
73 *The Complete Prose Works of John Milton*, ed. Don M. Wolfe (New Haven: Yale University Press, 1953), 1:930.
74 See Culmer, *Cathedrall newes*, 22; Hamon L'Estrange, *The reign of King Charles an history* (London, 1655), 217 (not an anti-Laudian polemic, but it relates the controversy over the cope); William Prynne, *A quench-coale* (Amsterdam, 1637), 108.
75 Peter Smart, *Canterburies crueltie* (London, 1643), 1–2.
76 Andrew Marvell, "The Rehearsall Transpros'd," in *The Prose Works of Andrew Marvell*, 1:188–189.
77 See Derek Hirst and Steven Zwicker, "High Summer at Nun Appleton, 1651: Andrew Marvell and Lord Fairfax's Occasion," *The Historical Journal* 36 (1993): 247–269, 267 for the lines' "inescapably sexual" meaning.
78 Kitty W. Scoular, *Natural Magic: Studies in the Presentation of Nature in English Poetry from Spenser to Marvell* (Oxford: Clarendon Press, 1965), 173.
79 Rosalie L. Colie, *"My Echoing Song": Andrew Marvell's Poetry of Criticism* (Princeton: Princeton University Press, 1970), 252.
80 A.D. Cousins, "Marvell's 'Upon Appleton House, to my Lord Fairfax' and the Regaining of Paradise," in *The Political Identity of Andrew Marvell*, ed. Conal Condren and A.D. Cousins (Aldershot: Scolar Press, 1990), 53–84, 77.

81 C.A. Patrides, "'Till prepared for longer flight': The sublunary poetry of Andrew Marvell," in *Approaches to Marvell: The York Tercentenary Lectures*, ed. C.A. Patrides (London: Routledge & Kegan Paul, 1978), 31–55, 46.
82 Hirst and Zwicker, *Orphan of the Hurricane*, 53.
83 Donald M. Friedman, *Marvell's Pastoral Art* (Berkeley: University of California Press, 1970), 241. See also Donald M. Friedman, "Rude Heaps and Decent Order," in *Marvell and Liberty*, ed. Warren Chernaik and Martin Dzelzainis (New York: St. Martin's Press, Inc., 1999), 123–144, 133.
84 Smith, *Andrew Marvell: The Chameleon*, 98.
85 Smith, *The Poems of Andrew Marvell*, 238n.
86 For further discussion of how Maria "corrects" the nuns' sexual impropriety, see Holstun, "'Will you Rent our Ancient Love Asunder?,'" 851–852.
87 See Melissa E. Sanchez's discussion of Marvell's allusion to the poem. "'She Straightness on the Woods Bestows,'" 91–92.
88 Robin Robbins (ed.), *The Complete Poems of John Donne* (Harlow: Longman, 2010).
89 For a contrasting reading of Maria, see Robert Wilcher, *Andrew Marvell* (Cambridge: Cambridge University Press, 1985), 162; Charles Molesworth, "Marvell's 'Upon Appleton House': The Persona as Historian, Philosopher, and Priest," *SEL* 13 (1973): 149–162, 158–159. I do not think this poem, as with Milton's *A Mask*, embraces nuptial inevitability. The apocalyptic vitrification of the world forestalls a conjugal teleology. See also John Rogers, who regards the poem's praise for Mary's future marriage as "compromised." "The Enclosure of Virginity: The Poetics of Sexual Abstinence in the English Revolution," in *Enclosure Acts: Sexuality, Property, and Culture in Early Modern England*, ed. Richard Burt and John Michael Archer (Ithaca: Cornell University Press, 1994), 229–250, 242. For interpretation that sees the poem moving from "celibacy to fruition," see Turner, *The Politics of Landscape*, 74.
90 See Stocker's discussion of this moment and its apocalypticism. Margarita Stocker, *Apocalyptic Marvell: The Second Coming in Seventeenth-Century Poetry* (Athens, OH: Ohio University Press, 1986), 60.
91 I am referring to Lady Fairfax's "outbursts" at the trial of Charles I. For gender and silence in the poem, see Cristina Malcolmson, "The Garden Enclosed/The Woman Enclosed: Marvell and the Cavalier Poets," in *Enclosure Acts: Sexuality, Property, and Culture in Early Modern England*, ed. Richard Burt and John Michael Archer (Ithaca: Cornell University Press, 1994), 251–269, 266; Sarah Monette, "Speaking and Silent Women in 'Upon Appleton House,'" *SEL* 42 (2002): 155–171.
92 Lynn Staley, "Enclosed Spaces," in *Cultural Reformations: Medieval and Renaissance in Literary History*, ed. Brian Cummings and James Simpson (Oxford: Oxford University Press, 2010), 113–133, 131.

93 About the elision of nature and the body, this is a poem in which the speaker refers to himself as an "inverted tree" (71.568) as he dissolves into nature during stanzas seventy-one to eighty-one. And the poem finds nature unchaste, thereby establishing a continuity between the corporal and natural.

94 Smith, *The Poems of Andrew Marvell*, 221n.

95 John Bunyan, *The Miscellaneous Works of John Bunyan*, ed. Roger Sharrock, vol. 3, *The Resurrection of the Dead*, ed. J. Sears McGee (Oxford: Clarendon Press, 1987), 3:224. All quotations of Bunyan's prose are from this edition unless otherwise noted. For ease of reading, I have de-italicized quotations.

96 David Evett calls this "esthetic piety." "'Paradice's Only Map': The 'Topos' of the 'Locus Amoenus' and the Structure of Marvell's 'Upon Appleton House,'" *PMLA* 85 (1970): 504–513, 508.

97 Bunyan, "The Resurrection of the Dead," in *The Miscellaneous Works of John Bunyan*, 3:224.

98 Elizabeth Grey, *A true gentlewomans delight* (London, 1653), 54. Grey connects amber and candying. In stanza eighty-five, the halcyon's effect on nature leaves "stupid fishes hang[ing], as plain/As flies in crystal overta'en" (85.677–79). Smith's note explains that the crystal "must in fact mean amber" (238n). Vitrification also crystalizes.

99 William Loe, *A sermon preached at Lambeth* (London, 1645), 9.

100 See also Ann E. Berthoff, *The Resolved Soul: A Study of Marvell's Major Poems* (Princeton: Princeton University Press, 1970), 194.

101 Kuzner, *Open Subjects*, 125.

102 Kuzner, *Open Subjects*, 141.

103 For discussion of unseriousness in the poem, see Kuzner, *Open Subjects*, 138.

104 John Wells, *A prospect of eternity* (London, 1654), 242–244.

105 Scoular, *Natural Magic*, 178. Vitrification may also denote such perfection. Thomas Browne argues that it presents "the world in its epitome or contracted essence." Thomas Browne, *Religio Medici*, ed. James Winny (Cambridge: Cambridge University Press, 1963), part 1, section 50, p. 62.

106 Colie, *"My Echoing Song,"* 270.

107 Ryan Netzley, "Sameness and the Poetics of Nonrelation: Andrew Marvell's 'The Garden,'" *PMLA* 132 (2017): 580–595, 593.

## 5. Self-Denial, Monasticism, and The Pilgrim's Progress

1 For discussions about the emergence of subjectivity during the Renaissance era, see Jacob Burckhardt, *The Civilisation of the Renaissance in Italy*, transl. S.G.C. Middlemore (New York: Macmillan, 1904), 129; Paul Oskar Kristeller, *Renaissance Thought II: Papers on Humanism and the Arts* (New York: Harper & Row, 1965), 65; Stephen Greenblatt, *Renaissance*

*Self-Fashioning from More to Shakespeare* (Chicago: University of Chicago Press, 1980; Chicago: University of Chicago Press, 2005), 2; Brian Cummings, *Mortal Thoughts: Religion, Secularity & Identity in Shakespeare and Early Modern Culture* (Oxford: Oxford University Press, 2013), 45; Udo Thiel, *The Early Modern Subject: Self-Consciousness and Personal Identity from Descartes to Hume* (Oxford: Oxford University Press, 2011), 67, 72. For critique of Renaissance individualism, see John J. Martin, *Myths of Renaissance Individualism* (New York: Palgrave Macmillan, 2004), 127.

2 John Bunyan, *The Pilgrim's Progress* (Hertfordshire: Wordsworth Editions Limited, 1996), xii.

3 John Bunyan, *The Pilgrim's Progress* (New York: Signet Classics, 1994; New York: Signet Classics, 2009), xiv. See Taylor's discussion of Bunyan's work as partially exhibiting a "new consciousness." Charles Taylor, *Sources of the Self: The Making of the Modern Identity* (Cambridge: Cambridge University Press, 1989), 287.

4 Jason Crawford, *Allegory and Enchantment: An Early Modern Poetics* (Oxford: Oxford University Press, 2017), 179.

5 Michael Davies, "Spirit in the Letters: John Bunyan's Congregational Epistles," *Seventeenth Century* 24 (2009): 323–360, 323. Bunyan has also been connected to the way in which Reformation practices helped facilitate the discovery of this inner domain. David L. Jeffrey, *House of the Interpreter: Reading Scripture, Reading Culture* (Waco, TX: Baylor University Press, 2003), 6.

6 Roger Pooley, "*Grace Abounding* and the New Sense of Self," in *John Bunyan and His England, 1628–88*, ed. Anne Laurence, W.R. Owens, and Stuart Sim (London: The Hambledon Press, 1990), 105–114, 114. See also J.C. Davis, "Living with the Living God: Radical Religion and the English Revolution," in *Religion in Revolutionary England*, ed. Christopher Durston and Judith D. Maltby (Manchester: Manchester University Press, 2006), 19–41, 31–35; Galen K. Johnson, *Prisoner of Conscience: John Bunyan on Self, Community, and Christian Faith* (Bletchley: Paternoster, 2003), 164. See also Thomas H. Luxon, *Literal Figures: Puritan Allegory and the Reformation Crisis in Representation* (Chicago: University of Chicago Press, 1995), 26.

7 Margaret Soenser Breen, "The Sexed Pilgrim's Progress," *SEL* 32 (1992): 443–460, 444. For similar claims, see Kathleen Swaim, *Pilgrim's Progress, Puritan Progress: Discourses and Contexts* (Urbana: University of Illinois Press, 1993), 295; Cynthia Marshall, *The Shattering of the Self: Violence, Subjectivity, and Early Modern Texts* (Baltimore: The Johns Hopkins University Press, 2002), 14, 30.

8 Linda Tredennick, "Exteriority in Milton and Puritan Life Writing," *SEL* 51 (2011): 159–179, 175.

9 For Bunyan's views of Catholic asceticism, see *The Miscellaneous Works of John Bunyan*, ed. Roger Sharrock, vol. 9, *A Treatise of the Fear of God*, ed. Roger Sharrock (Oxford: Clarendon Press, 1981), 9:29. For Bunyan's

complicated attitude towards women, see John Bunyan, *Grace Abounding to the Chief of Sinners*, ed. Roger Sharrock (Oxford: Oxford University Press, 1962), para. 315; Thomas H. Luxon, "One Soul Versus One Flesh: Friendship, Marriage, and the Puritan Self," in *Trauma and Transformation: The Political Progress of John Bunyan*, ed. Vera J. Camden (Stanford: Stanford University Press, 2008), 81–99, 85. See also Sharrock's discussion of Bunyan's first marriage in "Spiritual Autobiography in *The Pilgrim's Progress*," *RES* 24 (1948): 102–120, 111–112.

10 For Weber's discussion of the relation between the new asceticism and individualism, see *The Protestant Ethic and the Spirit of Capitalism*, ed. Richard Swedberg, transl. Talcott Parsons (New York: W.W. Norton & Company, 2009), 53.

11 See note 80 in the introduction.

12 James Kuzner, *Open Subjects: English Renaissance Republicans, Modern Selfhoods, and the Virtue of Vulnerability* (Edinburgh: Edinburgh University Press, 2011; Edinburgh: Edinburgh University Press, 2012), 30.

13 Timothy J. Reiss, *Mirages of the Selfe: Patterns of Personhood in Ancient and Early Modern Europe* (Stanford: Stanford University Press, 2003), 318, 315.

14 Reiss, *Mirages of the Selfe*, 45. See also 40.

15 Jerrold Seigel, *The Idea of the Self: Thought and Experience in Western Europe since the Seventeenth Century* (Cambridge: Cambridge University Press, 2005), 46–7.

16 Quotations of and references to the Bible are from *King James Study Bible*, ed. Kenneth Barker (Michigan: Zondervan, 2002).

17 See Brooke Conti's discussion of another of Bunyan's framing prefaces in *Confessions of Faith in Early Modern England* (Philadelphia: University of Pennsylvania Press, 2014), 161.

18 Unless otherwise noted, all quotations of Bunyan are from *John Bunyan, The Pilgrim's Progress*, 2nd ed., ed. James Blanton Wharey and Roger Sharrock (Oxford: Clarendon Press, 1928; Oxford: Clarendon Press, 1967). For ease of reading, I have de-italicized the introductory poem. In-text references are to page numbers.

19 John Milton, *Paradise Lost*, ed. Alastair Fowler, rev. 2nd ed. (Harlow: Longman, 1971; New York: Routledge, 2007).

20 *Oxford English Dictionary*, s.v. "come, v.," accessed November 10, 2018, http://www.oed.com.proxy.lib.siu.edu/view/Entry/36824?rskey=giiyH6&result=4. Eric Partridge, *Shakespeare's Bawdy*, 3rd ed. (London: Routledge, 1947; London: Routledge Classics, 2001), 102–103.

21 *The method of chemical philosophie and physic* (London, 1664), 110.

22 *Aristoteles Master-piece* (London, 1684), 74.

23 Randle Holme, *The academy of armory* (Chester, 1688), 104.

24 Joan Fitzpatrick, "'I Must Eat my Dinner': Shakespeare's Foods from Apples to Walrus," in *Renaissance Food from Rabelais to Shakespeare: Culinary*

*Readings and Culinary Histories*, ed. Joan Fitzpatrick (Surrey: Ashgate, 2010), 127–143, 138.

25 William Shakespeare, *Hamlet*, ed. Philip Edwards (Cambridge: Cambridge University Press, 1985; Cambridge: Cambridge University Press, 2003).

26 *The Complete Poems of John Donne*, ed. Robin Robbins (Harlow: Longman, 2010).

27 John Swan, *Speculum mundi* (Cambridge, 1635), 389.

28 John Bunyan, *The Miscellaneous Works of John Bunyan*, ed. Roger Sharrock, vol. 12, *The Acceptable Sacrifice*, ed. W.R. Owens (Oxford: Clarendon Press, 1994), 12:33. See also "A holy life, the beauty of Christianity," in *The Miscellaneous Works of John Bunyan*, 9:273–274.

29 John Bunyan, *The Miscellaneous Works of John Bunyan*, ed. Roger Sharrock, vol. 11, *The Advocateship of Jesus Christ*, ed. Richard L. Greaves (Oxford: Clarendon Press, 1985), 11:159. See also John Bunyan, *The Miscellaneous Works of John Bunyan*, ed. Roger Sharrock, vol. 8, *Come & Welcome to Jesus* Christ, ed. Richard L. Greaves (Oxford: Clarendon Press, 1979), 8:67.

30 "Come and Welcome," in *The Miscellaneous Works of John Bunyan*, 8:260.

31 This is consistent with Nigel Smith's observation that "*The Pilgrim's Progress* is often noted for its corporeality." Nigel Smith, "Bunyan and the Language of the Body in Seventeenth-Century England," in *John Bunyan and His England, 1628–88*, ed. Anne Laurence, W.R. Owens, and Stuart Sim (London: The Hambledon Press, 1990), 161–174, 166.

32 Christopher Wilson, *Self Deniall: or, A Christians Hardest Taske* (London, 1625), sig. E4[r].

33 See discussion of this moment in Daniel Shanahan, *Toward a Genealogy of Individualism* (Amherst: The University of Massachusetts Press, 1992), 73.

34 John Bunyan, *The Miscellaneous Works of John Bunyan*, ed. Roger Sharrock, vol. 3, *The Resurrection of the Dead*, ed. J. Sears McGee (Oxford: Clarendon Press, 1987), 3:278. See Christopher Hill's discussion of self-denial in *A Turbulent, Seditious, and Factious People: John Bunyan and his Church 1628–1688* (Oxford: Clarendon Press, 1988), 275–276.

35 "Instruction for the Ignorant," in *The Miscellaneous Works of John Bunyan*, 8:43.

36 John Stalham, *Vindiciae redemptionis* (London, 1647), 155.

37 *Grace Abounding to the Chief of Sinners*, para. 325.

38 "Instruction for the Ignorant," in *The Miscellaneous Works of John Bunyan*, 8:40.

39 Thomas Manton, *One hundred and ninety sermons on the hundred and nineteenth Psalm* (London, 1681), 337.

40 Erasmus, *The first tome or volume of the Paraphrase of Erasmus vpon the Newe Testamente* (London, 1548), fo. liii[v].

41 Cf. N.B., *A journal of meditations for every day in the year gathered out of divers authors* (s.l., 1669), 410; George Petter, *A learned, pious, and practical commentary, upon the Gospel according to St. Mark* (London, 1661), 459.

42 Erasmus, *The first tome or volume of the Paraphrase of Erasmus vpon the Newe Testamente*, fo. liiii^r^.
43 Thomas Watson, *Holsome and catholyke doctryne concerninge the seuen Sacramentes of Chrystes Church* (London, 1558), fo. xx^v^.
44 See Swaim, *Pilgrim's Progress, Puritan Progress*, 211.
45 John Bunyan, *The Miscellaneous Works of John Bunyan*, ed. Roger Sharrock, vol. 4, *A Confession of my Faith*, ed. T.L. Underwood (Oxford: Clarendon Press, 1989), 4:172.
46 "A Confession of My Faith," in *The Miscellaneous Works of John Bunyan*, 4:164.
47 Niels Hemmingsen, *A Postill, or, Exposition of the Gospels* (London, 1569), fo. 250^r^.
48 R.J., *Compunction or pricking of heart* (London, 1648), 316.
49 "A Holy Life," in *The Miscellaneous Works of John Bunyan*, 9:331.
50 Edward Polhill, *Precious faith considered in its nature, working, and growth* (London, 1675), 34.
51 Stalham, *Vindiciae redemptionis*, 170.
52 Thomas Watson, *The duty of self-denial* (London, 1675), 48.
53 Timothy Manlove, *Praeparatio evangelica* (London, 1698), 159.
54 Watson, *The duty of self-denial*, 48.
55 John Howe, *The blessednesse of the righteous* (London, 1668), 123.
56 Howe, *The blessednesse of the righteous*, 124–127.
57 Cf. Samuel Rutherford, *Christ dying and drawing sinners to himself* (London, 1647), 358.
58 Richard Baxter, *A Treatise of Self-Denial* (London, 1659), 67.
59 Richard Valantasis, *The Making of the Self: Ancient and Modern Asceticism* (Oregon: Cascade Books, 2008), 174.
60 For the mystical connotations of Baxter's illuminated soul, cf. Henry More, *Conjectura cabbalistica* (London, 1653), 56.
61 John Collinges, *A Lesson of Self-Deniall* (London, 1650), 62. For the use of a similarly graphic metaphor about spiritual mortification, see John Cotton, *A practicall commentary, or an exposition with observations, reasons, and vses upon the first Epistle generall of John* (London, 1656), 112.
62 Stalham, *Vindiciae redemptionis*, 164.
63 Wilson, *Self Deniall*, sig. F1^v^.
64 Thomas Reeve, *God's plea for Nineveh* (London, 1657), 83.
65 See also Samuel Smith, *The Character of A Weaned Christian. Or The Evangelical Art of promoting Self-denial* (London, 1675), 8.
66 Jeremiah Burroughs, *Moses his self-denyall* (London, 1641), 32–34.
67 Henry Burton, *A most godly sermon* (London, 1641), sig. A3^r^.
68 Thomas Beard, *A retractiue from the Romish religion* (London, 1616), 24–25.
69 Girolamo Piatti, *The happines of a religious state* (Rouen, 1632), 83–84.
70 This *kenosis* would undoubtedly have appealed to Everard's mystical interests, evidenced as they are by his translation of P-Dionysius and the influence the Dominican contemplative tradition and Henry Niclaes exerted on him.

71 John Everard, *The Gospel treasury opened* (London, 1657), 232–233.
72 Everard, *The Gospel treasury opened*, 238.
73 Everard, *The Gospel treasury opened*, 246.
74 Everard, *The Gospel treasury opened*, 238.
75 Robert Crofts, *The terrestriall paradise* (London, 1639), 57.
76 Weber, *The Protestant Ethic and the Spirit of Capitalism*, 80.
77 Richard Baxter, *The crucifying of the world by the cross of Christ* (London, 1658), 75.
78 Baxter, *A Treatise of Self-denial*, 83.
79 Jeremiah Burroughs, *The excellency of holy courage in evil times* (London, 1661), 153.
80 Anthony Burgess associates breaking a hard heart, melting, and crying tears "like the Fish-pools of Heshbon" with a "detestation of sin" during the process of conversion. Anthony Burgess, *Spiritual refining* (London, 1652), 487. He also uses similar imagery to detail the effects of humiliation. See Anthony Burgess, *An expository comment, doctrinal, controversal, and practical upon the whole first chapter to the second epistle of St. Paul to the Corinthians* (London, 1661), 180.
81 For discussion of Bunyan's allusions to The Song of Solomon in the allegory, see Brainerd P. Stranahan, "'With Great Delight': The Song of Solomon in *The Pilgrim's Progress*," *English Studies* 68 (1987): 220–227.
82 John Robotham, *An exposition on the whole booke of Solomons song* (London, 1651), 692.
83 *The Minor Poems of Joseph Beaumont, D.D., 1616–1699*, ed. Eloise Robinson (Boston: Constable & Company, 1914), 258.
84 Peter Hausted, *Ten Sermons* (London, 1636), 177.
85 Piatti, *The happines of a religious state*, 96.
86 Piatti, *The happines of a religious state*, 578.
87 For contemplative quiet, see Francis Godwin, *The succession of the bishops of England* (London, 1625?), 173; Galeazzo Gualdo Priorato, *The history of France* (London, 1676), 531. For solitude, see Serenus Cressy, *The church-history of Brittany* (Rouen, 1668), 632; Thomas Fuller, *The history of the worthies of England* (London, 1662), 331.
88 For a discussion of the relationship between secularity and allegory, see Jason Crawford, "Bunyan's Secular Allegory," *Religion & Literature* 44 (2012): 45–72.
89 Baxter, *The crucifying of the world by the cross of Christ*, 9.
90 Reiss, *Mirages of the Selfe*, passim.

## Conclusion

1 Sarah Apetrei, "'The Life of Angels': Celibacy and Asceticism in Anglicanism, 1660–c. 1700," *Reformation & Renaissance Review* 13 (2011): 247–274, 261.

2 Anthony Horneck, *The happy ascetick* (London, 1681), sigs. A7r-A8r.
3 Horneck, *The happy ascetick*, 317.
4 Horneck, *The happy ascetick*, 457.
5 Horneck, *The happy ascetick*, 438–439.
6 Horneck, *The happy ascetick*, 439.
7 Horneck, *The happy ascetick*, 462–463.
8 Horneck, *The happy ascetick*, 442.
9 Horneck, *The happy ascetick*, 404.
10 Horneck, *The happy ascetick*, 466–467.
11 John Donne, *The Sermons of John Donne*, 10 vols., ed. George R. Potter and Evelyn M. Simpson (Berkeley and Los Angeles: University of California Press, 1953–1962), 8:100–101.
12 Matthew Poole, *Annotations upon the Holy Bible* (London, 1685), 2:sig. Ccccc2r.
13 *An Account of marriage* (London, 1672), 52.
14 Horneck, *The happy ascetick*, 486. For a sense of the provocation Horneck's position offers, see John Jewel's criticism of the Fathers on this issue; *The Works of John Jewel*, ed. John Ayre (Cambridge: Cambridge University Press, 1848), 3:395.
15 See Daniel Rogers, *Matrimoniall honovr* (London, 1642), 11.
16 Richard Kidder, *The life of the Reverend Anthony Horneck, D.D.* (London, 1698), 35–36, 53.
17 Kidder, *The life of the Reverend Anthony Horneck*, 26.
18 Kidder, *The life of the Reverend Anthony Horneck*, 27.
19 Kidder, *The life of the Reverend Anthony Horneck*, 28.
20 Christopher Wilson, *Self Deniall* (London, 1625), sig. L2r.
21 Kidder, *The life of the Reverend Anthony Horneck*, 30.
22 Horneck, *The happy ascetick*, 449.
23 Kidder, *The Life of the Reverend Anthony Horneck*, 26–27.
24 William Prynne, *Canterburies doome* (London, 1646), 356.

# Bibliography


Abbot, George. *The reasons vvhich Doctour Hill hath brought, for the vpholding of papistry*. Oxford, 1604.

*An Account of marriage*. London, 1672.

Ainsworth, Henry. *Annotations upon the five bookes of Moses, the booke of the Psalmes, and the Song of Songs, or, Canticles*. London, 1627.

Albrecht, Roberta. "Alchemical Augmentation and Primordial Fire in Donne's 'The Dissolution.'" *Studies in English Literature* 45 (2005): 95–115.

Alleine, Joseph. *The way to true happiness*. London, 1675.

Amar, Joseph P. (transl). "On Hermits and Desert Dwellers." In *Ascetic Behavior in Greco-Roman Antiquity: A Sourcebook*, edited by Vincent L. Wimbush, 66–80. Minneapolis: Fortress Press, 1990.

Ambrose of Milan, Saint. *De Virginibus*. Vol. 16 of *Patrologia Latina*, 1st ser. Edited by J.-P. Migne. Paris: Garnieri Fratres, 1845.

– *A Select Library of Nicene and Post-Nicene Fathers*, 2nd ser. Edited by Philip Schaff and Henry Wace. Vol. 10, *Concerning Virgins*, translated by Rev. H. De Romestin. Grand Rapids, MI: Wm. B. Eerdmans Publishing Company, 1955. First published 1896 by the Christian Literature Company (New York).

Anderson, Judith H. *Words That Matter: Linguistic Perception in Renaissance English*. Stanford: Stanford University Press, 1996.

– *Translating Investments: Metaphor and the Dynamic of Cultural Change in Tudor-Stuart England*. New York: Fordham University Press, 2005.

Andrewes, Lancelot. *A learned discourse of ceremonies retained and used in Christian churches*. London, 1653.

– *Two Answers to Cardinal Perron, and Other Miscellaneous Works of Lancelot Andrewes*. Edited by Henry Isaacson. Oxford: John Henry Parker, 1854.

*The Annotated Book of Common Prayer*. Edited by John Henry Blunt. London: Longmans, Green, 1895.

Apetrei, Sarah. "'The Life of Angels': Celibacy and Asceticism in Anglicanism, 1660–c. 1700." *Reformation & Renaissance Review* 13 (2011): 247–274.

Appleford, Amy. "Asceticism, Dissent, and the Tudor State: Richard Whitford's Rule for Lay Householders." *Journal of Medieval and Early Modern Studies* 46 (2016): 381–404.

*Aristoteles Master-piece*. London, 1684.

*The Arminian Nunnery*. London, 1641.

Armstrong, Archie. *Archy's Dream*. London, 1641.

Attersoll, William. *Three treatises*. London, 1633.

Austin, William. *Devotionis Augustinianae flamma*. London, 1635.

– *Haec Homo*. London, 1637.

Babington, Gervase. *A very fruitfull exposition of the Commaundements*. London, 1583.

Bach, Rebecca Ann. "(Re)placing John Donne in the History of Sexuality." *ELH* 72 (2005): 259–289.

Bailey, Rebecca A. *Staging the Old Faith: Queen Henrietta Maria and the Theatre of Caroline England, 1625–1642*. Manchester: Manchester University Press, 2009.

Baillie, Robert. *Ladensium Autokatakrisis*. Amsterdam, 1640.

Baines, John. *The Life of William Laud, Archbishop of Canterbury, and Martyr*. London: Joseph Masters, 1855.

Baker, Stewart A. "Eros and the Three Shepherds of *Comus*." *Rice University Studies* 61 (1975): 13–26.

Bald, R.C. *John Donne: A Life*. Oxford: Oxford University Press, 1970.

Bale, John. *The image of bothe churches after reulacion of saynt Iohan the euangelyst*. s.l., 1545.

– *The apology of Iohan Bale agaynste a ranke papyst*. London, 1550.

Bancroft, Richard. *Articles, to be enquired of vvithin the dioces of London*. London, 1604.

Barbour, Reid. *English Epicures and Stoics: Ancient Legacies in Early Stuart Culture*. Amherst: University of Massachusetts Press, 1998.

– *Literature and Religious Culture in Seventeenth-Century England*. Cambridge: Cambridge University Press, 2002.

Basil of Caesarea, Saint. "Letter 2: To Gregory." Vol. 32 of *Patrologiae Graeca*, edited by J.-P. Migne. Paris: Imprimerie Catholique, 1857.

– *The Fathers of the Church*, edited by Roy Deferrari. Vol. 13, *Letters*, translated by Sister Agnes Clare Way. Washington, D.C.: The Catholic University of America Press, 1965. First published 1951 by The Catholic University of America Press (Washington, D.C.).

Bastwick, John. *The answer of John Bastvvick, Doctor of Phisicke, to the information of Sir Iohn Bancks Knight*. Leiden, 1637.

Baxter, Richard. *The crucifying of the world by the cross of Christ*. London, 1658.

– *A Treatise of Self-Denial*. London, 1659.

Beard, Thomas. *A retractiue from the Romish religion*. London, 1616.

Beaumont, Joseph. *The Minor Poems of Joseph Beaumont, D.D., 1616–1699*. Edited by Eloise Robinson. Boston: Constable & Company, 1914.

Beckwith, Sarah. *Signifying God: Social Relation and Symbolic Act in the York Corpus Christi Plays*. Chicago: University of Chicago Press, 2001.

Becon, Thomas. *A new postil*. London, 1566.

Bedingfield, M. Bradford. *The Dramatic Liturgy of Anglo-Saxon England*. Suffolk: The Boydell Press, 2002.

Beer, Anna. *Milton: Poet, Pamphleteer, and Patriot*. London: Bloomsbury, 2008.

Bell, Ilona. "Gender Matters: The Woman in Donne's Poems." In *The Cambridge Companion to John Donne*, edited by Achsah Guibbory, 201–216. Cambridge: Cambridge University Press, 2006.

Bell, Thomas. *The suruey of popery*. London, 1596.

Bellarmine, Robert, Saint. *An ample declaration of the Christian doctrine*. Roan, 1604.

Benet, Diane Treviño. "Sexual Transgression in Donne's Elegies." *Modern Philology* 92 (1994): 14–35.

Benson, Arthur Christopher. *William Laud Sometime Archbishop of Canterbury, A Study*. London: Kegan Paul, Trench, Trübner & Co., Ltd., 1897.

Bentley, Thomas. *The fift lampe of virginitie*. London, 1582.

Berkeley, David Shelley. *Inwrought with Figures Dim: A Reading of Milton's "Lycidas."* The Hague: Mouton, 1974.

Berkowitz, M.S. "An Earl's Michaelmas in Wales: Some Thoughts on the Original Presentation of *Comus*." *Milton Quarterly* 13 (1979): 122–125.

Berthoff, Ann E. *The Resolved Soul: A Study of Marvell's Major Poems*. Princeton: Princeton University Press, 1970.

Beza, Theodore. *A briefe and piththie summe of the Christian faith*. London, 1565.

Boas, Evert van Emde. *Language and Character in Euripides'* Electra. Oxford: Oxford University Press, 2017.

Bradbrook, M.C. "Marvell and the Poetry of Rural Solitude." *Review of English Studies* 17 (1941): 37–46.

Braithwaite, Richard. *The English gentlevvoman*. London, 1631.

Brand, John. Vol. 1 of *Observations on Popular Antiquities*. Revised by Sir Henry Ellis. London: F.C. and J. Rivington, 1813.

Breen, Margaret Soenser. "The Sexed Pilgrim's Progress." *Studies in English Literature* 32 (1992): 443–460.

Breeze, Andrew. "Donne's 'Blest Hermaphrodite' and Psalms 'More Harsh.'" *John Donne Journal* 22 (2003): 249–254.

Brightman, Thomas. *The Art of Self-Deniall: or, A Christian's First Lesson*. London, 1646.

Britland, Karen. *Drama at the Courts of Queen Henrietta Maria*. Cambridge: Cambridge University Press, 2006.

– "Recent Studies of the Life and Cultural Influence of Queen Henrietta Maria." *English Literary Renaissance* 45 (2015): 303–321.

Broughton, Richard. *The iudgement of the Apostles and of those of the first age.* Douai, 1632.

Brown, Cedric C. *John Milton's Aristocratic Entertainments.* Cambridge: Cambridge University Press, 1985.

Brown, Peter. *The Body and Society: Men, Women and Sexual Renunciation in Early Christianity.* New York: Columbia University Press, 1988.

Browne, John. *A discovery of the notorious proceedings of William Lavd Archbishop of Canterbury.* London, 1641.

Browne, Thomas. *Pseudodoxia Epidemica.* Vol. 2 of *The Works of Sir Thomas Browne,* new ed., edited by Geoffrey Keynes. Chicago: University of Chicago Press, 1964. First published 1928 by Faber and Faber (London).

– *Religio Medici.* Edited by James Winny. Cambridge: Cambridge University Press, 1963.

Bulkley, Edward. *An answere to ten friuolous and foolish reason.* London, 1588.

Bullinger, Heinrich. *The golde[n] boke of christen matrimony.* London, 1542.

– *Fiftie godlie and learned sermons.* London, 1577.

Bunyan, John. *Grace Abounding to the Chief of Sinners.* Edited by Roger Sharrock. Oxford: Oxford University Press, 1962.

– *The Miscellaneous Works of John Bunyan.* Edited by Roger Sharrock. Vol. 3, *The Resurrection of the Dead,* edited by J. Sears McGee. Oxford: Clarendon Press, 1987.

– *The Miscellaneous Works of John Bunyan.* Edited by Roger Sharrock. Vol. 4, *A Confession of My Faith,* edited by T.L. Underwood. Oxford: Clarendon Press, 1989.

– *The Miscellaneous Works of John Bunyan.* Edited by Roger Sharrock. Vol. 8, *Come & Welcome to Jesus Christ,* edited by Richard L. Greaves. Oxford: Clarendon Press, 1979.

– *The Miscellaneous Works of John Bunyan.* Edited by Roger Sharrock. Vol. 9, *A Treatise of the Fear of God,* edited by Roger Sharrock. Oxford: Clarendon Press, 1981.

– *The Miscellaneous Works of John Bunyan.* Edited by Roger Sharrock. Vol. 11, *The advocateship of Jesus Christ,* edited by Richard L. Greaves. Oxford: Clarendon Press, 1985.

– *The Miscellaneous Works of John Bunyan.* Edited by Roger Sharrock. Vol. 12, *The Acceptable Sacrifice,* edited by W.R. Owens. Oxford: Clarendon Press, 1994.

– *The Pilgrim's Progress.* Edited by James Blanton Wharey, revised by Roger Sharrock. Oxford: Clarendon Press, 1967. First published 1928 by Clarendon Press (Oxford).

– *The Pilgrim's Progress.* Hertfordshire: Wordsworth Editions Limited, 1996.

– *The Pilgrim's Progress.* New York: Signet Classics, 2009. First published 1994 by Signet Classics (New York).

Burckhardt, Jacob. *The Civilisation of the Renaissance in Italy*. Translated by S.G.C. Middlemore. New York: Macmillan, 1904.

Burdon, Pauline. "The Second Mrs Marvell." *Notes & Queries* 227 (1982): 33–44.

Burgess, Anthony. *Spiritual refining*. London, 1652.

– *A treatise of original ain*. London, 1658.

– *An expository comment, doctrinal, controversal, and practical upon the whole first chapter to the second epistle of St. Paul to the Corinthians*. London, 1661.

Burgwinkle, Bill. "Medieval Somatics." In *The Cambridge Companion to the Body in Literature*, edited by David Hillman and Ulrika Maude, 10–23. Cambridge: Cambridge University Press, 2015.

Burkert, Walter. *Homo Necans: The Anthropology of Ancient Greek Sacrificial Ritual and Myth*. Translated by Peter Bing. Berkeley: University of California Press, 1983.

Burroughs, Jeremiah. *Moses his self-denyall*. London, 1641.

– *The excellency of holy courage in evil times*. London, 1661.

Burrow, Colin. "Poems 1645: The Future Poet." In *The Cambridge Companion to Milton*, edited by Dennis Danielson, 54–69. Cambridge: Cambridge University Press, 1999. First published 1989 by Cambridge University Press (Cambridge).

Burton, Henry. *A tryall of priuate deuotions*. London, 1628.

– *Truth's triumph ouer Trent*. London, 1629.

– *For God, and the King*. Amsterdam, 1636.

– *A replie to a relation, of the conference between William Laude and Mr. Fisher the Jesuite*. Amsterdam, 1640.

– *A most godly sermon*. London, 1641.

– *A full and satisfactorie ansvvere to the Arch-bishop of Canterbvries speech*. London, 1645.

Butler, Martin. *The Stuart Court Masque and Political Culture*. Cambridge: Cambridge University Press, 2008.

Bynum, Caroline Walker. "The Female Body and Religious Practice in the Later Middle Ages." In *Fragments for a History of the Human Body*, edited by Jonathan Crary, Michel Feher, Hal Foster, Sanford Kwinter. Vol. 1, *Part One*, edited by Michel Feher, 160–219. New York: Zone Books, 1989.

– *Fragmentation and Redemption: Essays on Gender and the Human Body in Medieval Religion*. New York: Zone Books, 1992.

Calvin, John. *The institution of Christian religion*. Translated by Thomas Norton. London, 1561.

– *The sermons of M. Iohn Caluin vpon the fifth booke of Moses called Deuteronomie*. London, 1583.

Campbell, Gordon, and Thomas N. Corns. *John Milton: Life, Work, and Thought*. Oxford: Oxford University Press, 2008.

Canne, John. *A necessitie of separation from the Church of England, prooved by the nonconformists principles*. Amsterdam, 1634.

*Canterburie[s] pilgrimage*. London, 1641.

Carabine, Deirdre. *John Scottus Eriugena*. Oxford: Oxford University Press, 2000.

Carew, Richard. *The survey of Cornvvall*. London, 1602.

Carew, Thomas. *Coelum Britannicum*. London, 1634.

Carey, John. *John Donne: Life, Mind and Art*. New York: Oxford University Press, 1981.

Carlton, Charles. *Archbishop William Laud*. London: Routledge & Kegan Paul, 1987.

Cartwright, Thomas. *The holy exercise of a true fast*. [Scotland?], 1582.

Caussin, Nicolas. *The holy court*. London, 1650.

Chambers, Douglas D.C. "'To the Abbyss': Gothic as a Metaphor for the Argument about Art and Nature in 'Upon Appleton House.'" In *On the Celebrated and Neglected Poems of Andrew Marvell*, edited by Claude J. Summers and Ted-Larry Pebworth, 139–153. Columbia: University of Missouri Press, 1992.

Chambers, Humphrey. *A divine balance to weigh religiovs fasts in applyed to present vse in a sermon preached before the honourable House of Commons in S. Margarets Westminster at their publique fast Sept* 27, 1643. London, 1643.

Chapman, Alison A. *Patrons and Patron Saints in Early Modern English Literature*. New York: Routledge, 2013.

Charalampous, Charis. "Thinking (of) Feelings in Donne's Poetry: The Signifying Rift and 'The Evidence of Things Not Seen.'" *Religion & Literature* 47 (2015): 61–98.

Charke, William, and William Fulke. *A treatise against the Defense of the censure, giuen upon the bookes of W.Charke and Meredith Hanmer*. Cambridge, 1586.

Church of England. *Articles ecclesiasticall to be inquired of by the churchwardens and the sworne-men within the dioces of Hereforde* [Westfaling]. Oxford, 1592.

– *Articles ecclesiastical*. London, 1621.

– *Articles to be inquired of in the metropoliticall visitation of the most reverend father, VVilliam, by Gods providence, Lord Arch-bishop of Canterbury*. London, 1635.

Cirillo, A.R. "The Fair Hermaphrodite: Love-Union in the Poetry of Donne and Spenser." *Studies in English Literature* 9 (1969): 81–95.

Clements, Arthur L. *Poetry of Contemplation: John Donne, George Herbert, Henry Vaughan, and the Modern Period*. New York: State University of New York Press, 1990.

Cogan, Henry (transl.). *The court of Rome*. London, 1654.

Coiro, Anne. "'A Ball of Strife': Caroline Poetry and Royal Marriage." In *The Royal Image: Representations of Charles I*, edited by Thomas N. Corns, 26–46. Cambridge: Cambridge University Press, 1999.

– "Anonymous Milton, or, A 'Maske' Masked." *ELH* 71 (2004): 609–629.

– "'A thousand fantasies': The Lady and the *Maske*." In *The Oxford Handbook of Milton*, edited by Nicholas McDowell and Nigel Smith, 89–111. Oxford: Oxford University Press, 2009.

Colie, Rosalie L. *"My Echoing Song": Andrew Marvell's Poetry of Criticism*. Princeton: Princeton University Press, 1970.

Collinges, John. *A Lesson of Self-Deniall*. London, 1650.

Collins, Siobhán. *Bodies, Politics and Transformations: John Donne's Metempsychosis*. Surrey: Ashgate, 2013.

Conti, Brooke. *Confessions of Faith in Early Modern England*. Philadelphia: University of Pennsylvania Press, 2014.

– "Milton, Jerome, and Apocalyptic Virginity." *Renaissance Quarterly* 72:1 (2019): 194–230.

Cotterill, Anne. "Marvell's Watery Maze: Digression and Discovery at Nun Appleton." *ELH* 69 (2002): 103–132.

Cotton, John. *A practicall commentary, or an exposition with observations, reasons, and vses upon the first Epistle generall of John*. London, 1656.

Cousins, A.D. "Marvell's 'Upon Appleton House, to My Lord Fairfax' and the Regaining of Paradise." In *The Political Identity of Andrew Marvell*, edited by Conal Condren and A.D. Cousins, 53–84. Aldershot: Scolar Press, 1990.

Coverdale, Miles. *The newe testamente both Latine and Englyshe ech correspondent to the other after the vulgare texte, communely called S. Ieroms*. Southwarke, 1538.

Crawford, Jason. "Bunyan's Secular Allegory." *Religion & Literature* 44 (2012): 45–72.

– *Allegory and Enchantment: An Early Modern Poetics*. Oxford: Oxford University Press, 2017.

Creaser, John. "The Original Sabrina?" *Milton Quarterly* 46 (2012): 15–20.

Cressy, Serenus. *The church-history of Brittany*. Rouen, 1668.

Crewe, Jonathan. "The Garden State: Marvell's Poetics of Enclosure." In *Enclosure Acts: Sexuality, Property, and Culture in Early Modern England*, edited by Richard Burt and John Michael Archer, 270–289. Ithaca: Cornell University Press, 1994.

Crofts, Robert. *The Lover; or, Nuptiall love*. London, 1638.

– *The terrestriall paradise*. London, 1639.

– *The way to happinesse on earth*. London, 1641.

Cross, Claire, and Noreen Vickers. *Monks, Friars and Nuns in Sixteenth Century Yorkshire*. Yorkshire: The Yorkshire Archaeological Society, 1995.

Culmer, Richard. *Cathedrall newes from Canterbury*. London, 1644.

Cummings, Brian. "Donne's Passions: Emotion, Agency and Language." In *Passions and Subjectivity in Early Modern Culture*, edited by Brian Cummings and Freya Sierhuis, 51–74. Surrey: Ashgate, 2013.

– *Mortal Thoughts: Religion, Secularity & Identity in Shakespeare and Early Modern Culture*. Oxford: Oxford University Press, 2013.

Cyprian. *The discipline and habit of virgins*. London, 1697.

Daly, Peter M., and Mary V. Silcox. "William Marshall's *Emblems* (1650) Rediscovered." *English Literary Renaissance* 19 (1989): 346–374.

Datta, Kitty. "Love and Asceticism in Donne's Poetry: The Divine Analogy." *Critical Quarterly* 19 (1977): 5–25.

Davenant, William. *The temple of love*. London, 1634.

Davies, Julian. *The Caroline Captivity of the Church: Charles I and the Remoulding of Anglicanism* 1625–1641. Oxford: Oxford University Press, 1992.

Davies, Michael. "Spirit in the Letters: John Bunyan's Congregational Epistles." *Seventeenth Century* 24 (2009): 323–360.

Davis, J.C. "Living with the Living God: Radical Religion and the English Revolution." In *Religion in Revolutionary England*, edited by Christopher Durston and Judith D. Maltby, 19–41. Manchester: Manchester University Press, 2006.

Demaray, John G. *Milton and the Masque Tradition: The Early Poems, Arcades, and Comus*. Cambridge, MA: Harvard University Press, 1968.

Dent, Arthur. *The ruine of Rome: or An exposition vpon the whole Reuelation*. London, 1603.

Dickens, A.G. *Reformation Studies*. London: The Hambledon Press, 1982.

Dickey, David N. *A Study in the Place of Women in the Poetry and Prose Works of John Milton*. Lewiston, NY: The Edwin Mellen Press, 2000.

DiGangi, Mario. *Sexual Types: Embodiment, Agency, and Dramatic Character from Shakespeare to Shirley*. Philadelphia: University of Pennsylvania Press, 2011.

Dillon, John M. "Rejecting the Body, Refining the Body: Some Remarks on the Development of Platonist Asceticism." In *Asceticism*, edited by Vincent L. Wimbush and Richard Valantasis, 80–87. Oxford: Oxford University Press, 1998.

DiPasquale, Theresa M. "Ambivalent Mourning in 'Since she whome I lovd.'" In *John Donne's "desire of more,"* edited M. Thomas Hester, 183–195. Newark: University of Delaware Press, 1996.

– *Literature and Sacrament: The Sacred and the Secular in John Donne*. Pittsburgh: Duquesne University Press, 1999.

Disanto, John Michael. "Andrew Marvell's Ambivalence towards Adult Sexuality." *Studies in English Literature* 48 (2008): 165–182.

Donne, John. Vol. 2 of *The Poems of John Donne*, edited by Herbert J.C. Grierson. Oxford: Clarendon Press, 1912.

– *The Divine Poems*, edited by Helen Gardner, 2nd ed. Oxford: Clarendon Press, 1978. First published 1952 by Clarendon Press (Oxford).

– *The Sermons of John Donne*. 10 vols. Edited by Evelyn M. Simpson and George R. Potter. Berkeley: University of California Press, 1953–1962.

– *John Donne: The Complete English Poems*. Edited by A.J. Smith. London: Penguin Classics, 1986. First published 1971 by Penguin Books (London).

– *The Complete Poems of John Donne*. Edited by Robin Robbins. Harlow: Longman, 2010.

Doriani, Daniel. "The Puritans, Sex, and Pleasure." In *Christian Perspectives on Sexuality and Gender*, edited by Adrian Thatcher and Elizabeth Stuart, 33–52. Herefordshire: Fowler Wright Books, 1996.

Downame, George. *The Christians sanctuarie vvhereinto being retired, he may safely be preserued in the middest of all dangers*. London, 1604.

– *A godly and learned treatise of prayer*. London, 1640.

Dubrow, Heather. *A Happier Eden: The Politics of Marriage in the Stuart Epithalamium*. Ithaca: Cornell University Press, 1990.

Duffy, Eamon. *The Stripping of the Altars: Traditional Religion in England c. 1400–c. 1580*. New Haven: Yale University Press, 1992.

Du Moulin, Pierre. *The accomplishment of the prophecies*. Oxford, 1613.

Duncon, Eleazar. *Of worshiping God towards the altar*. London, 1660.

Durston, Christopher. "'For the Better Humiliation of the People': Public Days of Fasting and Thanksgiving during the English Revolution." *The Seventeenth Century* 7 (1992): 129–149.

Dwalphintramis [Richard Bernard]. *The anatomie of the service book*. s.l., 1641.

Edwards, Catharine. *Writing Rome: Textual Approaches to the City*. Cambridge: Cambridge University Press, 1996.

Elton, Edward. *An exposition of the Epistle of St Paule to the Colossians deliuered in sundry sermons*. London, 1615.

*Eniautos, or, A course of catechizing*. London, 1664.

Erasmus. *The first tome or volume of the Paraphrase of Erasmus vpon the Newe Testamente*. London, 1548.

Eriugena, John Scottus. *De divisione Naturae*. Vol. 122 of *Patrologia Latina*, 2nd ser., edited by J-.P. Migne. Paris: Garnieri Fratres, 1853.

Escobedo, Andrew, and Beth Quitslund (eds.). "*The Faerie Queene* at Ludlow." Special issue *Milton Quarterly* 37 (2003): 179–244.

Euripides. *Electra*. Vol. 2 of *Fabulae*, edited by J. Diggle. Oxford: Clarendon Press, 1981.

Evans, J. Martin. *The Road from Horton: Looking Backwards in "Lycidas."* Victoria, B.C.: University of Victoria Press, 1983.

– *The Miltonic Moment*. Lexington: The University Press of Kentucky, 1998.

Everard, John. *The Gospel treasury opened*. London, 1657.

Evett, David. "'Paradice's Only Map': The 'Topos' of the 'Locus Amoenus' and the Structure of Marvell's 'Upon Appleton House.'" *PMLA* 85 (1970): 504–513.

Fairfax, Edward. *Daemonologia: A Discourse on Witchcraft*. Edited by William Grainge. Harrogate: R. Ackrill, Printer and Publisher, Herald Office, 1882.

Featley, Daniel. *The Honour of Chastity*. London, 1632.

Fincham, Kenneth (ed.). *Visitation Articles and Injunctions of the Early Stuart Church*. 2 vols. Suffolk: Boydell & Brewer, 1994–1998.

– "William Laud and the Exercise of Caroline Ecclesiastical Patronage." *Journal of Ecclesiastical History* 51 (2000): 69–93.

Fincham, Kenneth, and Nicholas Tyacke. *Altars Restored: The Changing Face of English Religious Worship, 1547–c. 1700*. Oxford: Oxford University Press, 2007.

Fisher, John, Saint. *A sermon had at Paulis*. London, 1526.

Fitzpatrick, Joan. "'I Must Eat My Dinner': Shakespeare's Foods from Apples to Walrus." In *Renaissance Food from Rabelais to Shakespeare: Culinary Readings and Culinary Histories*, edited by Joan Fitzpatrick, 127–143. Surrey: Ashgate, 2010.

Fletcher, Anthony. "The Protestant Idea of Marriage in Early Modern England." In *Religion, Culture and Society in Early Modern Britain: Essays in Honour of Patrick Collinson*, edited by Anthony Fletcher and Peter Roberts, 161–181. Cambridge: Cambridge University Press, 1994.

Fletcher, Harris Francis. "John Milton's Copy of Lycophron's *Alexandra* in the Library of the University of Illinois." *Milton Quarterly* 23 (1989): 129–158.

Florio, John. *A vvorlde of wordes*. London, 1598.

Foucault, Michel. *The Hermeneutics of the Subject: Lectures at the Collège de France*, 1981–82. Edited by Frédéric Gros, translated by Graham Burchell. New York: Palgrave, 2005.

Foxe, John. Vol. 2 of *Actes and monuments*. London, 1583.

Friedman, Donald M. *Marvell's Pastoral Art*. Berkeley: University of California Press, 1970.

– "Rude Heaps and Decent Order." In *Marvell and Liberty*, edited by Warren Chernaik and Martin Dzelzainis, 123–144. New York: St. Martin's Press, Inc., 1999.

Frye, Roland Mushat. "The Teachings of Classical Puritanism on Conjugal Love." *Studies in the Renaissance* 2 (1955): 148–159.

Fulke, William. *A defense of the sincere and true translations of the holie Scriptures into the English tong*. London, 1583.

– *Praelections vpon the sacred and holy Reuelation of S. Iohn*. London, 1573.

Fuller, Thomas. *The history of the worthies of England*. London, 1662.

– Vol. 3 of *The Church History of Britain*. London: Thomas Tegg and Son, 1837.

Gearing, William. *The arraignment of pride*. London, 1660.

George, Charles H., and Katherine George. *The Protestant Mind of the English Reformation* 1570–1640. Princeton: Princeton University Press, 1961.

Giugni, Astrid. "The 'Holy Dictate of Spare Temperance': Virtue and Politics in Milton's *A Masque Presented at Ludlow Castle*." *Journal of Medieval and Early Modern Studies* 45 (2015): 395–418.

Godwin, Francis. *The succession of the bishops of England*. London, 1625?.

Goldberg, Jonathan. "Dating Milton." In *Soliciting Interpretation: Literary Theory and Seventeenth-Century English Poetry*, edited by Elizabeth D.

Harvey and Katherine Eisaman Maus, 199–220. Chicago: University of Chicago Press, 1990.

Golding, Arthur. *The vvarfare of Christians*. London, 1576.

Goodman, Godfrey. *Bishop Goodman his proposition in discharge of his own dutie and conscience both to God and man*. London, 1650.

Gouge, William. *Of domesticall duties*. London, 1622.

– *A learned and very useful commentary on the whole epistle to the Hebrews*. London, 1655.

Greenblatt, Stephen. *Renaissance Self-Fashioning from More to Shakespeare*. Chicago: University of Chicago Press, 2005. First published 1980 by University of Chicago Press (Chicago).

– *The Swerve: How the World Became Modern*. New York: W.W. Norton & Company, 2011.

Gregory of Nyssa. *De hominis opificio*. Vol. 44 of *Patrologiae Graeca*, edited by J.-P. Migne. Paris: Imprimerie Catholique, 1863.

– *A Select Library of Nicene and Post-Nicene Fathers of the Christian Church*, 2nd ser. Edited by Philip Schaff and Henry Wace. Vol. 5, *On the Making of Man*, translated by William Moore and Henry Austin Wilson. Grand Rapids, MI: Wm. B. Eerdmans Publishing Company, 1961. First published 1893 by the Christian Literature Company (New York).

Greteman, Blaine. "'All this seed pearl': John Donne and Bodily Presence." *College Literature* 37 (2010): 26–42.

Grey, Elizabeth. *A true gentlewomans delight*. London, 1653.

Griffin, Patsy. "'Twas No Religious House till Now': Marvell's 'Upon Appleton House.'" *Studies in Engish Literature* 28 (1988): 61–76.

Guibbory, Achsah. *Ceremony and Community from Herbert to Milton: Literature, Religion, and Cultural Conflict in Seventeenth-Century England*. Cambridge: Cambridge University Press, 1998.

– "Erotic Poetry." In *The Cambridge Companion to John Donne*, edited by Achsah Guibbory, 133–148. Cambridge: Cambridge University Press, 2006.

– *Returning to John Donne*. Surrey: Ashgate, 2015.

– "Reconsidering Donne: From Libertine Poetry to Arminian Sermons." *Studies in Philology* 114 (2017): 561–590.

Guillory, John. *Poetic Authority: Spenser, Milton, and Literary History*. New York: Columbia University Press, 1983.

Guy-Bray, Stephen. "Animal, Vegetable, Sexual: Metaphor in John Donne's 'Sappho to Philaenis' and Andrew Marvell's 'The Garden.'" In *Sex before Sex: Figuring the Act in Early Modern England*, edited by James M. Bromley and Will Stockton, 195–212. Minneapolis: University of Minnesota Press, 2013.

Hagman, Patrik. "The End of Asceticism: Luther, Modernity and How Asceticism Stopped Making Sense." *Political Theology* 14 (2013): 174–187.

Hall, Joseph. *The honor of the married clergie*. London, 1620.

– *Christian moderation*. London, 1640.

– *Three tractates*. London, 1646.

Haller, William, and Malleville Haller. "The Puritan Art of Love." *Huntington Library Quarterly* 5 (1942): 235–272.

Halpern, Richard. "The Lyric in the Field of Information: Autopoiesis and History in Donne's *Songs and Sonnets*." In *Critical Essays on John Donne*, edited by Arthur F. Marotti, 49–76. New York: G.K. Hall & Co., 1994.

Hamilton, Gary D. "Marvell, Sacrilege, and Protestant Historiography: Contextualizing 'Upon Appleton House.'" In *Religion, Literature, and Politics in Post-Reformation England, 1540–1688*, edited by Donna B. Hamilton and Richard Strier, 161–186. Cambridge: Cambridge University Press, 1996.

Hammond, Henry. *A practicall catechisme*. Oxford, 1645.

Hammond, Paul. "Marvell's Sexuality." *The Seventeenth Century* 16 (1996): 87–123.

Hanford, James Holly. "The Youth of Milton: An Interpretation of His Early Literary Development." In *Studies in Shakespeare, Milton and Donne*, 87–164. New York: Haskell House, 1964. First published 1925 by Macmillan (New York).

Hanmer, Meredith (transl.). *The auncient ecclesiasticall histories of the first six hundred yeares after Christ, wrytten in the Greeke tongue by three learned historiographers*. London, 1577.

Harpham, Geoffrey Galt. *The Ascetic Imperative in Culture and Criticism*. Chicago: University of Chicago Press, 1987.

Harvey, Susan Ashbrook (transl.). "Jacob of Serug, *Homily on Simeon the Stylite*." In *Ascetic Behavior in Greco-Roman Antiquity: A Sourcebook*, edited by Vincent L. Wimbush, 15–28. Minneapolis: The Fortress Press, 1990.

Hausted, Peter. *Ten Sermons*. London, 1636.

Hawkins, Harriett. "The Seductions of Comus." In *Style: Essays on Renaissance and Restoration Literature and Culture in Memory of Harriet Hawkins*, edited by Allen Michie, Eric Buckley, and Harriet Hawkins, 60–68. Newark: University of Delaware Press, 2005.

Hegel, G.F.W. *Phenomenology of Spirit*. Translated by A.V. Miller. Oxford: Oxford University Press, 1977.

Hemmingsen, Niels. *A Postill, or, Exposition of the Gospels*. London, 1569.

Herodotus. *Histories I*. Edited by J.H. Sleeman. London: Bristol Classical Press, 2002. First published 1909 by Cambridge University Press (Cambridge).

Heylyn, Peter. *Theologia veterum*. London, 1654.

– *Cyprianus anglicus*. London, 1668.

Heywood, Thomas. *Londini artium & scientiarum scaturigo*. London, 1632.

Hildersam, Arthur. *The doctrine of fasting and praier*. London, 1633.

Hill, Christopher. *Milton and the English Revolution*. New York: Faber & Faber, 1978.

– *A Turbulent, Seditious, and Factious People: John Bunyan and his Church 1628–1688*. Oxford: Clarendon Press, 1988.

Hill, John Spencer. *John Milton: Poet, Priest and Prophet: A Study of Divine Vocation in Milton's Poetry and Prose*. Totowa, NJ: Rowman and Littlefield, 1979.

Hillman, David. "Staging Early Modern Embodiment." In *The Cambridge Companion to the Body in Literature*, edited by David Hillman and Ulrika Maude, 41–57. Cambridge: Cambridge University Press, 2015.

Hindle, John. *Jacob Burckhardt and the Crisis of Modernity*. Montreal: McGill-Queen's University Press, 2000.

Hindle, Steve. "Beating the Bounds of the Parish: Order, Memory, and Identity in the English Local Community, c. 1500–1700." In *Defining Community in Early Modern Europe*, edited by Michael J. Halvorson and Karen E. Spierling, 205–228. Aldershot: Ashgate, 2008.

Hirst, Derek, and Steven N. Zwicker. *Andrew Marvell, Orphan of the Hurricane*. Oxford: Oxford University Press, 2011.

– "High Summer at Nun Appleton, 1651: Andrew Marvell and Lord Fairfax's Occasion." *The Historical Journal* 36 (1993): 247–269.

Hoard, Samuel. *The Churches Authority Asserted*. London, 1637.

Hodgson, Elizabeth M.A. *Gender and the Sacred Self in John Donne*. Newark: University of Delaware Press, 1999.

– "Milton Takes the Veil." In *Milton and Questions of History: Essays by Canadians Past and Present*, edited by Feisal G. Mohamed and Mary Nyquist, 311–326. Toronto: University of Toronto Press, 2012.

*The holie Bible*. Translated by Gregory Martin. Douai, 1609–1610.

Holme, Randle. *The academy of armory*. Chester, 1688.

Holstun, James. "'Will You Rent Our Ancient Love Asunder': Lesbian Elegy in Donne, Marvell, and Milton." *ELH* 54 (1987): 835–867.

Hooker, Thomas. *Heautonaparnumenos*. London, 1646.

Hopper, Andrew. *'Black Tom': Sir Thomas Fairfax and the English Revolution*. Manchester: Manchester University Press, 2007.

Hopton, Arthur. *A concordancy of yeares*. London, 1612.

Horneck, Anthony. *The happy ascetick*. London, 1681.

Houlbrooke, Ralph. "The family and pastoral care." In *A History of Pastoral Care*, edited by G.R. Evans, 262–293. London: Cassell, 2000.

Howe, John. *The blessednesse of the righteous*. London, 1668.

Howell, James. *Thērologia*. London, 1660.

Hoxby, Blair. "The Wisdom of Their Feet: Meaningful Dance in Milton and the Stuart Masque." *English Literary Renaissance* 37 (2007): 74–99.

Hutton, Ronald. *The Rise and Fall of Merry England: The Ritual Year 1400–1700*. Oxford: Oxford University Press, 1994.

– *The Stations of the Sun: A History of the Ritual Year in Britain*. Oxford: Oxford University Press, 2001.

I.F. *A sober inquiry*. London, 1660.

Jacob of Serug. "Jacob of Serug, *Homily on Simeon the Stylite*." Translated by Susan Harvey. In *Ascetic Behavior in Greco-Roman Antiquity: A Sourcebook*, edited by Vincent L. Wimbush, 15–28. Minneapolis: The Fortress Press, 1990.

James, Thomas. *A manuduction, or introduction vnto diuinitie containing a confutation of papists by papists, throughout the important articles of our religion*. London, 1625.

Jankowski, Theodora A. *Pure Resistance: Queer Virginity in Early Modern English Drama*. Philadelphia: University of Pennsylvania Press, 2000.

Jenkins, Hugh. "Two Letters to Lord Fairfax: Winstanley and Marvell." In *The English Civil Wars in the Literary Imagination*, edited by Claude J. Summers and Ted-Larry Pebworth, 144–168. Columbia: University of Missouri Press, 1999.

Jeffrey, David L. *House of the Interpreter: Reading Scripture, Reading Culture*. Waco, TX: Baylor University Press, 2003.

Jerome. *Adversus Jovinianum*. Vol. 23 of *Patrologia Latina*, 1st ser., edited by J.-P. Migne. Paris: Garnieri Fratres, 1845.

– *A Select Library of Nicene and Post-Nicene Fathers*, 2nd ser. Edited by Philip Schaff and Henry Wace. Vol. 6, *Against Jovinianus*, translated by W.H. Fremantle. Grand Rapids, MI: Wm. B. Eerdman's Publishing Company, 1954. First published 1892 by The Christian Literature Company (New York).

Jewel, John. *A defence of the Apologie of the Churche of Englande*. London, 1567.

– *Iniunctions giuen by the Reuerend Father in Christ John by Gods prouidence, Bishop of Sarisburie*. London, 1569.

– Vol. 3 of *The Works of John Jewel*. Edited by John Ayre. Cambridge: Cambridge University Press, 1845–1850.

Johnson, Bonnie Lander. *Chastity in Early Stuart Literature and Culture*. Cambridge: Cambridge University Press, 2015.

Johnson, Galen K. *Prisoner of Conscience: John Bunyan on Self, Community, and Christian Faith*. Bletchley: Paternoster, 2003.

Johnson, George W. (ed.). Vol 1 of *The Fairfax Correspondence*. London: Richard Bentley, New Burlington Street, 1848.

Johnson, Kimberly. *Made Flesh: Sacrament and Poetics in Post-Reformation England*. Philadelphia: University of Pennsylvania Press, 2014.

Johnson, Richard. *The pilgrimage of man*. London, 1635.

Johnson, Sarah E. *Staging Women and the Soul-Body Dynamic in Early Modern England*. Surrey: Ashgate, 2014.

Jones, William. *A commentary vpon the Epistles of Saint Paul to Philemon, and to the Hebrewes*. London, 1635.

Jonson, Ben. *Loues triumph through Callipolis*. London, 1631.

*Justa Edouardo King Naufrago*. Cambridge, 1638.

Kearney, Jillian. "Donne's *Devotions* in the Context of His Early Sermons: A Revelation of St John the Divine." D. Phil. Thesis, Oxford University, 1995.

Kelly, Kathleen Coyne, and Marina Leslie (eds.). *Menacing Virgins: Representing Virginity in the Middle Ages and Renaissance*. Newark: University of Delaware Press, 1999.

Kendrick, Christopher. "Milton and Sexuality: A Symptomatic Reading of *Comus*." In *Re-membering Milton: Essays on the Texts and Traditions*, edited by Mary Nyquist and Margaret W. Ferguson, 43–73. New York: Methuen, 1987.

Kerrigan, William. *The Sacred Complex: On the Psychogenesis of Paradise Lost*. Cambridge, MA: Harvard University Press, 1983.

– "What Was Donne Doing?" *South Central Review* 4 (1987): 2–15.

Kidder, Richard. *The life of the Reverend Anthony Horneck, D.D.* London, 1698.

Kilgour, Maggie. *Milton and the Metamorphosis of Ovid*. Oxford: Oxford University Press, 2012.

– "Virgil and Ovid." In *The Oxford History of Classical Reception in English Literature*, edited by David Hopkins and Charles Martindale. Vol. 2, (1558–1660), edited by Patrick Cheney and Philip Hardie. Oxford: Oxford University Press, 2015.

*King James Study Bible*. Edited by Kenneth Barker. Grand Rapids, MI: Zondervan, 2002.

Kittel, Gerhard (ed.). Vol. 4 of *Theological Dictionary of the New Testament*, translated by Geoffrey W. Bromiley. Grand Rapids, MI: Wm. B. Eerdmans Publishing Company, 1968. First published 1967 by Wm. B. Eerdmans (Grand Rapids, MI).

Klause, John. "Hope's Gambit: The Jesuitical, Protestant, Skeptical Origins of Donne's Heroic Ideal." *Studies in Philology* 91 (1994): 181–215.

Klawitter, George. *Andrew Marvell, Sexual Orientation, and Seventeenth-Century Poetry*. London: Rowman & Littlefield, 2017.

Kristeller, Paul Oskar. *Renaissance Thought II: Papers on Humanism and the Arts*. New York: Harper & Row, 1965.

Kuchar, Gary. *Divine Subjection: The Rhetoric of Sacramental Devotion in Early Modern England*. Pittsburgh: Duquesne University Press, 2005.

Kuzner, James. *Open Subjects: English Renaissance Republicans, Modern Selfhoods, and the Virtue of Vulnerability*. Edinburgh: Edinburgh University Press, 2012. First published 2011 by Edinburgh University Press (Edinburgh).

Lake, Peter. "Lancelot Andrewes, John Buckeridge, and Avant-garde Conformity at the Court of James I." In *The Mental World of the Jacobean Court*, edited by Linda Levy Peck, 113–133. Cambridge: Cambridge University Press, 1991.

Lamont, William. "The Religion of Andrew Marvell: Locating the 'Bloody Horse.'" In *The Political Identity of Andrew Marvell*, edited by Conal Condren and A.D. Cousins, 135–156. Aldershot: Scolar Press, 1990.

Laud, William. *Articles to be enquired of vvithin the dioces of London*. London, 1631.
– *Articles to be enquired of in the metropoliticall visitation of the most reverend father, VVilliam*. London, 1633.
– *Articles to be inquired of in the metropoliticall visitation*. London, 1635.
– *Articles to be inquired of in the first trienniall visitation of the most reverend father VVilliam*. London, 1637.
– (spurious). *The recantation of the prelate of Canterbury being his last advice to his brethren the bishops of England*. London, 1641.
– *The Works of the Most Reverend Father in God, William Laud, D.D.* 7 vols. New York: AMS, 1975. First published 1847–60 by John Henry Parker (Oxford).
Lawson, George. *Theo-politica*. London, 1659.
Lay, Jenna. *Beyond the Cloister: Catholic Englishwomen and Early Modern Literary Culture*. Philadelphia: University of Pennsylvania Press, 2016.
Le Comte, Edward. *Milton and Sex*. New York: Columbia University Press, 1978.
– "Translations: Obsequies for Edward King." *Milton Quarterly* 35 (2001): 198–217.
Leasure, Ross. "Milton's Queer Choice: *Comus* at Castlehaven." *Milton Quarterly* 36 (2002): 63–86.
Leigh, Edward. *A systeme or body of divinity consisting of ten books*. London, 1654.
Leonard, John. "Saying 'No' to Freud: Milton's *A Mask* and Sexual Assault." *Milton Quarterly* 25 (1991): 129–140.
– "Milton's Vow of Celibacy: A Reconsideration of the Evidence." In *Of Poetry and Politics: New Essays on Milton and His World*, edited by P.G. Stanwood, 187–202. Binghamton: State University of New York Press, 1995.
– *The Value of Milton*. Cambridge: Cambridge University Press, 2016.
Leslie, Marina. "Evading Rape and Embracing Empire in Margaret Cavendish's *Assaulted and Pursued Chastity*." In *Menacing Virgins: Representing Virginity in the Middle Ages and Renaissance*, edited by Kathleen Coyne Kelly and Marina Leslie, 179–197. London: Associated University Presses, 1999.
L'Estrange, Hamon. *The reign of King Charles an history*. London, 1655.
Lessius, Leonardus. *The treasure of vowed chastity in secular persons*. Saint-Omer, 1621.
Leupin, Alexandre. *Barbarolexis: Medieval Writing and Sexuality*. Translated by Kate M. Cooper. Cambridge, MA: Harvard University Press, 1989.
Lewalski, Barbara. "Milton's *Comus* and the Politics of Masquing." In *The Politics of the Stuart Court Masque*, edited by David Bevington and Peter Holbrook, 296–320. Cambridge: Cambridge University Press, 1998.
– *The Life of John Milton: A Critical Biography*. Oxford: Blackwell, 2003.
Lifshitz, Felice. *The Norman Conquest of Pious Neustria*. Toronto: PIMS, 1995.

Lilburne, John. *An Answer to nine arguments*. London, 1645.

Lindheim, Nancy. "Milton's Garden of Adonis: The Epilogue to the Ludlow Masque." *Milton Studies* 35 (1997): 21–41.

Lindsell, Augustine. *Theophylaktou Archiepiskopou Boulgarias Exegesis ton Epistolon tou Hagiou Paulou*. London, 1636.

Lloyd, Michael. "Justa Edouardo King." *Notes and Queries* 5 (1958): 432–434.

Loe, William. *A sermon preached at Lambeth*. London, 1645.

Lupton, Donald. *The glory of their times*. London, 1640.

Lupton, Thomas. *The Christian against the Iesuite*. London, 1582.

Luxon, Thomas H. *Literal Figures: Puritan Allegory and the Reformation Crisis in Representation*. Chicago: University of Chicago Press, 1995.

– "One Soul Versus One Flesh: Friendship, Marriage, and the Puritan Self." In *Trauma and Transformation: The Political Progress of John Bunyan*, edited by Vera J. Camden, 81–99. Stanford: Stanford University Press, 2008.

Lycophron. *Lycophronos tou Chalkideōs Alexandra*. Edited by Isaac Tzetzes. Geneva, 1601.

– *Lycophronis Alexandra*. Edited by L. Mascialino. Leipzig: B.G. Teubneri, 1964.

Mackintosh, W.L. *Life of William Laud*. London: Masters & Co. Ltd., 1907.

Malcolmson, Cristina. "The Garden Enclosed/The Woman Enclosed: Marvell and the Cavalier Poets." In *Enclosure Acts: Sexuality, Property, and Culture in Early Modern England*, edited by Richard Burt and John Michael Archer, 251–269. Ithaca: Cornell University Press, 1994.

Mallet, Charles Edward. Vol. 2 of *The Sixteenth and Seventeenth Centuries*, in *A History of the University of Oxford*. London: Methuen, 1924.

Malpezzi, Frances M. "Adam, Christ, and Mr. Tilman: God's Blest Hermaphrodites." *The American Benedictine Review* 40 (1989): 250–260.

Manlove, Timothy. *Praeparatio evangelica*. London, 1698.

Manton, Thomas. *One hundred and ninety sermons on the hundred and nineteenth Psalm*. London, 1681.

– *A fourth volume containing one hundred and fifty sermons on several texts of Scripture in two parts*. London, 1693.

Marchant, Ronald A. *The Puritans and the Church Courts in the Diocese of York, 1560–1642*. London: Longmans, 1960.

Marcus, Leah S. *The Politics of Mirth: Jonson, Herrick, Milton, Marvell, and the Defense of Old Holiday Pastimes*. Chicago: University of Chicago Press, 1986.

Marshall, Cynthia. *The Shattering of the Self: Violence, Subjectivity, and Early Modern Texts*. Baltimore: The Johns Hopkins University Press, 2002.

Marshall, Peter. *The Catholic Priesthood and the English Reformation*. Oxford: Oxford University Press, 1994.

Martin, Catherine Gimelli. "The Erotology of Donne's 'Extasie' and the Secret History of Voluptuous Rationalism." *Studies in English Literature* 44 (2004): 121–147.

– *Milton among the Puritans: The Case for Historical Revisionism*. Surrey: Ashgate, 2010.
– *Milton's Italy: Anglo-Italian Literature, Travel, and Religion in Seventeenth-Century England*. New York: Routledge, 2017.
Martin, John J. *Myths of Renaissance Individualism*. New York: Palgrave Macmillan, 2004.
Marvell, Andrew. *Miscellaneous Poems*. London, 1681.
– Vol. 1 of *The Complete Works in Verse and Prose of Andrew Marvell*, edited by Rev. Alexander B. Grosart. New York: AMS Press, 1966. First published 1872 by Robson and Sons, Printers (London).
– *The Poems of Andrew Marvell*. Revised edition, edited by Nigel Smith. London: Longman, 2007. First published 2003 by Longman (London).
– Vol. 1 of *The Prose Works of Andrew Marvell*, edited by Annabel Patterson, Martin Dzelzainis, N.H. Keeble, and Nicholas von Maltzahn. New Haven: Yale University Press, 2003.
Mason, Henry. *Christian Humiliation*. London, 1625.
– *The epicures fast*. London, 1626.
Mason, Thomas. *Christs victorie ouer Sathans tyrannie*. London, 1615.
Masson, Cynthea. "Text as Stone: Desire, Sex, and the Figurative Hermaphrodite in the *Ordinal* and *Compound of Alchemy*." In *Sexual Culture in the Literature of Medieval Britain*, edited by Amanda Hopkins, Robert Allen Rouse, and Cory James Rushton, 111–126. Cambridge: D.S. Brewer, 2014.
McColley, Diane Kelsey. *Poetry and Ecology in the Age of Milton and Marvell*. Hampshire: Ashgate, 2007.
McDowell, Nicholas. "'Lycidas' and the Influence of Anxiety." In *The Oxford Handbook of Milton*, edited by Nicholas McDowell and Nigel Smith, 112–135. Oxford: Oxford University Press, 2009.
– "How Laudian was the Young Milton?" *Milton Studies* 52 (2011): 3–33.
McDuffie, Felecia Wright. *"To Our Bodies Turn We Then": Body as Word and Sacrament in the Works of John Donne*. New York: Continuum, 2005.
McGerr, R.P. "Donne's 'Blest Hermaphrodite' and the *Poetria Nova*." *Notes and Queries* 33 (1986): 349.
McGrath, Patrick J. "A Religious House: 'Upon Appleton House,' Laudianism, and Exodus." *The Andrew Marvell Society Newsletter* 5 (2013): 4–16.
McGuire, Maryann Cale. *Milton's Puritan Masque*: Athens: University of Georgia Press, 1983.
Merbecke, John. *A booke of notes and common places*. London, 1581.
*Mercuries message, or, The coppy of a letter sent to William Laud, late Archbishop of Canterbury, now prisoner in the Tower*. London, 1641.
*The method of chemical philosophie and physic*. London, 1664.
Methodius of Olympus. *The Symposium*. Edited and translated by H. Musurillo. New York: Paulist Press, 1958.

– *Le banquet*. Edited by V.H. Debidour and H. Musurillo. *Sources chrétiennes* 95. Paris: Cerf, 1963.

Miller, Jeffrey Alan. "Milton and the Conformable Puritanism of Richard Stock and Thomas Young." In *Young Milton: The Emerging Author, 1620–1642*, edited by Edward Jones, 72–106. Oxford: Oxford University Press, 2013.

Miller, Patricia Cox. "Dreaming the Body: An Aesthetics of Asceticism." In *Asceticism*, edited by Vincent L. Wimbush and Richard Valantasis, 281–300. Oxford: Oxford University Press, 1998.

Milton, Anthony. *Catholic and Reformed: The Roman and Protestant Churches in English Protestant Thought*, 1600–1640. Cambridge: Cambridge University Press, 1995.

– *Laudian and Royalist Polemic in Seventeenth-Century England: The Career and Writings of Peter Heylyn*. Manchester: Manchester University Press, 2007.

Milton, John. Vol. 1 of *Paradise Lost*, edited by Thomas Newton. London, 1750.

– Vol. 1 of *The Complete Prose Works of John Milton*, edited by Don M. Wolfe. New Haven: Yale University Press, 1953.

– *Paradise Lost*. Rev. 2nd ed. Edited by Alastair Fowler. New York: Pearson/ Longman, 2007. First published 1971 by Longman (Harlow).

– *John Milton: Complete Shorter Poems*. Edited by Stella Revard. Oxford: Wiley-Blackwell, 2009.

*A mis-led King, and a memorable Parliament*. London, 1643.

Molesworth, Charles. "'Upon Appleton House': The Persona as Historian, Philosopher, and Priest." *Studies in English Literature* 13 (1973): 149–162.

Monette, Sarah. "Speaking and Silent Women in 'Upon Appleton House.'" *Studies in English Literature* 42 (2002): 155–171.

Montagu, Richard. *Immediate addresse vnto God alone*. London, 1624.

More, Henry. *Conjectura cabbalistica*. London, 1653.

Mosley, Nicholas. *Psychosophia*. London, 1653.

Mueller, Janel. "Women among the Metaphysics: A Case, Mostly, of Being Donne For." *Modern Philology* 87 (1989): 142–158.

– "The Saints." In *Cultural Reformations: Medieval and Renaissance in Literary History*, edited by Brian Cummings and James Simpson, 166–187. Oxford: Oxford University Press, 2010.

Muir, Edward. *Ritual in Early Modern Europe*. Cambridge: Cambridge University Press, 2005. First published 1997 by Cambridge University Press (Cambridge).

Murray, Molly. *The Poetics of Conversion in Early Modern English Literature: Verse and Change from Donne to Dryden*. Cambridge: Cambridge University Press, 2009.

Nabbes, Thomas. *Microcosmus*. London, 1637.

N.B. *A journal of meditations for every day in the year gathered out of divers authors*. s.l., 1669.

Negus, William. *Mans actiue obedience.* London, 1619.

Netzley, Ryan. *Reading, Desire, and the Eucharist in Early Modern Poetry.* Toronto: University of Toronto Press, 2011.

– "Sameness and the Poetics of Nonrelation: Andrew Marvell's 'The Garden.'" *PMLA* 132 (2017): 580–595.

*The New Testament.* Translated by Gregory Martin. Douai, 1582.

Nipperdey, Thomas. "The Reformation and the Modern World." In *Politics and Society in Reformation Europe: Essays for Sir Geoffrey Elton on his Sixty-Fifth Birthday*, edited by E.I. Kouri and Tom Scott, 535–552. London: Macmillan, 1987.

Norbrook, David. *Writing the English Republic: Poetry, Rhetoric and Politics, 1627–1660.* Cambridge: Cambridge University Press, 1999.

North, Thomas. *The Church Bells of Northamptonshire.* Leicester: Samuel Clarke, 1878.

*Novum Testamentum Graece.* Stuttgart: Deutsche Bibelgesellschaft, 1993.

Oliphant, Hughes Old. Vol. 4 of *The Reading and Preaching of the Scriptures in the Worship of the Christian Church.* Grand Rapids, MI: William B. Eerdmans, 2002.

Orme, Nicholas. *The Saints of Cornwall.* Oxford: Oxford University Press, 2000.

Ortiz, Joseph M. *Broken Harmony: Shakespeare and the Politics of Music.* Ithaca: Cornell University Press, 2011.

Osiander, Lucas. *A manuell or briefe volume of controuersies of religion betweene the Protestants and the Papists.* London, 1606.

*Oxford Dictionary of National Biography.* Oxford University Press, 2004; online ed., 2007. http://www.oxforddnb.com/

Papazian, Mary Arshagouni. "The Augustinian Donne: How a 'Second S. Augustine?'" In *John Donne and the Protestant Reformation: New Perspectives*, edited Mary Arshagouni Papazian, 66–89. Detroit: Wayne State University Press, 2003.

Parish, Helen. *Clerical Marriage and the English Reformation.* Surrey: Ashgate, 2000.

– *Clerical Celibacy in the West: c. 1100–1700.* Surrey: Ashgate, 2010.

Parker, Charles H. "Diseased Bodies, Defiled Souls: Corporality and Religious Difference in the Reformation." *Renaissance Quarterly* 67 (2014): 1265–1297.

Pareus, David. *A commentary upon the divine Revelation of the apostle and evangelist, Iohn.* Amsterdam, 1644.

Parkhurst, John. *Iniunctions.* London, 1569.

Parry, Graham. *Glory, Laud and Honor: The Arts of the Anglican Counter-Reformation.* Suffolk: The Boydell Press, 2006.

Partridge, Eric. *Shakespeare's Bawdy.* 3rd ed. London: Routledge Classics, 2001. First published 1947 by Routledge & Kegan Paul (London).

Patrides, C.A. "'Till prepared for longer flight': The sublunary poetry of Andrew Marvell." In *Approaches to Marvell: The York Tercentenary Lectures*, edited by C.A. Patrides, 31–55. London: Routledge & Kegan Paul, 1978.

Patterson, Annabel. "'Forc'd fingers': Milton's Early Poems and Ideological Constraint." In *"The Muses Common-Weale": Poetry and Politics in the Seventeenth Century*, edited by Claude J. Summers and Ted-Larry Pebworth, 9–22. Columbia: University of Missouri Press, 1988.

Patton, Brian. "Preserving Property: History, Genealogy, and Inheritance in 'Upon Appleton House.'" *Renaissance Quarterly* 49 (1996): 824–839.

Perkins, William. *A treatise vnto a declaration whether a man be in the estate of damnation or in the estate of grace*. London, 1590.

– *A golden chaine*. London, 1591.

– *A commentarie or exposition, vpon the fiue first chapters of the Epistle to the Galatians*. Cambridge, 1604.

– *Christian oeconomie*. London, 1609.

Petter, George. *A learned, pious, and practical commentary, upon the Gospel according to St. Mark*. London, 1661.

Phillips, Joshua. "Monasticism and Idleness in Spenser's Late Poetry." *Studies in English Literature* 54 (2014): 59–79.

Piatti, Girolamo. *The happines of a religious state*. Rouen, 1632.

Pocklington, John. *Altare Christianum*. London, 1637.

Polhill, Edward. *Precious faith considered in its nature, working, and growth*. London, 1675.

Poole, Matthew. *Annotations upon the Holy Bible*. London, 1685.

Pooley, Roger. "*Grace Abounding* and the New Sense of Self." In *John Bunyan and His England, 1628–88*, edited by Anne Laurence, W.R. Owens, and Stuart Sim, 105–114. London: Continuum, 1990.

Pratt, Anne. Vol. 1 of *The Flowering Plants of Great Britain*. London: Society for Promoting Christian Knowledge, 1855.

Priorato, Galeazzo Gualdo. *The history of France*. London, 1676.

*A prophecie of the life, reigne, and death of VVilliam Laud, Archbishop of Canterbury*. London, 1644.

Prynne, William. *A briefe suruay and censure of Mr Cozens his couzening deuotions*. London, 1628.

– *Histriomastix*. London, 1633.

– *A quench-coale*. Amsterdam, 1637.

– *Lord bishops, none of the Lords Bishops*. Amsterdam, 1640.

– *The fourth part of The soveraigne povver of parliaments and kingdoms*. London, 1643.

– *A breviate of the life, of VVilliam Laud Arch-Bishop of Canterbury*. London, 1644.

– *Canterburies doome*. London, 1646.

– *Diotrephes catechized*. London, 1646.

– *A short sober pacific examination of some exuberances in, and ceremonial appurtenances to the Common prayer.* London, 1661.

Purchas, Samuel. *Purchas his pilgrims.* London, 1625.

Purkiss, Diane. "Thinking of Gender." In *The Cambridge Companion to Andrew Marvell,* edited by Derek Hirst and Steven N. Zwicker, 68–86. Cambridge: Cambridge University Press, 2011.

Quantin, Jean-Louis. *The Church of England and Christian Antiquity: The Construction of a Confessional Identity in the 17th Century.* Oxford: Oxford University Press, 2009.

Quint, David. "Expectation and Prematurity in Milton's 'Nativity Ode.'" *Modern Philology* 97 (1999): 195–219.

Radden, Jennifer (ed.). *The Nature of Melancholy from Aristotle to Kristeva.* Oxford: Oxford University Press, 2000.

Rajan, Balachandra. "Ludlow Revisited: Milton and Eco-Justice." In *Milton and Questions of History: Essays by Canadians Past and Present,* edited by Feisal G. Mohamed and Mary Nyquist, 379–393. Toronto: University of Toronto Press, 2012.

Rawlinson, John. *The foure summons of the Shulamite.* Oxford, 1606.

Raymond, Joad. *Milton's Angels: The Early-Modern Imagination.* Oxford: Oxford University Press, 2010.

Read, Sophie. *Eucharist and the Poetic Imagination in Early Modern England.* Cambridge: Cambridge University Press, 2013.

Reiss, Timothy J. *Mirages of the Selfe: Patterns of Personhood in Ancient and Early Modern Europe.* Stanford: Stanford University Press, 2003.

Reeve, John. *Hymnes and spiritual songs extracted from Scripture.* London, 1682.

Reeve, Thomas. *God's plea for Nineveh.* London, 1657.

Revard, Stella P. *Milton and the Tangles of Neaera's Hair: The Making of the 1645 Poems.* Columbia: University of Missouri Press, 1997.

R.H. [Abraham Woodhead]. *Two discourses.* Oxford, 1687.

Richeome, Louis. *The pilgrime of Loreto.* Saint-Omer, 1629.

Rist, Thomas. "Topical Comedy: On the Unity of *Love's Labour's Lost.*" *Ben Jonson Journal* 7 (2000): 65–87.

Ristuccia, Nathan J. *Christianization and Commonwealth in Early Medieval Europe.* Oxford: Oxford University Press, 2018.

R.J. *Compunction or pricking of heart.* London, 1648.

Robartes, Foulke. *Gods holy house and service.* London, 1639.

Robinson, Benedict S. "The 'Turks,' Caroline Politics, and Philip Massinger's *The Renegado.*" In *Localizing Caroline Drama: Politics and Economics of the Early Modern English Stage, 1625–1642,* edited by Adam Zucker and Alan B. Farmer, 213–238. New York: Palgrave, 2006.

Robinson, Richard. *The vineyarde of virtue.* London, 1579.

Robotham, John. *An exposition on the whole booke of Solomons song.* London, 1651.

Rogers, Daniel. *Matrimoniall honovr.* London, 1642.
Rogers, John. "The Enclosure of Virginity: The Poetics of Sexual Abstinence in the English Revolution." In *Enclosure Acts: Sexuality, Property, and Culture in Early Modern England,* edited by Richard Burt and John Michael Archer, 229–250. Ithaca: Cornell University Press, 1994.
– *The Matter of Revolution: Science, Poetry, and Politics in the Age of Milton.* Ithaca: Cornell University Press, 1996.
Rogers, John. *A Treatise of Love.* London, 1629.
Rosendale, Timothy. *Liturgy and Literature in the Making of Protestant England.* Cambridge: Cambridge University Press, 2007.
Ross, Alexander. *Pansebeia.* London, 1655.
Rumrich, John. *Milton Unbound: Controversy and Reinterpretation.* Cambridge: Cambridge University Press, 1996.
Rutherford, Samuel. *Christ dying and drawing sinners to himself.* London, 1647.
Sanchez, Melissa E. *Erotic Subjects: The Sexuality of Politics in Early Modern English Literature.* Oxford: Oxford University Press, 2011.
– "'She Straightness on the Woods Bestows': Protestant Sexuality and English Empire in Marvell's 'Upon Appleton House.'" In *Atlantic Worlds in the Long Eighteenth Century: Seduction and Sentiment,* edited by Toni Bowers and Tita Chico, 81–96. New York: Palgrave Macmillan, 2012.
Saunders, Ben. *Desiring Donne: Poetry, Sexuality, Interpretation.* Cambridge, MA: Harvard University Press, 2006.
Saurat, Denis. *Milton: Man and Thinker.* New York: Haskell House, 1970. First published 1924 by J. Cape (London).
Schoenfeldt, Michael C. *Bodies and Selves in Early Modern England: Physiology and Inwardness in Spenser, Shakespeare, Herbert, and Milton.* Cambridge: Cambridge University Press, 1999.
Schücking, Levin L. *The Puritan Family: A Social Study from the Literary sources.* Translated by Brian Battershaw. London: Routledge & Kegan Paul, 1969.
Schwartz, Louis. *Milton and Maternal Mortality.* Cambridge: Cambridge University Press, 2009.
Schwartz, Regina. *Sacramental Poetics at the Dawn of Secularism: When God Left the World.* Stanford: Stanford University Press, 2008.
Schwarz, Kathryn. "Chastity, Militant and Married: Cavendish's Romance, Milton's Masque." *PMLA* 118 (2003): 270–285.
Scodel, Joshua. *Excess and the Mean in Early Modern English Literature.* Princeton: Princeton University Press, 2002.
Scoular, Kitty W. *Natural Magic: Studies in the Presentation of Nature in English Poetry from Spenser to Marvell.* Oxford: Clarendon Press, 1965.
Seigel, Jerrold. *The Idea of the Self: Thought and Experience in Western Europe since the Seventeenth Century.* Cambridge: Cambridge University Press, 2005.
Sellin, Paul R. "The Mimetic Poetry of Jack and John Donne: A Field Theory for the Amorous and the Divine." In *Sacred and Profane: Secular*

*and Devotional Interplay in Early Modern British Literature*, edited Helen Wilcox, Richard Todd, and Alasdair MacDonald, 163–172. Amsterdam: VU University Press, 1996.

Semler, L.E. "Who Is the Mother of 'Eliza's Babes' (1652)? 'Eliza,' George Wither, and Elizabeth Emerson." *JEGP* 99 (2000): 513–536.

– "The Creed of Eliza's Babes (1652): Nakedness, Adam, and Divinity." *Albion* 33 (2001): 185–217.

– (ed). *Eliza's Babes: or The Virgin's Offering*. Madison: Fairleigh Dickinson University Press, 2001.

Sensabaugh, G.F. *The Tragic Muse of John Ford*. Stanford: Stanford University Press, 1944.

Sergeant, John. *Of devotion*. London, 1678.

Shagan, Ethan H. *Popular Politics and the English Reformation*. Cambridge: Cambridge University Press, 2003.

Shakespeare, William. *Hamlet*. Edited by Philip Edwards. Cambridge: Cambridge University Press, 2003. First published 1985 by Cambridge University Press (Cambridge).

Shanahan, Daniel. *Toward a Genealogy of Individualism*. Amherst: The University of Massachusetts Press, 1992.

Sharpe, Kevin. "Archbishop Laud." In *Reformation to Revolution: Politics and Religion in Early Modern England*, edited by Margo Todd, 71–77. London: Routledge, 1995.

Sharrock, Roger. "Spiritual Autobiography in *The Pilgrim's Progress*." *Review of English Studies* 24 (1948): 102–120.

Shelford, Robert. *Five Pious and Learned Discourses*. Cambridge, 1635.

Shell, Alison. *Oral Culture and Catholicism in Early Modern England*. Cambridge: Cambridge University Press, 2007.

Shohet, Lauren. "Figuring Chastity: Milton's Ludlow Masque." In *Menacing Virgins: Representing Virginity in the Middle Ages and Renaissance*, edited by Kathleen Coyne Kelly and Marina Leslie, 146–164. Newark: University of Delaware Press, 1999.

Shuger, Deborah. "Laudian Feminism and the Household Republic of Little Gidding." *Journal of Medieval and Early Modern Studies* 44 (2014): 69–94.

Shullenberger, William. *Lady in the Labyrinth: Milton's Comus as Initiation*. Cranbury, NJ: Associated University Presses, 2008.

Sibbes, Richard. *Bovvels opened*. London, 1639.

Sikes, George. *The life and death of Sir Henry Vane*. London, 1662.

Simpkinson, C.H. *Life and Times of William Laud, Archbishop of Canterbury*. London: John Murray, Albemarle Street, 1894.

Sirluck, Ernest. "Milton's Idle Right Hand." *Journal of English and Germanic Philology* 60 (1961): 749–785.

Skinner, Robert. *A Sermon Preached Before the King at White-Hall*. London, 1634.

Smart, Peter. *Canterburies crueltie*. London, 1643.

Smith, Nigel. "Bunyan and the Language of the Body in Seventeenth-Century England." In *John Bunyan and His England, 1628–88*, edited by Anne Laurence, W.R. Owens, and Stuart Sim, 161–174. London: The Hambledon Press, 1990.

– *Andrew Marvell: The Chameleon*. New Haven: Yale University Press, 2010.

Smith, Samuel. *The Character of A Weaned Christian. Or The Evangelical Art of promoting Self-denial*. London, 1675.

Smuts, R. Malcolm. *Court Culture and the Origins of a Royalist Tradition in Early Stuart England*. Philadelphia: University of Pennsylvania Press, 1987.

– "Force, Love and Authority in Caroline Political Culture." In *The 1630s: Interdisciplinary Essays on Culture and Politics in the Caroline Era*, edited by Ian Atherton and Julie Sanders, 28–49. Manchester: Manchester University Press, 2006.

Spenser, Edmund. *The Faerie Queene*. Edited by A.C. Hamilton. New York: Longman, 1977.

Stafford, Anthony. *Staffords Niobe*. London, 1611.

– *The femall glory*. London, 1635.

Staley, Lynn. "Enclosed Spaces." In *Cultural Reformations: Medieval and Renaissance in Literary History*, edited by Brian Cummings and James Simpson, 113–133. Oxford: Oxford University Press, 2010.

Stalham, John. *Vindiciae redemptionis*. London, 1647.

Starke, Sue P. *The Heroines of English Pastoral Romance*. Cambridge: D.S. Brewer, 2007.

Stieg, Margaret. *Laud's Laboratory: The Diocese of Bath and Wells in the Early Seventeenth Century*. Lewisburg, PA: Bucknell University Press, 1982.

Stocker, Margarita. *Apocalyptic Marvell: The Second Coming in Seventeenth Century Poetry*. Athens: Ohio University Press, 1986.

Stockton, Will, and James M. Bromley. "Introduction: Figuring Early Modern Sex." In *Sex before Sex: Figuring the Act in Early Modern England*, edited by James M. Bromley and Will Stockton, 1–24. Minneapolis: University of Minnesota Press, 2013.

Stoughton, John. *XI. choice sermons*. London, 1640.

Stranahan, Brainerd P. "'With Great Delight': The Song of Solomon in *The Pilgrim's Progress*." *English Studies* 68 (1987): 220–227.

Strier, Richard. "The Refusal to Be Judged in Petrarch and Shakespeare." In *A Companion to Shakespeare's Sonnets*, edited by Michael Schoenfeldt, 73–89. Oxford: Blackwell Publishing Ltd., 2007.

– "Radical Donne: 'Satire III.'" *ELH* 60 (1993): 283–332.

– *The Unrepentant Renaissance: From Petrarch to Shakespeare to Milton*. Chicago: University of Chicago Press, 2011.

Strode, William. *The Floating Island*. London, 1655.

– *A sermon preached at a visitation held at Lin in Norfolk, June the 24th anno 1633*. London, 1660.

Sugimura, N.K. *"Matter of Glorious Trial": Spiritual and Material Substance in Paradise Lost*. New Haven: Yale University Press, 2009.

Swaim, Kathleen M. *Pilgrim's Progress, Puritan Progress: Discourses and Contexts*. Urbana: University of Illinois Press, 1993.

Swain, Joseph Ward. *The Hellenic Origins of Christian Asceticism*. New York: The New Era Printing Company, 1916.

Swan, John. *Speculum mundi*. Cambridge, 1635.

Targoff, Ramie. "Facing Death." In *The Cambridge Companion to John Donne*, edited by Achsah Guibbory, 217–232. Cambridge: Cambridge University Press, 2006.

– *John Donne, Body and Soul*. Chicago: University of Chicago Press, 2008.

Taverner, Richard. *The Epistles and Gospelles with a brief postil vpon the same from after Easter tyll Aduent*. London, 1540.

Taylor, Charles. *Sources of the Self: The Making of the Modern Identity*. Cambridge: Cambridge University Press, 1989.

Taylor, Jeremy. *The great exemplar of sanctity and holy life according to the Christian institution*. London, 1649.

– *The rule and exercises of holy living*. London, 1650.

Teskey, Gordon. *The Poetry of John Milton*. Cambridge, MA: Harvard University Press, 2015.

Theodoret of Cyrrhus. *A History of the Monks of Syria*. Translated by R.M. Price. Kalamazoo: Cistercian Publications, 1985.

– *Théodoret de Cyr. L'histoire des moines de Syrie*. 2 vols. Edited by P. Canivet and A. Leroy-Molinghen. Paris: Cerf, 1977–1979.

Thiel, Udo. *The Early Modern Subject: Self-Consciousness and Personal Identity from Descartes to Hume*. Oxford: Oxford University Press, 2011.

Thomas, Catherine. "Chaste Bodies and Poisonous Desires in Milton's *Mask*." *Studies in English Literature* 46 (2006): 435–459.

*Threnoikos*. London, 1640.

Tibullus. *The Elegies of Albius Tibullus*. Edited by Kirby Flower Smith. New York: American Book Company, 1913.

Tillyard, E.M.W. *Milton*. London: Chatto & Windus, 1946. First published 1930 by Chatto & Windus (London).

Tombes, John. *Fermentvm Pharisaeorvm*. London, 1643.

Townshend, Aurelian. *Tempe restord*. London, 1632.

Tredennick, Linda. "Exteriority in Milton and Puritan Life Writing." *Studies in English Literature* 51 (2011): 159–179.

Trevor-Roper, H.R. *Archbishop Laud, 1573–1645*: London: Macmillan & Co. Ltd., 1963.

Troughton, William. *The mystery of the marriage song and mutuall spirituall embraces between Christ & his spouse opened*. London, 1656.

Tully, George. *An answer to a discourse concerning the celibacy of the clergy*. Oxford, 1688.

Turner, James. *The Politics of Landscape: Rural Scenery and Society in English Poetry 1630–1660*. Cambridge, MA: Harvard University Press, 1979.

Turner, James Grantham. *One Flesh: Paradisal Marriage and Sexual Relations in the Age of Milton*. Oxford: Clarendon Press, 1987.

Tyacke, Nicholas. *Anti-Calvinists: The Rise of English Arminianism c. 1590–1640*. Oxford: Oxford University Press, 1987.

Tyndale, William. *An answere vnto Sir Thomas Mores dialoge*. Antwerp, 1531.

– *The vvhole workes of W. Tyndall, Iohn Frith, and Doct. Barnes*. London, 1573.

Ursinus, Zacharias. *The summe of Christian religion*. London, 1645.

Valantasis, Richard. *The Making of the Self: Ancient and Modern Asceticism*. Eugene, OR: Cascade Books, 2008.

Vane, Henry, Sir. *The retired mans meditations*. London, 1655.

Veevers, Erica. *Images of Love and Religion: Queen Henrietta Maria and Court Entertainments*. Cambridge: Cambridge University Press, 1989.

Virgil. *Virgil: Georgics I and IV*. Edited by H.H. Huxley. London: Methuen & Co. Ltd., 1963.

Vives, Juan Luis. *A very frutefull and pleasant boke called the Instructio[n] of a Christen woma[n]*. London, 1529.

Von Maltzahn, Nicholas. *An Andrew Marvell Chronology*. New York: Palgrave Macmillan, 2005.

Waldron, Jennifer. *Reformations of the Body: Idolatry, Sacrifice, and Early Modern Theater*. New York: Palgrave Macmillan, 2013.

Wall, Kathleen. "*A Mask Presented at Ludlow Castle*: The Armor of Logos." In *Milton and the Idea of Woman*, edited by Julia M. Walker, 52–65. Urbana: University of Illinois Press, 1988.

Wallace, David. "Nuns." In *Cultural Reformations: Medieval and Renaissance in Literary History*, edited by Brian Cummings and James Simpson, 502–526. Oxford: Oxford University Press, 2010.

Walsham, Alexandra. *The Reformation of the Landscape: Religion, Identity, & Memory in Early Modern Britain & Ireland*. Oxford: Oxford University Press, 2011.

Walton, Izaak. *The lives of Dr. John Donne, Sir Henry Wotton, Mr. Richard Hooker, Mr. George Herbert*. London, 1675.

Ward, Richard. *Theologicall questions, dogmaticall observations, and evangelicall essays, vpon the Gospel of Jesus Christ, according to St. Matthew*. London, 1640.

Warnke, Frank J. "The Meadow-Sequence in 'Upon Appleton House': Questions of Tone and Meaning." In *Approaches to Marvell: The York Tercentenary Lectures*, edited by C.A. Patrides, 234–250. London: Routledge & Kegan Paul, 1978.

Warren, Austin. *Richard Crashaw: A Study in Baroque Sensibility*. Ann Arbor: University of Michigan Press, 1957. First published 1939 by University of Michigan Press (Ann Arbor).

Watson, Thomas. *The duty of self-denial*. London, 1675.

Watson, Thomas. *Holsome and catholyke doctryne concerninge the seuen Sacramentes of Chrystes Church*. London, 1558.

Watts, William. *Mortification apostolicall*. London, 1637.

Weber, Max. *The Protestant Ethic and the Spirit of Capitalism*. Edited by Richard Swedberg, translated by Talcott Parsons. New York: W.W. Norton & Company, 2009.

Webster, Tom. "Early Stuart Puritanism." In *The Cambridge Companion to Puritanism*, edited by John Coffey and Paul C.H. Lim, 48–66. Cambridge: Cambridge University Press, 2008.

Wells, John. *A prospect of eternity*. London, 1654.

Whalen, Robert. *The Poetry of Immanence: Sacrament in Donne and Herbert*. Toronto: University of Toronto Press, 2002.

Wharton, Henry. *A treatise of the celibacy of the clergy*. London, 1688.

Whately, William. *A Bride-Bush*. London, 1619.

Whiting, Robert. *The Blind Devotion of the People: Popular Religion and the English Reformation*. Cambridge: Cambridge University Press, 1991. First published 1989 by Cambridge University Press (Cambridge).

Wilcher, Robert. *Andrew Marvell*. Cambridge: Cambridge University Press, 1985.

Willet, Andrew. *Synopsis papismi*. London, 1592.

– *Tetrastylon papisticum*. London, 1593.

– *A catholicon*. Cambridge, 1602.

Wilson, Christopher. *Self Deniall: or, A Christians Hardest Taske*. London, 1625.

Wilson, Thomas. *A Christian dictionarie*. London, 1612.

– *A commentarie vpon the most diuine Epistle of S. Paul to the Romanes*. London, 1614.

Wither, George. *The hymnes and songs of the Church*. London, 1623.

Wotton, Anthony. *A defence of M. Perkins booke, called A reformed Catholike*. London, 1606.

Yost, John K. "The Reformation Defense of Clerical Marriage in the Reigns of Henry VIII and Edward VI." *Church History* 50 (1981): 152–165.

Young, Patrick. *Catena Graecorum patrum in beatum Iob collectore Niceta Heracleae*. London, 1637.

Younge, Richard. *A counterpoyson*. London, 1641.

Zwicker, Steven N. "The Day that George Thomason Collected His Copy of the *Poems of Mr. John Milton, Both English and Latin, Compos'd at Several Times*." *Review of English Studies* 64 (2012) 231–245.

# Index

www.ingramcontent.com/pod-product-compliance
Lightning Source LLC
LaVergne TN
LVHW090157080826
844660LV00013B/839/J